BISON
BOOKS

MALINDA JENKINS

Gambler's Wife

The Life of

Malinda Jenkins

as told in coversations to
Jesse Lilienthal

Introduction to the Bison Books Edition
by Paula Mitchell Marks

UNIVERSITY OF NEBRASKA PRESS
LINCOLN AND LONDON

⊛ The paper in this book meets the minimum requirements of American
National Standard for Information Sciences—Permanence of Paper for
Printed Library Materials, ANSI Z39.48-1984.

First Bison Books printing: 1998
Most recent printing indicated by the last digit below:
10   9   8   7   6   5   4   3   2   1

Library of Congress Cataloging-in-Publication Data
Jenkins, Malinda, 1848–
Gambler's wife: the life of Malinda Jenkins / Malinda Jenkins, as told in
conversations to Jesse Lilienthal; introduction to the Bison books edition
by Paula Mitchell Marks.
p.   cm.
Originally published: Boston and New York: Houghton Mifflin, 1933.
Includes bibliographical references.
ISBN 0-8032-7607-9 (pbk.: alk. paper)
1. Jenkins, Malinda, 1848–   . 2. Gambler's spouses—United
States—Biography.   3. Frontier and pioneer life—United States.
I. Lilienthal, Jesse, b. 1887.   II. Title.
CT275.J552A3   1998
973.8′092—dc21
[B]
98-10455   CIP

Reprinted from the original 1933 edition by Houghton Mifflin Company,
Boston.

Introduction

Paula Mitchell Marks

Malinda Plunkett was born to a farming family in northern Indiana in 1848, the year American women's-rights advocates entered the public political arena with a convention in Seneca Falls, New York. Throughout her long and eventful life, Plunkett (later Page, Chase, and finally Jenkins) did not engage politically in the women's-rights cause; if anything, she appears to have remained noncommittal or ambivalent about some of the changes the reformers brought about. At the same time, she actively exemplified the independence for which they fought.

Her life story effectively undercuts any remaining traditional assumptions about westering women as simply "helpmates," "genteel civilizers," or "oppressed drudges."[1]

In fact, the narrative in *Gambler's Wife*, recorded by Jesse Lilienthal in the early 1930s, provides one of the best examples to date of a phenomenon recognizable to students of nineteenth-century American women's history: the extent to which individual women acted from both necessity and choice in ways that challenged the era's "True Womanhood" ideology, with its emphasis on female piousness, passivity, domesticity, submissiveness, self-sacrifice, and purity.

The bare bones of Jenkins's story as detailed in the narrative are as follows: she was the eighth of nine children born to Abram Mosley Plunkett and Malinda Goben Plunkett, who had moved from Kentucky to Indiana. When the younger Malinda was five, a brother died of typhoid, and the grieving mother soon succumbed as well. Malinda's father then married a widow named Mary Huffman, and Malinda lived alternately with the couple and with one or another older married sister.

In April 1865, Malinda married Willie Page, the youngest son of a prosperous local farming family, and they lived on the Page holdings. A son, Ollie, was born the following year. In late 1867 or early 1868, the young family moved to Boone County in central Indiana, near a sister of Willie's. Here daughter May and son William were born.

When her father's death left Malinda with a small inheritance, the family used it to move to Kansas. Crop failures drove them back to Boone County, where Malinda, exasperated with what she perceived as Willie's laziness, left him and the children. She journeyed to Fort Worth (probably in 1875) and began a series of business enterprises—boardinghouse keeper, millinery-store owner—her industry and success hampered only by periodic bouts of typhoid fever. Meanwhile, Willie divorced her.

In Fort Worth, Malinda, in her late twenties, met and married a man of about fifty, a cotton broker and commission merchant referred to only as "Mr. Chase."[2] Chase offered funds to help her try to win her children from Willie, and she succeeded in obtaining May. She and Chase also launched a grocery-store business in Wichita Falls, Texas, and it boomed. But Chase soon died, on a trip to Galveston to visit relatives.

Malinda then met and in 1883 married William Graham Jenkins, twelve years her junior. With Jenkins a restless young "sporting man," the couple would experience numerous ups and downs, but as Malinda noted, "he kept me guessing and going over the jumps for forty-three years. There was too much to know about that man." The two often lived apart, Jenky gambling, Malinda pursuing a variety of business ventures, from running another boardinghouse to operating a beauty parlor. Malinda also provided the initiative for some of the saloon enterprises in which Jenky engaged.

The couple gravitated to the West Coast, where Malinda, with an eye for real estate, began buying property, in part to have "something for Jenky to come to." They participated in the Klondike gold rush by traveling separately to Dawson and mounting separate business ventures there, using their profits to buy ranches and other property up and down the West Coast. The two continued to live apart for long periods, especially when Malinda moved to Oakland, California, to provide a place for May's son and Ollie's children to go to school, and Jenky remained on an Oregon ranch. But Malinda and Jenky stayed a couple until his death in 1929, their mutual love for horse racing infusing their later years with excitement.

Malinda had moved from a conventional farm-family existence to life as an independent urban businesswoman, then as the wife of a cotton broker on Fort Worth's "Quality Hill," and again as a business-woman and something of a "sporting woman," in that her enterprises included providing whiskey to miners and finery to boomtown dance-hall girls. Thus, she seemed to move across social and economic class lines. With her lack of formal education and affinity for hard physical labor and some of the jobs she held—such as logging-camp cook—she might have identified herself as working class. But she was enough of an entrepreneur to establish herself repeatedly in business. And in the relatively open society of the Yukon, she indicates that she joined other women in the role of genteel civilizer—while doctoring whiskey for sale and holding "spook meetings," or seances.

Malinda had no "upper-class" aspirations. As she put it, "I be-lieve in knowin' what you ain't jes' the same as knowin' what you are." She rejected a blue-blood suitor from Kentucky who wanted to train her for his kind of society and later commented of her time with Mr. Chase on "Quality Hill" that she disliked going "into soci-ety," in part because the women "would say nice things to your face and belt you one when you wasn't looking!"

In his interviews with Malinda, Jesse Lilienthal found her "to the extent that one of us can judge another, entirely truthful." Of course, no account based on memory and subject to the perceptions and story-shaping techniques of another human being can be taken entirely at face value. We cannot know, for example, whether Lilienthal accu-rately recorded Malinda's vernacular speech, but the patterns are fresh and immediate, with delightfully creative word choices—"that stificating heat," "a gaunt woman . . . mighty stray-looking," "never seen such a glumpy person," "looked at me in surprisement."

When the book first appeared in 1933, reviewers responded warmly—if with class consciousness—to this naturally disarming and vivid voice, one citing the apparent veracity of "the intonations, the grammar, the colloquialisms, the curiously good-hearted peas-ant point of view," another the "uncouth . . . but always expressive" and "redolent" English.[3]

In the narrative, Malinda's views on life are strongly and consis-tently expressed in five interrelated themes: industry, education, mo-rality, mysticism, and independence.

From childhood, Malinda showed a propensity for hard work and enterprise. Raised in the old domestic artisan tradition in which almost everything a family needed was produced at home, she became justly proud of her homemaking abilities. She indicated that she was more than ready to farm with husband Willie as well, but "dodging work . . . pretty near kept him busy. He was a good man, he never give me a cross word in his life, but he didn't like work." One reason for Malinda's subsequent lasting union with Jenky was the fact that, despite his soft white gambler's hands, he showed he could do hard manual labor when the situation demanded.

Malinda herself easily made the transition from home production work to the marketplace, becoming adept at buying and selling land, goods, and services. Her confidence in her ability to work and make money was undimmed after eighty-two years of living: "Do you know what I'd do if I was to get broke-up? I'd go into business tomorrow. Yes, sir . . . and I'd make good like I always done."

The soul of practicality, Malinda saw formal education as unnecessary except for professional people because "education gets people to trying for a living without work. Anyhow, too easy. To live off their education, there ain't jobs enough of that kind." She adored her father, who lacked "book learning" but could figure complicated sums in his head. Too prideful at age seven to continue attending a local school in which she felt her relative poverty, she was instead tutored by her brother Alfred and expressed no regrets about her lack of formal education.

Nonetheless, Malinda viewed her whole life as a series of educational experiences. Childhood lessons included learning to take care of her own needs, not to lie, and not to behave spitefully. In choosing to leave the familiar communities and settings of her youth and early married life, she "went out and learned something" through "seeing and remembering." Her subsequent marriage to Jenky brought a further broadening of horizons: "I learned more from Jenky than all the others put together." Jenky's wandering spirit fed Malinda's own: "Jenky wanted to go as far west as the train would take him. He's always been that way, and that's why I say it was Jenky educated me, instead of me him. I was narrow; it took him to open my eyes."

As a mature woman, Malinda experienced other pivotal events in her own education, including the journey to Alaska and the Klondike that impressed upon her "the nothingness of small things": "I never knew nothing until I went to Alaska. That's where I learned—it will learn anybody. There was so much I couldn't understand. . . . In Alaska everything is big."

Part of Malinda's education involved an examination of the moral and religious values she imbibed as a member of a Bible-believing farming family and community. Again, she took her cue from her father—"Me and papa didn't have no regular religion and didn't belong to no church." By contrast, the rest of her extended family had "too much religion . . . ministers galore and religion crazy." Malinda was partially soured on religion by her sister Susan, who repeatedly told her she was "going to the devil." Malinda also deeply resented being singled out at about age twelve by the preacher at a Baptist revival who asked her in front of everyone why she had not come forward during the invitation. She responded, "That's my business!" and refused ever to attend a Baptist meeting again.

On her own, Malinda rejected a hellfire-and-brimstone God: "I say find the Heaven that's inside you and you've found everything you'll ever need or want for. God is all in the world that is good, all and everything."

Malinda also rejected some of the moral strictures under which she had been brought up. She left Willie Page at a time when divorce was becoming more common, reflecting a general challenge to the long-suffering model of "true womanhood," but the dissolution of a marriage still stigmatized women—and, of course, Malinda had chosen to at least temporarily leave her children as well.[4] And she acknowledged that she entered the marriage with Jenky considering divorce if it didn't work out.

Malinda claimed to be so naive that she did not even realize she was marrying a "sporting man," and Jenky's gambling initially caused friction in the relationship. But she eventually determined that "Jenky had as good a right to gamble as I had to pray. . . . everything we take hold of is a gamble—everything we go into." Further, she took pride in her husband's being "a square gambler."

While Malinda looked askance at preachers' interpretations of both immorality and immortality, she did subscribe to the popular spiritualist beliefs of her day. The year of her birth was marked not only by the Seneca Falls convention but by the "spirit rapping" claims of the Fox sisters of Rochester, New York, claims that touched off an American spiritualism movement.

From a young age, Malinda felt herself tuned to "messages . . . voices and dreams." The sense of clairvoyance was dramatically demonstrated for her by the two visits she describes receiving as an adolescent from her dead suitor Henry Fuel. But it was not until Malinda visited a medium in Washington State many years later that she began to focus on her own apparent powers in this area. For six years, she worked on concentrating, first beholding "tiny lights," then hearing "faint tappings on the table," then seeing people emerge gradually from a dimness, then hearing voices. She used these powers in her "spook meetings" in Dawson, giving answers to miners wondering about family and friends back home. "I never took no money for it," she reported, "I was agreeable and glad to help them lonely souls."

Malinda held the meetings over Jenky's objections. In fact, she showed no signs of the passivity and submissiveness considered prize characteristics of a woman brought up in the Victorian era. In a small but telling incident, on her arrival in Dawson, Jenky—who had preceded her and established a saloon—greeted her with the words, "Why didn't you put on a dress?" She responded, "I come the whole way in pants." Jenky, showing the power of gender stereotypes even in a frontier environment, insisted, "You could a-put a dress on to land in." Malinda's response? "Aw, shut up, will you?"

Despite the title of the narrative, Malinda never subsumed her own identity in the marriage relationship. In Dawson, she required Jenky to pay the same for her doctored liquor as other saloon keepers were paying, and on the West Coast she bought land "that he would be so crazy about that he'd buy it from me!" She also evinced a lifelong wanderlust totally at odds with the female stereotypes of the time. In this sense, she found soulmates in Jenky, who "wanted to go as far as the train would take him," and in her youngest child, Willie, "a tramp and a wanderer all his life."

It should be noted, however, that Malinda did show an adherence to the traditional female role of wife and mother. As Robert Griswold has noted, western women "might exhibit behavior and attitudes that simultaneously confirmed and seemingly contradicted the ideology

of domesticity," and Malinda would insist that all three of her husbands failed to provide her with the domestic role—in a nice home,
surrounded by children—that she professed to want.[5] Further, many
of her apparently independent actions were undertaken for the good
of her family—especially Jenky, May, and May's son Billie. For example, her business ventures were often mounted to offset Jenky's
gaming losses and shore up his fortunes as well as her own. Like a
more famous chronicler of western women's experience, Elinore Pruitt
Stewart, Malinda combined a self-reliant outlook with "actions [that
revealed] the importance of family and cooperation."[6]

Malinda apparently demonstrated no awareness of or affinity for
women's increasing political and social gains in the Progressive Era.
As an old woman, she decried the rising divorce rate, harking back
to her youth, when "there wasn't no idle women and mighty few
divorces." Of a childhood neighbor who "said that a woman that
read a newspaper wasn't fit to be a wife," Malinda simply commented,
"I wish she could see some of the young gals around here today."

If Malinda failed to recognize or acknowledge the similarities to
her own actions and desires—to be free of a bad marriage, to learn
about the ways the world worked—she nonetheless exhibited the vi-
brant confidence in her own identity and abilities that women's-rights
advocates sought for all women. Her legacy is not one of political
activism or unbridled freedom, but it demonstrates the extent to which
a self-reliant woman could and did chart her own course in the late-
nineteenth-century and early-twentieth-century American West.

NOTES

1. Elizabeth Jameson discusses the insufficient nature of these images
in "Women as Workers, Women as Civilizers: True Womanhood in the American West," Susan Armitage and Elizabeth Jameson, eds., *The Women's West*
(Norman: University of Oklahoma Press, 1987), p. 146.

2. Although Malinda was vague about dates, one might expect to find
Chase listed in the 1877 Fort Worth business directory, which provides
sketches of prominent businessmen and listings for others. He is not included, indicating that he was not a prominent businessman at the time,
although Malinda reported that they lived on "Quality Hill."

3. Stanley Walker, review in *Books*, April 23, 1933, p. 5; F. F. Kelly, review in the *New York Times*, April 23, 1933, p. 10.

4. See Janet Lecompte, ed., *Emily: The Diary of a Hard-Worked Woman* (Lincoln: University of Nebraska Press, 1987), p. 9. Lecompte reports that "divorce increased . . . fourfold in the United States between 1860 and 1900," although the percentage was still small. By 1890, she notes, "divorce was still a stigma for a woman . . . but too common to be a social disaster."

5. Griswold qtd. in Sherry L. Smith, "Single Women Homesteaders: The Perplexing Case of Elinore Pruitt Stewart," *Western Historical Quarterly* 22, no. 2 (May 1991), p. 181.

6. See Smith, "Single Women Homesteaders," pp. 163–83. She provides a fascinating analysis of Stewart's public stance in relation to her private actions.

Preface

WE WERE on our way back from Agua Caliente. My friend and I wandered into the club car for a smoke. The talk was aimless and disjointed. Eventually we got on the subject of biography and I said that I hoped, some time or other, to write the life of a plain, earthy sort of person. 'Biography of the Real Thing' was the way I put it.

A few months later I had a phone call from this same friend. He asked me to lunch. 'Bill Jenkins from Portland, Oregon, is stopping with me,' he said, 'and I think you ought to meet him. His grandmother's eighty-two. She lives in southern California, in a small town down by the Mexican border. She's the honest-to-God American you've been looking for!' 'A woman?' I asked. *'Some woman!'* he laughed. *'Wait till you hear!'*

Bill Jenkins talked all afternoon. More than once he wanted to stop but I wouldn't let him. 'It's a great story,' I told him at the end of it, 'but how do you know that your grandmother will see me?' Bill said, 'She'll see you, don't worry! She's been waiting for you to show up. About twenty-five years ago she dreamt that someone was going to write her life!'

Which is just the way it was. Malinda was a mystic. 'Something give it to me,' she'd explain. She had her voices and her dreams. 'They are voices to me, not to no one else. The air is full of what's happenin', things keep goin' on, nothin' is lost... messages... voices and dreams. But it don't matter what you call 'em.'

I think of Malinda, first of all, as a sage counselor. Here was that rare human that talked most of the time and most of the time knew what she was talking about. And why not? How much she had seen and how much she remembered of it all! 'Fifty years back I wasn't as wise, by a lot. It was all

work and no play for Malinda.   Since then I've had time to
think on it. I didn't know the word them days...'

Malinda was substance, quality and type. Malinda was
dramatic. But she was steady and sure with it all. And a.
great story-teller who knew her climaxes. 'I'll commence at
the top,' she liked to say, 'but the bottom ain't far off.' She
knew how to keep to her promise, too.

A hard trader — she had to be. But she was no money-
lover. 'Money has its uses, it's the most curiful way outen
the kind of trouble people gets into.... Most of what I liked
in my life, though, money wouldn't buy.'

Malinda had her own way of sizing up people. 'Smiles,' she
told me, 'and pleasant ways don't come from good dispositions
so much as from good digestions. Too much smile's as bad
as too much grouch. I like to know where everybody stands:
for me or against me. Give me the man that knows how to
get mad.... Make your mind up slow — then get as mad as
you want.'

An amazingly accurate person. And, to the extent that
one of us can judge another, entirely truthful. Her approach
to that was original: 'You got to have too good a memory to
be a liar!' She had an aversion to exaggeration. 'Stretchin''
she called it.

Like most of us she resented criticism. But she knew her
own limitations: 'I believe in knowin' what you ain't jes'
the same as knowin' what you are.' She was stubborn as a
mule and slow to change her mind. She sincerely believed
she knew how to forgive but I never saw any proof of it. She
liked to talk of her cowardice, but Malinda was brave. She
'blinked' at nothing; saw everything straight, and said what
she had to say.

She loved life. But not for its quiet moments. She liked it
'off the griddle.' Contemplating the past, she told me: 'I'm
satisfied with life — everything except what I missed.' And
she was grateful to it: 'I believe in stoppin' once in a while
and lookin' back to bad times. It don't pay to get too smart
Aleck!'

'Time don't mean nothin' — what's age? 'Tain't how old you are, it's keepin' on that counts.' Malinda didn't resent her years, she simply didn't recognize them. . . . 'I want to climb, I want to climb always. Do you know what I'd do if I was to get broke-up? I'd go into business tomorrow. Yes sir, at eighty-two, and I'd make good like I always done.'

Of her clothes there was no end. The photographer came out one afternoon to take her picture. She had on a red dress — red doesn't take well. At his suggestion Malinda changed to something else. In due course she appeared wearing a dress that I hadn't seen before. 'Gee,' I said, 'that's pretty! You've been holding out on me, haven't you?' 'Holdin' out on you!' she exclaimed. 'Have you seen the same rig on me twice? Ain't I worn something different for you each time you been here?'

So Bill Jenkins wrote his grandmother to say that he had found someone to write her life. And, a few days later, I wrote, too. A cautious, tactful letter asking Mrs. Jenkins if I might visit her and when it would suit her best to see me. That was July of 1930. I looked for an answer in a month or two. Something on ruled paper, written in pencil. But the mails were too slow for Malinda. She wired. Here it is:

Glad to see you forenoons   At races every afternoon

She was standing on the porch of her little cottage when I drove up. She was down the steps and half-way to my car before I could untangle myself. Her arms were outstretched to the heavens. 'Well,' she said, 'you sure been a long time a-comin', ain't you?'

And then, as an afterthought: 'Say, son, in another twenty years I mightn't 'a' been here!'

J. L.

San Mateo, California

GAMBLER'S WIFE

. .

Chapter I

PAPA never worked none that I can remember. He was crippled by sciatic rheumatism and had to walk with a crutch. He got so heavy the big scales wouldn't weigh him so he must have gone over three hundred pounds. I was crazy about him; I used to set on a little homemade stool at his feet and listen to him talk.

I mind well what he told me about the people we come from. They was English and belonged to a titled family by the name of Mosley. Jesse Mosley — that was my grandfather — married against his old man's wishes. Left his people after the rumpus and lit out. He changed his name to Jesse Plunkett and come over with his wife to America.

By and by old Mosley showed up in America. He'd got hold of a big tract of land in Kentucky — across the Indiana line, six thousand acres of the finest blue grass country that later on was the town of Cynthiana. They was still on bad terms, him and his son, but old Mosley swallowed his pride and visited Plunkett where he was settled in Indiana.

Jesse Plunkett had a raft of children. The youngest was my father, Abram Mosley Plunkett, and it was this middle name that raised a big to-do and cost the family a fortune, papa first and then us.

That's so. Here's the way it was. Mosley went home to England, to die. Then come a letter saying as how he hadn't remembered nobody in America except the four year old Abram, the only one of the breed that had the family name. Yes sir. Left my papa the whole of that tract in Kentucky.

Strange as that was, wasn't it more strange that papa never

knew about his inheritance until grandpa Jesse Plunkett, an old man over ninety, lay there dying in our Indiana house? He told papa then about the lands that was his'n. Kept the news back all them years — cheated his own son out of hate for another. Said he couldn't bear the idea of his flesh and blood taking substance from old Mosley.

Don't think that papa didn't try to get what was due him. Crippled as he was, he made that long trek to Kentucky. This was long before the Civil War, and before there was any rail-roads. He started for Kentucky but didn't get no further than the state line. Them days the states had different kinds of money, and all papa carried with him was Indiana money. I reckon it wasn't no good in Kentucky, and after going all that distance he had to turn back. Papa tried it a second time but he fell sick on the way. He was awful bad with rheumatic fever, I can just remember it.

A long time after, when I was growed up, I begun to think of the rights we had in Kentucky. There'd been lots of joking that we was all going to be millionaires, so I said, 'Well, let's find out!' First I talked to my brother Alfred and we agreed we ought to do something. We all put up some money to pay his expenses to go to Cynthiana and search out the records.

When Alfred come back his report was pretty short. The town was there, every bit of it — all but the old court house that burned down in the Civil War. The records was gone with the court house, up in smoke. There was plenty of people knowed this story from beginning to end. They remembered grandpa Jesse Plunkett, but that didn't do no good neither....

Anyway, it wasn't just talk. It was worth something to prove up everything papa told us.... Ay, we all got the same. Nothing.

Papa was proud of his ancestry. 'No scandals,' he'd say, 'and no bastards!'

I recollect that one of my father's sisters come on from

Crawfordsville, Indiana, about thirty miles away. Her name was Sarah Wilheit. A praying Christian! Sing, my Lord! I never heard a sweeter voice. She come to visit and the family was eating breakfast. Some one went in to wake up grandpa and he was dead.... Sarah Wilheit sung a hymn that made me cry. I sure was too young to cry over old Jesse Plunkett, and death didn't bother me none. It was the way Aunt Sarah sung it.

My mother's maiden name was Goben. I was only five years old when she died. It must have been in 1853, as I was born in 1848. If mother had lived I would have known her people, too, but as it was I never knew none of them except her brother, Uncle Jess Goben, that was a preacher. I don't know what denomination he belonged to but they preached that everybody is saved and nobody goes to hell — perdition they called it.

Papa and my mother was married in Kentucky. When sister Betty come three years old they moved over to Indiana and took up a homestead in Putnam County. Betty used to tell me how they cut down the trees and built the house that the rest of us was born in. They tied a small cow-bell on Betty's neck to keep track of her. But she would hold the clapper so's she could play and go where she wanted. Another baby had come and they wanted Betty to stay close and sometimes rock the cradle. But Betty wanted to play.

The second child was Nancy. Susan was the next, and after Susan come Mary and brother Alfred. Then Abram and James but they died young. Then me. William Thomas Jefferson was the youngest. People had families them days.

The only thing that was wrong with us was too much religion. The whole family was that way, the cousins and the rest of them; ministers galore and religion crazy. My brother-in-law was a preacher, and my cousin was the famous Abram Plunkett of the Christian Church in Indiana.

I was religious too, until I found out you couldn't pray for things — that you had to work for them to get what you wanted.... I was the wild one, if you could call me that, because I left the old homestead and pulled out. Left behind everything, all their prayers and old beliefs, and went out and learned something. That's just what I done. I had no education in school but books ain't everything, seeing and remembering is important, too.

All my people and the things I seen in my early days didn't count for long. They passed by and was gone. Mostly you live and die with them you growed up with. Not me. I cleared out too young.

The family made everything that could be made at home. When anything come from a store it was because there wasn't no other way to get it. My sisters was spinning and weaving half the time.

The spinning wheel and hand loom stood in the kitchen. That was a separate house, about eighteen by twenty foot in size. It was a big one for them parts, with a chimney and fireplace, and the regulation crane and kettle to het the water in. Twelve foot away stood another house of the same size, that we lived in. Both of them was log houses. They was cold and full of cracks and took a deal of heating.

I remember one fall day. I don't suppose I was much over three years old. Susan was weaving on the big loom over by the window. Mary set at the spinning wheel on the other side of the room, making thread out of wool rolls. There wasn't no dinner cooked that day, everybody was out except my two sisters and me.

I was begging for something to eat. 'Let's feed her,' one of them said, 'and when she gets enough maybe she'll let us alone and we can have a little quiet.' They told me they had the fireplace full of potatoes, roasting under the coals. After a while they set them in a pan outside by the kitchen door where the salt gourd stood.

I et potatoes — and salt by the handful. That night I had a regular spasm. I guess it was the salt that done it. The whole family was scared. They kept passing me around the room from one to another. First one took me, trying to do for me, and then the next.

Something was in my mouth I was trying to get shut of, see. A spoon handle to keep me from chewing my tongue. They put salt on my tongue too, the very thing that had made me sick! But salt was all they knowed to break a spasm. Me fighting them all, and them passing me around with the salt gourd chasing after me. At last I was so sick I spewed up over everything and everybody.... I must have fell asleep then. When I woke up later I was in my little trundle bed and somebody was setting by me. For awhile they thought it was all over with Linney. From that day to this, and it's eighty years ago, I ain't et a potato with a speck of salt on it.

My brothers and sisters strung along at all ages. Some of them was growed up and married when I was just a little kid. My sister Betty's first was named Jeby. When she was four years old I was only five. Jeby was the biggest coward, but I loved her best in all the world. That didn't keep me from trying to scare her in all sorts of ways. As for me, I wasn't scared of nothing. Not then. But later on in life I knowed what it was to be scared of things, too. You get wiser as you grow older, and the wiser you get the more scary and careful you are.

Papa had a good size sugar orchard. They'd tap the maple trees with an elder spile and catch the sweet water in a trough. There was birch trees there with great spreading branches that come very near to the ground. The boys went out Sundays and lapped the limbs over, wrapping them with bark. It made a wonderful swing.

One day I was in the orchard with Jeby and I seen the swing. 'Jeby,' I said, 'we're goin' to swing!'

I made her climb an old broken root sticking up about ten foot. I was too little to lift her but she worked her way out and onto the branches alone, until she must have been fifteen foot off the ground.

I had it in my mind what I was going to do. Holler 'booger!

booger!' and run. The grown-ups used to say that when they wanted to scare us children; and, Lord, how that little thing was frightened at the word.

Jeby took hold of the guide rope to get over to the swing. Now for the first time I seen what happened. The boys had cut the swing, down by the seat, so's we couldn't get in and get hurt.

Jeby climbed up over. She had her hands and arms up high as she could reach, ready to slide down to the seat that wasn't there.... It was still in my mind to frighten her, to holler 'booger!' Then it come to me she would be hurt sure, so I kept still and let her slide quiet to the ground. She burnt her hands a little, that was all. To myself I was saying: 'God, take care of Jeby!'

Wasn't I a little girl to be thinking of God? It seemed to me that God could save her, if he only would. Maybe he did.

Brother Alfred was growed up. He come riding down the road toward the house, one day, and as he got nearer I could see that something was lying, like a sack of meal, across the horse's neck. It was my little brother Abram, about four years older than me. Mother run out and lifted Abram off the horse. He was deathly sick, all white and pale. Abram was her favorite of us all.

He was hot with fever, I reckon, for she was putting cold water on his head. She told me to run to the spring with the gourd and fill it. It was only twenty yards off but like a bad child I didn't want to do it.

She had to tell me twice. I didn't want no water; I didn't see why I should go. I went but I brought it sulky.

Five days more and Abram was dead of typhoid. Then I got my punishment. Young as I was I wet my pillow with tears because I didn't fetch that water right off.... I done a wrong act — it seemed to me to be very serious and I never could forget it. You can't lie to your conscience when it comes to a thing like that; you can't make the wrong look right.

Next day — he was still lying there in the house — I was

looking around for mother. I found her outside on her knees with her hands lifted before her face and praying: 'Oh sweet Jesus, take my little darlin' into your arms.'

Then I happened to look up and I seen a man dressed in white and I thought it was an angel coming! I let out a yelp and run for the house. We had one of them old-fashion footboards with the draperies hanging down to hide the trundle bed underneath. Mother had to pull me out from under it; I thought the angel had come to take us all.

It wasn't an angel, but Mr. Gelty, a friend, that come to see if he could help. It was right in the middle of summer, terrible hot, and he was dressed in homemade linen. Them Geltys was queer folk — strait-laced even for then. The daughters looked it; one of them said that a woman that read a newspaper wasn't fit to be a wife. I wish she could see some of the young gals around here today.

Mother put in a month praying and grieving for her child. Then she took down, her and little Jeby. I don't remember nothing that happened until one night Uncle John Dean waked me up. He took me out of mother's bed. I was cold and all crumpled up. I reckon I was right sleepy.

Come sun up. When I set up in bed I seen a long white sheet, spread over a board, on two chairs about six foot apart. Mother had died in the night. Across over to the door, on the opposite side of the room, was another sheet and two chairs but something much shorter.

I run to papa's bed and shook him. He wasn't asleep, he just had his eyes shut.

'Daddy, daddy, what are them things?' I was crying already.

'Don't cry,' he said, and put his hands on my shoulders and patted me. 'She's left us and went to a better place....'

'But how can we do without her?'

'We have to. I'll take care of you and be good to you like always.'

I asked him, 'Who is the other one?'

'It's Jeby.'

We had three deaths in the family in about a month.

It wasn't more than a week and papa had the typhoid. My sister Susan took him over to her house, and my little brother Tommy. They moved papa in a wagon, on a mattress.

Papa got over it all right. Meanwhile Tommy — we called him Buddy, his name was Thomas Jefferson — took down with it. He got over it, too.

Buddy just commenced to walk. He had to learn it all over after the sickness. Not long afterward he was outside when somebody come along on a horse to talk to Susan's husband, Albert Fields, the shoe-maker preacher. The man tied his horse to a locust bush in front of the house. It got tangled up in its bridle and fell. Buddy run in as fast as he could and hollered, 'Mister, your horse is chokin'!'

They got the bridle off but the horse couldn't get up at first. It was a close call, Buddy was right. The man said, 'Well son, you sure saved my horse.' He turned to Albert, 'You make him a pair of shoes and I'll pay the damage.'

But Buddy piped up: 'I don't want no shoes, I wants a pair of boots with red tops!' They had a big laugh over that. Albert made him a beautiful pair which the man paid for.... In them days you couldn't give a little boy nothing in the world that would please him so much as a pair of red top boots.

Papa called me Sinney, little Sinney. He got that from Linney that everybody else called me. Malinda was my mother's name. I was named after her.

When my mother was dying she asked papa to let sister Mary take and raise me. Mary was the only one of the girls that had married pretty well off and had a good home of her own. But papa kept me until he married again a year later. Then he took me to Mary the way mother wanted.

I was very happy there but papa wouldn't let me stay. He missed me and wanted me back, but I was too little to understand how that could be. I knew that he was married to a woman I didn't know, and I wanted to stay where I was.

My stepmother was Mary Huffman. She had been a widow for years. The thing I remember best about her was her sewing; she was a fine seamstress. Children don't like stepmothers, as a rule, but I thought the world of Mary Huffman. She had her peculiarities but never was a better stepmother, I guess, that ever lived. I loved her truly; we all did.

So Papa come and took me away from my sister Mary's. I went kicking and screaming. I was a red-head kid with a temper. When he got me home I wouldn't eat, and I wouldn't go to bed. They left me alone to see what I would do. I set by the fire and slept there with my head up against the jamb of the fireplace. I never left it, only for the seconds when I had to. I stayed there two days and nights crying myself to sleep.

The third day I heard papa say, 'I can't stand this, I can't see Sinney cryin' and unhappy. I can't stand no more of it; it's best to take her back to Mary's. When she gets ready to come home it will be time enough.' That day they took me back. It was kind of like the hunger strikes you hear of these days.

A year later they sent my little brother to fetch me home to go to school. When I got there they asked me a thousand questions about Mary's house, and how she lived, and so on. You see, she was better off than us, and they was curious. I didn't like that but I told them everything I knew. They wasn't satisfied; they kept asking me more questions. Not papa, but Alfred wouldn't let me alone.

The first thing I noticed to home was an old umbrella. It's hard to believe, but up to that time— and I was seven years old — I hadn't never seen one. I was always playing with it, opening it and trying to make the wind lift me off the ground. I played this way with Tiny Owens, another little girl that got hold of a second umbrella over to her place.

So one day I told them how me and Tiny was up to the hay loft and opened our umbrellas and jumped out. And that the wind carried us away off, and a farm hand come running up to see if we was hurt, and we said no, that everything was fine.

I knew that was a whopper of a lie but I don't know to this day why I told it, only that Alfred had been pestering me some more and I was mad. Maybe that was the reason, or maybe not. When children tell lies I think they just sort of come out.

I said to myself, 'It's a lie but I don't believe they will ever find it out.' I worried about it a lot though.

Papa spoke about it when he come in and I heard him. It frightened me terrible. 'Sinney's a good child and don't seem to be the lyin' sort but there's something about it I don't understand at all.'

Alfred just said, 'It's a lie!'

It didn't seem like I slept much that night. Papa catched on to it mighty quick, I thought. I was pretty near sick over it.

Next morning I heard him say to my stepmother: 'She never told me a lie and I can't believe she'd make up a bald-face one like that without a reason. Maybe the child dreamed it.'

Oh what glory, the child dreamed it! When papa said that I knew I was saved. And I was cured from lying. It made me fearful of a lie and was one of the best things that ever happened to me. I don't like to think about it even today. I hate lying and I hate liars.

Chapter II

I WAS going on eight when they started me off to school —
with a psalm book. It had big letters on the outside edge
in the song, commencing with A and going right down to Z.

Well now, in the first place, there's a streak of pride in me
that I can't and never could subdue. It crops up. I am proud.
I can't bear nothing that ain't the way it should be and I
knew it wasn't right for me to use a psalm book for my A.B.C's.

I cried nearly all the way to school. The other children had
spelling books, and McGuffey's First Reader and Second
Reader, and all that. I had nothing but my old song book,
and I was terribly ashamed of it.

I had two stepbrothers that was going to school with me
and Buddy. Buddy was big enough to go along, so I was pretty
old to start in. Maybe I wouldn't have been so humiliated if
I hadn't been that old.

This here stepbrother of mine, the biggest of the two, was
named Drury Staton. We called him Drew. His brother Joe
was cross-eyed and homely but an awful good boy. Drew was
all right enough but a glutton. He'd eat up every mouthful
of his lunch and most of ours before we ever got to school.
Just think of that. In the morning, right after breakfast, he'd
eat up the lunch. It didn't matter which was going to carry
the lunch, Drew took it away. So we got in the habit of eating,
too, to keep him from getting it all.

That was my start in school. The boys went out to play —
they didn't care so much — but I had to set there with the
girls at recess, watching them eat lunch and me with nothing.

I have thought of it many times since — I used to pray to
die to keep from having to go to school. With the wrong
schoolbook and no lunch. I begged so hard to keep from
going that my stepmother interfered. 'If she don't want to
go to school let her stay home and learn herself,' she told papa.
'Alfred's advanced, he can learn her.'

Alfred had a good education. All of them had — but me. Alfred taught school later, and my sister Betty was a practicing doctor.

When papa said, 'All right, you don't have to go no more,' I hugged and kissed him. I couldn't have stood it much longer without running away.

I commenced to learn at home, studying at night with Alfred. Papa said this, he put his hand on my head: 'Sinney, you have the will power, I think, to do what you set out for. There ain't nothin' to keep you busy round here. You don't have to do no chores. You can study and learn, and no one to bother you. Now you'll have to show us.'

My brother Alfred learned me to write. He set copies for me. I was a diligent scholar. I gathered hickory and piled it in the corner inside of the house. It was school time in the fall of the year. I'd put the hickory in the fire, a little at a time. Papa got me the right books and I lay there on my stomach night after night until ten o'clock. That was real studying. I owe most to Alfred for what I learned; he had lots of patience, showing me, and putting me right when I asked him.

I pestered papa but he liked it. Alfred said it was papa, with all his lack of book learning, that educated him in arithmetic. When he was doing his sums and problems papa would give him the answer before he was able to figure it on paper — to show you what a head could do.

Papa was a good reader but he never learned to write. He made a mark for his name. But papa knowed a hawk from a handsaw! Here's a little thing to show you how smart he was.

One fall he had a lot of fattening hogs. Alfred was the only other growed-up man on the place so papa would have a hand or two working for him at fattening time, being too heavy to do anything hisself. The wagons brought the corn up already husked and papa set there and watched it fed to the hogs. He let them sleep just so long and then he would have more corn thrown in to make them get up and feed. I seen him fatten as many as a hundred of the critters in one pen, quicker than anything. Them was to sell. The young 'uns he took his time with.

Papa went and fell sick now with that old sciatic hip trouble. He was in bed when some strange buyer come around but he sold him a drove of hogs just the same. The buyer paid papa in gold; three hundred dollars — fifteen twenty dollar gold pieces.

When papa was well enough he started out to buy more hogs. He'd buy them from people that didn't know the fattening business.

About a month later, not more than that, along come two men riding, and one of them was the constable.

'Is this the man?' he asked the other fellow, and he pointed at papa.

'It is.'

'What's all this?' papa wanted to know. 'Well,' the constable said, 'I'm compelled to arrest you.' 'What for?' papa asked, and the constable replied: 'For passin' counterfeit money.'

Papa said then, 'I ain't passed no counterfeit money that I know of.'

'Did you buy some hogs from this man and pay for 'em in gold?'

'I certainly did.'

The constable turned around to the other man: 'Give me that money here that you got from Plunkett. This,' he said, 'is a silver dollar; it ain't gold.'

He handed it over to papa. 'I never paid for it in silver, it was all in gold,' papa told him.

The constable turned up the silver dollar. 'Do you see that yellow stuff in there? You can scrape it off. That's what you paid him, silver dollars with washed-in gold.'

'I got over a hundred dollars of it yet,' papa said. 'We'll take a look.'

The constable wanted to know how he come by it. 'A man give it to pay me for my hogs.'

Well now, papa went with them, they'd swore out a warrant.

Alfred hitched up the buggy and went along to give a bond.

Later on the case come up. I don't remember very much about that, only the day of his trial and my sisters running around in front of our place like a flock of geese. Susan was in hysterics, and me trying to get her to tell what it was all about, and her saying I was too little. And finally telling me that my papa was going to the penitentiary Then, my God, I begun to squeal and howl. Their crying was nothing to when I got started. They had to quit their squalling to try to make me stop.

It was around sundown when papa come driving up, smiling and looking pretty jolly. Later on I heard them talking about it and here is what happened, the way it was explained to me.

The judge said: 'This is a very serious matter, Mr. Plunkett. How is it you haven't no attorney? I would advise you to get you the best there is.'

And papa said, 'I won't need no attorney.'

'Do you mean to say you intend to plead your own case?'

'That's what I'm aimin' to do. I am innocent and I can prove it, and that's all, I guess, that is necessary.'

He said, when the time come, 'I have been arrested for handlin' counterfeit money. I am defendin' myself because I was deceived the same as the next man, but that ain't the question here. The charge is that I handled counterfeit money and I deny it. This ain't counterfeit money. The evidence consists of legal American dollars!'

It was that cleared him right off. They brought the wrong charge. Later on they found the man that tried that slick trick; he acknowledged it and went to jail for a year.

Now how did papa, an uneducated man, ever think of anything so cute as that?

They said the judge dismissed the case; in ten minutes it was all over with.

Papa made good them hogs, boughten with silver dollars. He used to tell me, 'All I got was fifteen silver dollars for three hundred dollars worth of pork!'

I believe in book learning, but I don't believe in too much of it except you're going to be a doctor or a lawyer. Education gets people to trying for a living without work. Anyhow, too easy. To live off their education, there ain't jobs enough of that kind.... Education is all right if you know what you want it for and where you're heading with it.

I wasn't inside a store until I was nine years old. That was in 1857. I wanted some nice things but my folks didn't know much about buying them, so I decided that I had better earn some money. There wasn't no sense telling papa because there hadn't been one in the family to work a day of their lives for wages away from home.

I asked him, 'Papa, won't you hire me to do something round here?'

Yes, he would, but he figured to stump me with a hard job. Our whole place was railed in with a worm fence. Rails of split walnut and poplar, about ten foot long. A lot of them was knocked off and lying on the ground.

'I'll pay you, if you'll lay up all them knocked down rails.'

'What will you pay me?'

'Oh, I reckon about a cent a piece.'

He didn't have no idea that I could lift a ten foot rail. And he didn't know that I was doing it until it was done.

Buddy was a delicate child and he couldn't do much. But he come along, day after day, trying to help. We had a hard time. It was an eight rail fence, crossed one over the other. I'd grab one end of a rail and climb the fence with it, hoisting with my hands and feet until I had it in place. I kept on until I put eleven hundred rails in place. Every ten I marked a cross down — we kept count in a little book.

Papa couldn't believe it. 'Do you mean to tell me there ain't no rails down?'

'If you'll get in the buggy you can come and see.' He was tickled but he was flabbergasted.

The damper comes in here, when I asked him for the eleven dollars due me. 'You don't want the money,' he said, 'one of these days I'll get you something for it.'

No sir, I wanted the money then and there.

He said, 'I ain't got but two dollars spendin' money on me.'

'You can drive me down to the store and I'll buy what I'm wantin'. When you get ready you can pay for it.'

'No,' he said, 'we'll wait for it to cool down.' Oh, it was awful hot, too. I answered him: 'It wasn't too hot for me to work in the sun puttin' up them rails!' And to show how determined I was to get what was coming to me: 'I'm a-goin' to walk to town and buy the clothes I want and you will have it to pay for!' He didn't answer me.

It was seven miles to town. I went to my stepmother and I was crying. She said she'd ask papa to take me. But he told her he would handle it his own way and that he'd pay me when he got ready.

Papa was setting there in the doorway in the shade when I started off. Buddy told him I was gone; Buddy was crying because he didn't want me to go. In a few minutes papa told Buddy to harness up the horse and buggy. Papa had to drive about a mile around where I cut across. I walked about two miles, I guess; the sweat was running down and I was fanning away with my palm-leaf fan. I was wishing I hadn't started but I was resolved to go — only I was wondering whatever would happen in that stificating heat, and fourteen miles to cover.

Then I heard the buggy catching up behind me. Papa come along and stopped the buggy. 'Jump in,' he said, 'I'll take you.' But I was stubborn. No sir, I wouldn't; I just walked on.

He set a while, then he come on and done the same thing again. And I pulled back a second time. He stopped there in the shade of a tree by the side of the road watching me, and I reckon he was laughing to hisself.... I begun to wonder if he'd gone back. Good lord, I knew I couldn't make it.

I looked around and I seen him coming and I said to myself, 'If he asks me this time you bet I'm goin' to climb in!'

It was a whole lot for papa to humble down like that and I had sense enough to know it. I seen I was wrong and I was awful sorry and I thought, sometime I'll tell him but I won't tell him now.

The town was Ashby Station, named after Mr. Ashby that owned the store. He come out and shook hands with papa. There was a platform about three foot high that I could step on to, from the buggy. Yep.

Papa couldn't get out; he was too fleshy. Mr. Ashby asked him to come in. Papa said, 'No, but I brought my little girl down to get some things and you give her what she wants.'

What a bonanza! I bought everything that I could think of that I needed from my feet up — shoes, stockings, and I don't know how many colored pieces of goods for dresses. Then I got my stepmother just as much again. And papa, two pairs of socks and two shirts. I asked Mr. Ashby what size papa wore and I got him fine ones with pleated bosoms.

I didn't stop so long as I could think of anything — lace and ribbons, and the craziest stuff like pins and needles.... Papa didn't chastise me at all. He paid the bill and I don't know how much it was. My stepmother told me she never found out. All papa said was that he guessed we needed it.

But that wasn't my first business transaction. The first money I ever earned sister Susan paid me. She'd had a baby and needed somebody around the house, but I reckon she thought I wasn't big enough to help with the work. She hired a girl that nearly ruined all the bed clothes. Didn't know nothing about washing them — put them in hot water and set the stains. Susan wouldn't keep her after that so she sent Albert to fetch me.... I never seen such a mess of soiled clothes. Every day I washed for four days.

When I got ready to start for home Susan paid me. She give me two ten cent pieces. That's a fact. That was five cents a day for the four days of washing.

It was the first money I ever had that I could call my own and I tied it up in a little bag and hung it around my neck.

I invested that twenty cents. I'll tell you how. When papa brought up his fattening hogs in the fall he had one little sandy-sided, pot-bellied pig in the lot. It wasn't thriving and I asked him what he'd take for it.

'You ain't got nothin' to buy pigs with.'

'I has, too!'

'How'd you come by it?'

'Susan paid me twenty cents for the washin' I done for her.'

'Where is it?'

And I said, throwing out my chest, 'Right here around my neck!'

I opened up the bag and there was my two dimes. Papa took them. 'All right,' he agreed, 'the pig's your'n!'

Well, sir, I went and built a pen, and I buried a little trough down in the ground so the pig couldn't root it up. Then I got me a pan and some homemade soap. I took a corn cob and I started to scrubbing on my pig. He squealed all the time but I didn't care. He was mine, boughten and paid for, and I was going to get him clean.

I asked papa, 'You ain't goin' to charge me for nothin' that pig eats?'

'No,' he said, 'you can help throw corn to the hogs for the feed your'n gets, but I don't reckon it will live long the way it squealed today. I reckon you near killed it.'

I never seen nothing thrive like that runt pig. It hadn't had no chance amongst them big brutes. After a few weeks I got papa to come and look him over.

'Are you sure that's the boughten pig? Ain't you turned it out and got one of my pigs in there?'

'No sir! Don't you see it ain't got no tail hardly?' Its tail was sore and I cut it off.

Well, my pig went on getting bigger and bigger until it weighed three hundred pounds, and pork was worth three cents a pound. How much of that did papa pay me? Shucks, I never got a sniff at it....

It ain't strange, now, my wanting that eleven dollars for fence fixing. Is it?

Chapter III

BESIDES raising hogs, papa was a cattle dealer and horse
trader. He kept fat cattle on hand, feeding them in the
blue grass pasture in the summer time, selling them off when
anybody came along. Raised mules, too. It was a great country for mules. He shipped them to Kentucky and Tennessee.
They was much better for plowing than horses. A mule can live
as long again as a horse and he eats less. A good mule that cost
you a hundred dollars fetched three times that. For a span of
mules papa got five hundred dollars, maybe six hundred.

We growed everything that we had and most everything you
could think of. Wheat, barley and rye. We raised clover and
threshed the seeds and took the hay of it for the cattle; it was
the main feed for the horses and mules. We sold the seeds.

We growed flax and made our own sheets and towels and
pillow cases; everything that was pertaining to the household.
We raised sheep, and the wool was made into clothing for the
men and women both. There wasn't never a yard of cloth
boughten, we made it all. But cotton — we couldn't grow
cotton in Indiana.

Papa sent me when I was ten to live with my sister Susan to
learn spinning and weaving; making bedspreads, throwing the
yarn up and making posy designs, like carpets today. Susan
taught me everything but she was awful mean about it.
Treated me worse than a stranger and she was the same to her
own kids. My other sisters wasn't that way.

Susan was counted the belle of Putnam County and took
prizes for her looks. I don't know, but it may have turned her
head. I look like papa, but Susan had dark hair and eyes like
my mother, from what they told me. She was the only one of
the family that wore store clothes. She had silk dresses, and
a big silk cape.

Anyhow, that was it. Susan couldn't be good to none of the

youngsters. She was a worker herself and didn't seem to understand why us children wouldn't work as much as she did.

I was still at Susan's after three years. When I was in my thirteenth year Abram Plunkett, my cousin, come to visit papa. He was papa's namesake. Abram was a young man just out of theological college but hadn't done no preaching yet. The Plunketts was mostly fair but Abram took after his mother, my uncle William's wife. They settled across the line from Kentucky where Uncle William took up some homestead land. We lived up around the northern part of Indiana but they lived way south, about a quarter of a mile from the Ohio River.

Of course I wasn't home when young Abram visited at papa's, but he called round to see the whole family in time. We all lived within a ten mile radius. And his coming to see Susan got me out of bondage. I called it that and it wasn't nothing else. Abram stayed at Susan's for three or four days. And he seen me drudging....

Susan used to call me 'wall eyes' from the way I'd look at her when she was scolding. That made her mad and finally she got me so I wouldn't look up at all. Abram noticed it when he was talking to me. I was drawing water out of the well, with the old sweep and bucket. Had my tub there filling it full of rinse water. There was a curbing about three foot high that you leaned against to balance you when you was pulling up the water. It was topped with big slabs and Abram was on the other side of the well, setting there and talking.

'Linney,' he said, 'why don't you look at me? You don't have to watch the bucket, it's comin' up by itself.'

I kind of half flashed my eyes up and dropped them back again. I didn't want him to see my wall eyes; that was Susan's doing. I felt blushful about it, too.

Abram knowed me when I was small but I'd forgot. I didn't think of him as kin; he was like any young man to me and I was getting to the age when pretty soon I was going to be interested in men. I was ashamed — I thought how terrible I must look to this educated young minister in my linsey-woolsey dress....

It was all I had and it was half wore out. I lay in bed that night and cried myself to sleep, thinking with shame how Susan was treating me after the way our mother took care of us. Susan with her silks to wear and me with nothing.

When Abram went back to papa's place he asked him why he kept me with Susan. 'Susan is undoin' her,' Abram said. 'She bids fair to be a nice young girl but Susan's got her cowed so bad I couldn't get her to look me in the face — even when I asked her to.' The next day papa sent my brother Alfred over and fetched me home....

Betty, my oldest sister, had allowed me to save up some of her wore-out togs, for barter with the huckster when he come around. I got two yards of calico goods that way. It was dark red, peppered with little white acorns. That was all I had to take back, the calico, and an extra set of underclothing. I tied them up in Alfred's bandanna and hung them on the horn of the saddle that was once my mother's. My shoes was a pair of brogans that Albert Fields made me.

My stepmother loaned me a dress while I was making a waist out of the calico piece. I cut it out and finished it with a ruffle around the neck. I had to use my old linsey skirt but I felt dressed up just the same. I'll have to die to forget the looks of that peppered calico!... Susan's training was wearing off quick. When Abram spoke to me I wasn't afraid to look up at him and have my say. Don't that show what getting away from somebody that has you cowed can do?

For a religious woman Susan had a queer way of showing it. Albert Fields, her husband, was different; a shoemaker week times and a hard-shell Baptist preacher on Sunday. With all this unkindness around him, still he was a kind man.

There was family prayer every night — all of us kneeling and praying. Them was silent prayers except when Susan would let go, raising off her knees, slapping her hands together and thanking the Lord for a husband that had prayers at home. I don't know what all she wouldn't pray, and abusing us children betwixt times.

Even child that I was I thought of that but I dasen't say

nothing, with Susan telling me how wicked I was and how I was going to the devil; and me praying and thinking it wasn't no fault of mine being born with the devil in me!

Bless me, I was so scared over that notion. I used to run up a corn row in the back of the yard in the middle of my work a half dozen times a day, to pray aloud, where they couldn't see me nor hear me, to rid the devil out of me! I joked about it in after years — how I'd knock down a row of corn a-praying my heart out.

And Susan thought I was lazy! She made complaint to Albert and I heard her.

Albert said, 'I ain't never seen nothin' lazy about Linney.'

'What's she doin' out there in the corn?'

'Why don't you try to find out?' he told her.

One night, no more than a week later, when I was laying in the trundle bed with their youngest, Julie, I heard Albert over on the other side of the room: 'I found out what Linney goes to the cornfield for. She's a-prayin' out there, a-prayin' out loud, and a mighty pitiful prayer it is. She's askin' her mother to come to her and help bear her burden more meek than she's a-doin'. And she's askin' God to take the load of wickedness away from her that she's a-carryin'. Susan,' he said, 'I want you to stop bein' so hard on her. It ain't Christian, you must learn to be more humble.'

If Susan answered him I didn't hear it. 'I never seen such prayin' by a child,' he said. Then he told her, 'We believe that people is forgive when they joins up. Linney ought to know that she is forgive after such prayers as that.'

That's a sample of old-fashioned religion — doing the best you know how and wondering how you're going to keep out of Hell when it's all over.

I say find the Heaven that's inside you and you've found everything you'll ever need or want for. God is all in the world that is good, all and everything. People ought to get rid of the idea of praying their hearts out. Yes, and thinking that when they die they're up against the judgment seat.

It's like the Irishman that come home one night and seen his dog Fido laying by the fire. 'Fido,' he said, 'I wish I was you and you was me! Sure, and don't I have to cook supper or go hungry? And milk the cow or go dry? And scrap with the wife a bit before I turn in? You just sleep all day. I even has to fix your supper for you. I got all this to do down here, and when I die I'll have to go to Hell yet to finish up!'

I wasn't a Baptist and wouldn't join up like the rest of the family. Me and papa didn't have no regular religion and didn't belong to no church.

I'm like a lot of people — the best way to get something out of me ain't ordering me about. A year after I was back home with papa and had nice clothes so's I could go to church — women used to ride side-saddle and I had my riding skirt — I went with Susan and Albert to a big Baptist meeting that was held in the Pennington Grove — a maple sugar grove with blue grass all around. It was the prettiest place ever, with a church set in the middle of it. This day the meeting was out of doors to hold the crowd. And benches for the people to set on and hear Jack Case, the famous traveling Baptist.

From the way he bellowed and the noises he made you could have heard him a quarter of a mile off; he sounded more like a donkey braying than a minister.

Here's what happened. Just as the meeting broke up he hollered out, 'Brother Fields!' We was starting to our horses and when Albert turned around, he said, 'No, it ain't you, it's the young lady I want to see.'

I stood there rooted. I felt small when I seen the whole congregation looking at me.

I wouldn't go over to him but he come to me. 'Why didn't you come forward today?' said he. 'You are ready to join the church. I waited and waited and kept lookin' right at you.'

'I know it,' I said. Everybody had been looking to see what was the matter that I didn't go forward.

'Well, why didn't you?'

I lost my head then. 'That's my business!' I told him.

Wasn't Susan mad! Albert was hurt but Susan was furious.

'You'll pay for that when you do join later on,' was one of the things she said.

And I answered her, 'Don't you go to worryin' about it. I'll never put my foot inside a Baptist church again!' And I never did. I ain't been to a Baptist meeting in seventy years.

Sometimes, when a great calamity comes upon a person, it makes them over. That's what changed Susan.

She had a boy born and the child was a cripple. He was a brilliant boy, too. His name was Gideon, after his father's middle name.

He lived to be forty years old and never walked a step in his life and never et a meal of vittles that wasn't fed to him. It was Gideon, I think, that changed my sister. In a few years she was just as different as if she was born again, kind-hearted and tender.

When Gideon come I went back to visit there. I was fourteen. I went for a week but I stayed all summer and a hat was the cause of it.

Susan bought herself a scoop bonnet, made out of green silk trimmed with lace. It was the prettiest thing; it was wonderful. I tried it on and it looked lovely. I asked her would she sell it to me. I hadn't no money to buy nothing with but I was willing to work my nails off to pay for it.

She told me she'd take ten dollars for it; but I knew it hadn't cost her half that because I asked my sister Betty and she told me.

I said to Susan, 'I can't buy it but I would love to work for it.'

That was all right with her, she said she'd pay me fifty cents a week. Five months work for a hat! Well, we compromised. I worked three months to get it. Though it was agreed I was to have it right off so I could wear it Sundays.... I never thought it was dear, I was sure proud of that bonnet of mine.

Alfred was always willing to take me to church Sundays. Even when I was a little tike he'd hold the halter and ride away to church with me, or sometimes we'd ride double. Alfred was a fine looking young man that all the girls was after and

I couldn't make out why he was willing to waste time on me.
I found out when I got older. They wouldn't have been allowed
to hang round him the way they done if I hadn't been along,
them pretending it was me they was wanting to talk to. But
it wasn't me; it was him.

My stepmother was as kind as a mother could have been but
she had one failing. She took brooding spells and wouldn't talk
to no one for a week or two at a time. Wore her sunbonnet tied
under her chin and wouldn't let you see her face. For a good
woman I never seen such a glumpy person.

She had a spell one time when wash day come. The water
had to be carried from the spring to the house and I went to
fetch it like always. That was my chore, and hanging up the
clothes, too.

This time she took the bucket out of my hands and went after
the water herself. Then I knew there was something wrong,
but I wasn't sure until she went to sorting out the clothes. She
throwed all papa's clothes aside, his shirts and things, and
didn't wash them. So the row was with him. But why was she
throwing mine out, too? Whatever I done wrong, I've forgot.
All I recollect is the way I felt, knowing I wasn't going to have
no clean clothes fixed and layed out ready for church.

Sunday morning come and Alfred asked me wasn't I going.
I told him I couldn't; I hadn't no clean clothes.

'Haven't you no extras?'

I was blubbering and couldn't answer.

Next wash day my stepmother was still pouting. She went
to searching out the clothes like the week before. But she
never made a move I didn't watch. I seen everything she done
until I knew that I could do it, too.

Come morning, I gathered up my own things — my little
short dress, my white pantalettes that went down to the ankles,
and my white aprons with armholes in them and little ruffles
round the neck — and I went to it. I washed my clothes, and
I made some starch and starched them. She'd be looking at me
but she never opened her mouth. I hanged my clothes out to

dry but I took plenty of time off to watch her with the ironing.

I sprinkled my things next day like she done, and I put the irons on and I ironed them without a wrinkle. All that time she never spoke a word.... I never done nothing that pleased me more. I showed papa and Alfred; I told everybody that come in and would listen to me. I knew that I was independent now and wouldn't have to stay home from church because I hadn't no clean clothes!

When I've been stumped in after life I've said to myself 'You made out with the washin' and you can make out to do this!' A little thing like that learned me. It changed my whole life.

Chapter IV

I GUESS my mind was set on the boys from now on. Susan wouldn't let me have no company but papa was different. He had confidence in me. And when Nancy, the second of my sisters — she had big children nearly as old as me — come visiting us and wanted me to go home with her, papa said as it was all right.

It was fall time and there was a lot of work to do at Nancy's. Her husband, Henry Stacker, was a fine farmer and a toilsome worker. Nancy told me about his having so many young men working on the farm but I soon seen I didn't want none of them farm-hands sparking around. They was piddling country boys working out by the day. But there was another fellow visiting near there. Nancy said, 'Wait till you see Henry Fuel, you will fall for him!'

Henry Fuel come along and I was right away shy. I could talk to them other boys but I wanted to steer away from him. I run out and went to playing with Nancy's kids; it made Nancy kind of sore on me.

'What's the matter with you?' she said. 'I thought you wanted to get acquainted with Hennie.' That's what everybody called him.

'I ain't goin' to break my neck over him! I don't see nothin' so grand about him.'

The next time, on Sunday evening, I knew that Hennie come as a suitor. He was all dressed up in a nice black suit; he had cologne or something on his hair and he smelled awful good. I wondered about it since, what made me say the things to him that I did. I treated him mean, as mean as I knew how. Once he come walking up right close, not more than a foot away. I stepped back very indignant. 'Say, don't you know, young man, it's the height of bad manners to walk in front of a girl and look at her like that?'

'I beg your pardon,' he said, 'I didn't mean nothin'.'

Ho! but it made a hit with him anyway. He said, 'Can I call on you regular and be a suitor?'

'Well,' I told him, 'I ain't seen nothin' so far to make me say that you couldn't.'

'Can I come around about seven o'clock on Friday night?'

I said I thought that sweethearts always went to see a girl on Sunday night.

'I reckon I'd call every night if I was allowed to!'

He come and he kept coming. And say, I fell for him good and plenty, I'll bet I did. I thought he was just about IT. The swellest fellow, and he did put the nicest smelling stuff on his hair.

But I wouldn't let him put his arm around me. I was dead in love with him; I would have loved for him to kiss me but he didn't dare try.

Well now, when I was in that condition — and I guess he was with me, too — there was a big Dunkard meeting going on about four or five miles away in a large sugar orchard. People come from a hundred miles off. The brethren put up tents to stay there for a week at a time, and killed beef and had a barbecue. It was an old habit but it was new to me. They done it once a year. Everybody was welcome to come and they fed them all. Dunkards are awful good people, nice Christian people.

Hennie was a city fellow. He worked in Ladoga, over in Montgomery County, but he put up with the Macdonalds when he was calling on me. Their place was about a half of a quarter away from Sarah's. They had a jerkey — that was a sort of carriage — with three big seats in it, for they was quite a family. Hennie come to ask me to go along with him and them and spend the day at the Dunkard meeting. They was the sect that wash your feet. They humbled themselves like the Savior done. They was good people. But I didn't know the Dunkards was some sort of Baptists or I wouldn't have gone. No sir.

We got to a good spot for the horses and hitched them to

a tree. Then we went to the meeting. When noon come Hennie told Mrs. Macdonald that he would go back and tend the horses. We had fine seats to hear, a bench where Hennie could find us easy. He said as he'd be back quick.

Willie Macdonald, the oldest boy, was right smart; he went along with Hennie. It was him that brought the news back: 'Say! Hennie's found a fly looker he's crazy over! They shook hands and she throwed her arms around his neck!'

By God, but wasn't I jealous! I thought: She can do that if she wants to but I won't!

After about an hour Hennie hadn't come back. Mrs. Macdonald said, 'I can't understand that boy.'

'I can,' I said. 'He's found someone that looks good to him!'

Then Willie come up. He'd been trying to keep track of Hennie. 'He lied to me!' he said. 'He was to wait there till I got back but he's gone.'... It was getting late. Hennie was going to take us over to the barbecue. Mrs. Macdonald was worried, thinking we wouldn't get nothing to eat.

I was all broke up, just as jealous as anybody ever gets.

Next time Willie come back I seen he'd been crying. 'Hennie's done us a dirty trick,' he said, 'but never mind, I'll take you all to dinner. I'll tell you what I think, Linney; he ain't treatin' you none too good. I don't think it's much of a nice woman he's with, neither.'

The rest of them et but I couldn't get nothing down. I was thinking of a dozen things. I was in love with him, that's it. And for my first sweetheart to take me out and ditch me! I was studying on it and getting hotter and hotter, wondering what to do about it.

Mrs. Macdonald was awful fond of us both and thought that me and Hennie was going to make a go of it. She was sending her Willie all over the place to look for Hennie. Every time Willie got back she'd send him off again. The sun was sinking in the west. It was only about an hour high when Hennie comes up to where he left us setting.

'He looked like a sheep-killing dog!' I told my sister when I got home. He couldn't look me in the face. A sheep-killing dog.

Mrs. Macdonald: 'Where have you been and why have you treated us like this?'

Hennie: 'I will explain to you....'

Mrs. Macdonald: 'You'll have a deal of explainin' to do before you get through with this. Sakes alive! Let's go. It will be dark before we get back, even leavin' now.'

Hennie tried to help me into the jerkey but I stepped round to the other side. He tried to talk to me but I never opened my mouth. He jumped out to help me off at Nancy's but I wouldn't let him. I thanked Mrs. Macdonald and said good-bye to them all, but not to him.

Nancy told me I looked pale and worried.

'Maybe I am,' I said, 'but I am riled more'n anything else. What do you think that sneak-bill done?' I asked her. 'I'm through with him,' I said, 'forever!'

'You think you are, but it's only a lover's quarrel.'

'There ain't been no quarrel. I don't want nothin' to do with him. When he comes in here I'm a-goin' to walk out!'

That went on for three weeks. Hennie come and talked to Nancy and tried his best to talk to me. Then he got Mrs. Macdonald to come down to tell me how he couldn't sleep nor eat, and begging my pardon, and saying he'd do anything I asked if only I would talk to him.

Now here's the part where I done wrong. Yes, it was a warning never to spite nobody, but it come too late. I'm not saying I wasn't right to square accounts, but there is ways and ways to get even and I went at it wrong.

I had it studied out. I decided that I would give him something to remember me by, as much as he give me: I'll be nice to him, then I'll throw him down like an old busted jug! Get even with him, that's what I wanted!

We made up. Hennie proposed to me and I took him. He become quite anxious to set the time. I said there wasn't no hurry to get married, but Hennie was determined to rush it along; he was fixing to speak to papa. When it got that far I made up my mind — I made up my mind fast for a kid not yet fifteen. I went to Nancy and I told her I never had no intention of marrying Hennie.

'What did you do that for then?' I said I done it to get even. Nancy said, 'Don't you know that's wrong?'

'I dunno. You wouldn't leave me alone, and he wouldn't, and Mrs. Macdonald wouldn't. I give him a dose of his own medicine.'

When Hennie come and I told him, gorry, he was broke up terrible. He bawled like a calf. But when Nancy told her husband, Henry Stacker, he said, 'Why, he's nothin' but a brayin' jackass anyhow!' Henry Stacker didn't like him at all, he wore too fine clothes to suit him and was from the city. He liked plain, ordinary people that would get in and work like hisself.

There had been two young fellows boarding at Nancy's — Joe Gribben and Bill Young. The uncle of Bill Young lived about a quarter of a mile from us. Both them boys come from well-fixed Kentucky people and they liked it that our family was from Kentucky, too. I didn't have much to say to them because I thought they was fresh; besides I was going on with this other thing and had plenty on my mind.

One evening, about this time, Willie Macdonald come down and told me that his kid sister was sick, and that Mr. Macdonald was away, and would I come over that night and help nurse her. Of course I went. About an hour after I got there, in come Hennie Fuel.

It was just a put-up job on me. But I was too big a coward to go home in the dark. I set up and talked to him the whole night through. It ain't easy to believe but I done it.

Hennie said I wouldn't make up with him because I was in love with Bill Young. 'I'm goin' to kill him,' he said, 'and I'll show you what with!' He raised up his vest and right in there he had a big long knife in a scabbard. 'I'm goin' to give him this!' he said.

I tried to laugh and talk him out of it but there was no laughing about it. I could see it in his face — it was changed somehow and his eyes scared me.

After a while, as a josh — there was apples setting there — I said, 'Give me that bloodstained knife of your'n to peel an apple.' I was laughing; but not Hennie, no laugh come from him.

I asked him, 'Don't you know you're actin' daft to talk to me like that?'

'I don't have no idea that I will be livin' two weeks from now,' he said, 'so what's the difference?' He give me the craziest answers, no matter what I'd say.

The night passed and it come daybreak. The moment I could see to go through the woods I told him I was leaving. When I was about twenty yards away from Macdonald's I turned around. Hennie stood there in the yard with his head down. I called back, 'You ain't licked so long as you can laugh!' He looked up then. I throwed my hand up to wave but he didn't wave back.

It's all very strange but it's written just as it happened. A week after I dreamed that Hennie come and was standing by my bed. He looked sick.

'I have come to say goodbye to you,' he said. 'I will be with you all the time for a year. I won't bother you none after that.' After a second or two he said, 'Yes, I am goin' away.'

I woke up and I must have screamed out. Nancy come over to my bed and shook me.

'I ain't asleep. I'm wide awake,' I said. I was shaking all over. 'Henry Fuel's been here.... I think he's dead.'

Nancy told me to turn over and go to sleep. 'You're jes' foolish,' she said.

Next morning I was good and sick. My heart was beating so hard it scared me. Is this retribution? I thought. Am I going to be sick and die? Then I turned to my old ways, I went to praying!

About eight o'clock — maybe it was nine — I heard someone come in, and Nancy starting half way up the stairs, calling me. 'Linney, Linney, come down, Mrs. Britts is here.' She was one of the neighbors. 'She's got something to tell you.'

I thought she looked kind of concerned. 'What is it?' I asked her.

'It's bad news. Henry Fuel got hurt yesterday afternoon.

He died at one o'clock this morning.... Your sweetheart is
dead.'

It was all in the paper later. It happened over at the McFarland place. McFarland's two boys, ten and eleven years old,
was standing by watching the hired man trimming off a tree
he'd felled. He was about half way up the butt when Hennie
come along. Him and this fellow was friends. He said howdy
to him but Hennie never answered nothing; he was acting
crazy, they all said so.

Hennie got up on the butt, cussing and threatening. The
fellow warned him: 'I ain't done nothin' to you, you better go
tend to your business!' It didn't do no good. Hennie pulled
out his knife and started edging up on him. The farm-hand
tried his best to ward him off, swinging his axe and ordering
him to stand back. But Hennie kept on coming.

The little boys testified to it. Hennie took a couple of steps
more and made a lunge with his knife. He was trying it again
when the axe catched him. Struck the handle of Hennie's knife
and sort of turned down and went in, right across where his
belt was. He fell off the log and the little boys and the hired
man run for it. When they got to the house they told what
had happened.

Mr. McFarland went to New Maysville, about two miles
away, for the doctor as quick as he could. They carried Hennie over to the house.

He could talk. 'Doctor,' he said, 'when you get back to
town tell the boys I say there ain't many can say he's seen his
own entrails!' He was bright as a dollar. That's when he
asked one of them to fetch me. But there wasn't nobody there
that knew me, nor nothing else.

This was midnight. They thought he was going to get well
and he thought so, too. There was no vital cut inside. He was
washed up and cleaned, and the doctor said he didn't see no
reason why he wouldn't be up and about in ten days.

It wasn't an hour before he asked for me again. And sudden
like he said, 'I am goin'; I want someone to pray for me.' In a
few minutes he was dead.

There's no telling exactly what happened. Hennie might have been drinking. But one thing is sure, he never would have touched the farm-hand for no right reason. He wanted to die and that's all there was to it.

When Mrs. Britts told me what she heard, that awful feeling left me. Then I just set down and thought about everything. And I didn't do much more than set for a whole year. I put in a year of repentence, I guess you might call it. Believe me, I wanted nothing more to do with boys.

At Nancy's they was all busy. I wanted to go home to papa but Henry Stacker couldn't pick up and drive me twenty miles — just to suit my whim. I longed to get away, to leave my troubles behind me.

I told my sister I was going. 'There's no one to take you,' she said.

'I'm a-goin' anyhow, I'm a-goin' to hoof it.'

She asked me, 'How will you get across Haw Creek?'

And when I started I was wondering, too, how was I going to get across? But I wouldn't turn back. I told myself, I'll stay there till someone comes along with a wagon.

I waited an hour by Haw Creek but nobody come and it was getting down along to the afternoon and I had ten miles to go yet. There was a kind of fence across the creek from one bank to the other, to keep the cattle from straying. I was afraid to start through the current — it could have knocked me down. But I had to chance it, there wasn't nothing else to do.

I took my shoes and stockings off and stuck them in my bosom, and I lifted my clothes around my middle and waded in, holding tight to the fence. The water come way up and pretty near upset me more than once but I made it taking it slow. I looked around to see that there was nobody watching me before I climbed out. I stayed like that and let the wind and sun dry me off.

When I walked into our house they was sure surprised to see me. My stepmother was just so glad that her eyes filled with tears. And papa was took back so he didn't know what to do I loved them and they loved me.

'Papa,' I said, 'I want you to drive me over tomorrow for my clothes; I'm a-comin' home to stay.' Then I up and told them all my troubles. They didn't know a thing about it. Twenty miles was like ten thousand miles today.

I stayed right at home the whole year and had nothing to say to no one nor nobody. All I done was to walk my horse around the place, though at first I wouldn't go outside hardly. I was scared to move two steps. I was sure Hennie was with me; I felt it. Papa used to make me get on my horse and go here and there. Riding was supposed to be good for me and they kept me at it as much as they could.

But nothing interested me. I was afeared — thinking of Hennie in his grave, and that he had done it a-purpose for what I done to him. They all thought I was losing my senses.

It was just a year after. Papa was away with my stepmother. I had Hennie's picture with a white muffler around his neck. I was standing in the middle of the floor. I was looking right at it, imagining I seen Hennie's lips moving though I couldn't hear the words. Then suddenly his voice come plain: 'It's all gone now, it's past and I'm a-leavin' you.'

I commenced to scream. And I couldn't let loose of the picture, I couldn't move. I don't know how long that lasted but outside, way off, Alfred heard me. He rushed in and jerked that thing away from me. I didn't stop squealing until he slapped my jaw on one side and then the other, just as hard as he could slap with his open hand.

He said, 'You get on your bonnet. Me and you are goin' to my place right now!' I hadn't spoke to his wife Rebecca for near a year. We'd quarreled over my saddle and horse. But Alfred made me go. I give in.

Alfred told Rebecca to be good to me; he thought I was cracked. But after that I come out of it. The scar's on me — I'll always have the scar on my mind. It left something for me to study on. It took a lot of poison out of me, and revenge. It made me so that I never tried again to get even.

I learned how to forgive; nobody can do nothing to me, I don't care what it is, that I won't forgive them.

It was the best thing that could have happened to me, though Hennie Fuel had to die for it. It learned me not to hurt people, doing things evil to bring suffering to others. Spite work falls on yourself.

Chapter V

I WENT back to sister Susan's. Now that I was bigger I liked to be with her. She was a worker and so was I.

Williamson Page lived five miles away. I had seen him but I hadn't never talked to him before. We walked from church a time or two....

I didn't stay at Susan's long. Alfred come after me one night. He said somebody at papa's wanted to see me but he teased and wouldn't tell me who. It was Bill Young that I hadn't seen for a year. Him and Joe Gribben was back from Kentucky and boarding at Nancy's.

I took to Bill Young because I knew he had people that amounted to something — his uncle lived close by — while this other fellow, Gribben, hadn't nobody that I knew of. Don't that show how calculating a young girl can be when she ain't really in love with a man?

I got to going with Bill. What I mean is, that when the time come for bed, Bill would be asking me to sit up with him an hour or so after the others turned in. Bill was all right.

Nancy said to me, 'I think you have made your choice but I would have taken the other one. He's got more brains, he talks best and he's best lookin'.'

'I know something about Bill,' I answered, 'and I don't know nothing about Joe.'

'Bill Young says he's all right.' Bill told Nancy he thought Joe's people had plenty of money.

It went on this way for some time and I was beginning to like Bill pretty well — he was more lively than Joe. Joe Gribben was certainly a gentleman but awful serious.

In about a month Joe had a bad accident. They was cutting wood and shipping it away by the carload. Him and Bill was doing this. Joe's axe slipped and slit his foot wide open. He near bled to death before they got the doctor. They had to cord up his leg to stop the bleeding. The doctor dressed it every day for two weeks. He wanted Joe to go to the hospital in Ladoga.. But no sir, Joe just stayed on.

Well, I reckon I fell in love with Joe. Bill Young was there, too. They got so's they wouldn't speak to each other hardly. Bill was always nice and courteous to me. But he told me, 'I step out — Joe's the one you are in love with.'

Joe asked me to marry him. I said I wouldn't give him his answer until I seen my dad. There's where I know now that I wasn't in love with him. Love ain't like that.

Papa and my stepmother come to visit Nancy about this time. Papa said as it was all right, he thought Joe was a gentleman. I told papa I didn't like the idea of leaving him and living in Kentucky. 'Never mind,' he said, 'you can work Joe to come and buy round these parts.'

Well sir, it sure is strange when you think about it, how scary a child can be when it comes to taking her out of her element. Joe told me he was going home to make arrangements for us to live in Lexington. 'We'll get married here, then I'm takin' you to my sister's. I want you to have a governess that'll learn you everything that is pertainin' to a lady, to take your place in life where you belong.' I begin to think on that. What I had to go through with, me that had never been to school. The more I studied on it the worse afeared I got. I talked to papa and to Nancy. There wasn't nothing I'd keep from them and my stepmother.

Long after I found out that Joe's people was stylish and went in Lexington society. Joe didn't want to rush me into that without he felt I could be happy there, knowing as much as everybody else knew. He was trying to make it easy for me. He didn't want me to grieve and sicken.

He went home to fix everything while I was having time to think. And thinking about it sure enough made me sick — just what Joe didn't want to happen. I begun to get pale and lose my appetite. My stepmother told papa I was fretted. He called me to him and asked me to talk it out, papa did. 'It's simple,' I said, 'I don't want to go.'

'It's goin' to be all right, Sinney, me and ma will go with you a bit.'

'But you won't stay,' I went on. 'You'll leave me and come back here, and I'll be shut up with a woman that's goin' to teach me. I can't do it!'

'It seems to me like, Sinney, you ain't in love with Joe.'

'Yes, I love him, I love him plenty if he'd stay here. I want to be his wife — if I can live like other women and go to house-keepin' like my sisters.'

Papa said: 'You're goin' into a great deal higher company than your sisters ever traveled in. You're goin' to be made a lady of, a Southern lady. I know their class and they is sweet women.'

I went home with papa; and when Joe come back to Nancy's he borrowed a horse and rode over. It was near winter. We had a big fire going. First supper. We set round after; then me and Joe walked out through the trees. If I go to Kentucky with Joe, I thought, I'll never see them old leaves fallin' again.

But there wasn't a word said about it then. When it come bedtime, me and him went outdoors to let the family turn in. They was sound asleep when we come back and set down by the fire. Sure, when I had a beau, I had to do my sparking in front of the old folks. It was all done in the same room. They turned their backs.

Well, I up and told Joe. He tried everything but I stuck to my point. Joe had to go back to Nancy's; he was finishing up his business around there. Nancy took a hand in it, too. She told me how much better I'd be off than her and the rest of the girls. 'You are missin' the best thing that you'll ever come up against in your life. You'll never have to work none.'

'I ain't afraid of work!'

But Nancy didn't feel that way about it. 'I'd marry him; I'd marry him quick!' she said.

It ended up just as I say. Joe had to go home but he'd be back in three months. He come back; I should say he did. I was over to Susan's meanwhile. And inside that time I got to going with Williamson Page and getting very much interested in him. Willie was about twenty-nine years old and a plain kind of country boy, one of my own class. A farm boy.

My brother Alfred took me to my father's. Joe was waiting for me; we set and hashed it all out but it wasn't no use. He loved me, Joe did; he knew I was an innocent girl and he'd seen a lot of the other kind in his twenty-four years, like them city boys does. Joe was always giving advice. 'Don't ever let no man lollygag you,' he used to say.

Joe was leaving and he looked pretty blue. Going back he'd have to travel by the graveyard where Hennie Fuel was buried. 'Joe,' I said, 'stop and look over the wall and think to yourself, would you rather be layin' there like him, or turned loose, with a blessin' for your happiness?'

'I can tell you now,' he said, 'I'd rather be as I am.... But I care a lot, and I'd have liked to have proved it to you.' He turned around and took me in his arms and hugged me.

'Remember what I told you about other men,' he said. Joe wasn't thinking about himself, he was like that.

I mightn't have married Willie Page if it hadn't been for all I heard around there about the Page name. Specially old man Page. He was very wealthy and give them all a home — every one of his ten children — eighty acres of land each, there in Hendricks County.

I'd be hearing, too, what Willie Page said, when I was only a child, that he was 'goin' to wait till that little red-head sister of Alfred's grows up.' He said it the day brother Alfred married Rebecca McCloud. Rebecca's mother was Willie Page's sister.

Willie waited on me for a year even after I was growed up. Alfred told him to take it cool. 'She's red-headed, you can't drive her, but she'll come round!' Alfred was strong for Willie. ... But my stepmother's nephew, Harry Staton, come mighty close to busting in on Willie. 'Uncle' Joe Staton was the richest man in them parts and Harry was his only child.

One of the neighbor girls was out in our yard seeing if I'd go to church with her next day, over to Haw Creek. I was in the shade washing my go-to-meeting dress. We had a cow in the clover patch, right close by the house, and next to it was a cornfield but no fence between. Papa was setting on the porch and he sung out, 'Sinney, the cow's in the corn, run her out!' I started off flying but I stepped in a hole and fell down.

'Goddamn that old post-hole, anyway!' Hearing me say that, not over twenty foot off, was two young men dismounting by the gate! And there I was, a young girl, swearing and cussing. Sure, I felt ashamed.

They was going into the house, but I cut across the clover patch, up to sister Betty's as fast as I could travel.

Betty told me, 'It serves you right, Linney, a-cussin'.'

'Aw,' I said, 'it jes' slipped out.'

I waited at Betty's quite a while and kept watching. Them horses still stood there. Then somebody come out and started leading them over to the barn.

'You're in for it now,' Betty said, 'it must be some kin of mother's and they're stayin' for the night. Streak for home and get on some nice clothes. Jes' walk down bold-like and be introduced.'

I done it and it worked fine. This young fellow, Harry Staton, asked me could he go with me next day to church. Sunday evening he asked me could he come back in a week. I told him no, he could come the Sunday after that. Willie Page had been coming to see me every second Sunday and this happened to be Willie's off Sunday. No, I didn't want no tangle.

It went on for five months like that and I was kind of up against it. Willie Page or Harry Staton? I couldn't decide which. Willie was always rubbing up against me and filching kisses, but the other one — never.

I told my stepmother I didn't know which I liked best.

'In accordance with that I don't believe you're much in love with either of them.'

And truthfully I don't believe I was myself, when I come to find out what love is.

Willie asked me to marry him but I wouldn't give him no decision. And the next week I said something to Harry that hurt his feelings — I accused him of going with some other girl — and land sakes, if he didn't propose to me!

I believe now it would have been best if I had married Harry. Harry was a goer; he was a money-maker and out of a fine family. Not that Willie wasn't of good stock too, but he was the baby and spoilt. He hadn't been made to work; he didn't know what it was like....

In about a month, I guess it was, I told Willie Page I'd marry him. It was right after the end of the Civil War. Papa had just bought my sister Susan's place and give Alfred the old homestead. We was married at Alfred's, on a Sunday forenoon, by old Adam Feathers. Then he goes over to the church after he marries us and tells the congregation about it. 'I'm come from joinin' Abe Plunkett's Linney,' he said, 'and Williamson Page!'

After meeting they all come over to papa's house where the wedding cake was baked and everything set for a big dinner. Me and Willie wasn't there. We lit out. We knew they'd be fixing for a shivaree and we dodged them. Jumped our horses and went to my husband's sister's place for the night. We was hiding out. We was ten miles from the old homestead.

Next day when we got back my sister Betty come up to me. 'I got something to tell you,' she said. 'Everybody was happy, and wishin' you much joy, and eatin' the cake, but one.'

'Who was that?'

'Sammy Booker!'

Sammy had been trying to go with me, and papa and his father had talked it all over and wanted us to get hitched. They promised each to give us forty acres of their land that joined. Eighty acres, quite a temptation for two young 'uns. But I didn't take to Sammy. He was a fine boy but he had ground-hog teeth. His upper lip wouldn't cover them. I never seen so many teeth put together in one mouth!

One time papa asked me, 'What have you got against Sammy? Is there somebody you like better?'

I answered him, 'Don't you think a woman wants to be kissed by her husband? How the devil's Sammy goin' to do it?' Wasn't that an awful thing to throw up against anybody? God a'mighty's truth, I did think of that!

Chapter VI

I WAS Malinda Page now, married to the youngest of the
Page children. Willie was the last one home and it was
supposed he would bring his wife to stay with the old folks
so that they wouldn't be alone. But mama Page had her
heart set on Willie marrying a cousin, to keep the Page lands
in the family, for one thing. And she was so vexed the way
it turned out she wouldn't have me in the house with her.
Bob Page was Willie's brother; him and Liz, his wife, was
living about a half mile north of the old folks. Mama Page
made Bob and Liz move over with them and give us Bob's
place — just as they left it exactly. Liz didn't move a stick
of furniture.

Mama Page was raising a little boy that Agatha, her
daughter, had adopted. Agatha died and the old lady kept
the child. It was him she sent over two days later to see what
kind of girl her Willie had married. He was a cute little cuss
about ten years old. He stayed a few minutes.

'What's she like?' she asked him when he come back. I
hadn't met Mrs. Page but that didn't keep her from hating
me.

'Pretty!' he told her. 'You'd sure like her — I jes' wish,
grandma, you could see her!'

'What are you talkin' about?'

'About her that's married Uncle Willie — what did you
send me for otherwise?'

That was the first time that my sister-in-law knew that
Mrs. Page had sent him. Liz was standing there and heard it.

The old lady said, 'Don't you be tellin' me she's pretty....'

'Well, she is! If I was a man and seen her first Bid wouldn't
never got her.' Bid was my husband's nickname.

Now there was a heavy ordeal come upon me. A week
after we was married papa Page took sick, awful bad too,

and of course Willie had to go down nights. I got it into my head, the way I'd heard, that the old man wasn't going to get well. And I made up my mind that I didn't care whether Mrs. Page spoke to me or not. I was going with Willie to see his father and do all I could to help nurse him.

'Mother is ornery,' Willie said. 'She won't speak to you. Are you goin' to let it hurt you very much?'

'It don't matter, I'm a-goin' anyway,' I answered. I felt sorry for Willie. I done it, too. I went the next evening after supper — about sundown; it was light yet.

We walked in and Willie introduced me to both of them. His father was in bed and the way he pulled me towards him I knew where I stood with him. I kissed him on the forehead.

He was seventy years old. It was dropsy that was killing him fast. He was all puffed out and couldn't breathe hardly.

Every time Willie went, I went along. I set with the old man by the hour. Him and Willie wanted me to eat there but that I wouldn't do. I stayed by him right to the last, though the old lady never spoke to me.

The corn was setting there in Bob Page's field, in the shock, all bunched together and tied. Bob was still cultivating around our house. Willie's corn was three-quarters of a mile away and he kept putting off the time for getting it in.

'The summer rains is comin',' I told Willie, 'I'll go with you and help.'

'You couldn't if I'd let you, account of the Spanish needles and the cockle-burrs. 'Tain't woman's work.'

A cockle-burr is a rough, sticky leaf that talls up two to three foot. And Spanish needles, they're a curse for horses that run out in pasture if they ain't cut down

I told Willie straight out: 'You sure don't cultivate right if that's true. Why didn't you kill 'em out when they was green? You got 'em in there now and they'll come up worse'n ever.'

But he wasn't thinking about burrs. Dodging work was all that was bothering Willie; it pretty near kept him busy. He was a good man, he never give me a cross word in his life, but he didn't like work.

'I'll wear a calico dress,' I said, 'in place of this worsted thing.' I took and turned it up short — there wasn't no short dresses them days. I went there with Willie, and legged it home again at noon and got dinner, and legged it back again. I worked right along with him. I never thought about making the old lady mad.

It was about a week when I seen Liz. Mrs. Page had told her: 'There she is provin' to me she ain't no good, with her dress pretty near up to her garters!'

Liz tried to explain: 'It's to keep from gettin' her skirt full of burrs.'

But it didn't make no difference. Mama Page had all kinds of excuses to dislike me.

I give up. I said to Willie, 'I ain't a-goin' there no more. She hates me and I'll jes' stay away.'

Willie would beg me to go with him when he went over but most times I kept away. 'Get your mother to come to us and eat a dinner up here. Then I'll forget everything,' I said. I had my reasons for wanting the old lady to eat a meal at my house. Not that I wished to put any detriment on Liz, because I liked her. But this house of hers and Bob's, that we'd moved into the next day after we was married, was the dirtiest I ever seen. I cleaned it proper and I didn't much mind who knew it, including my mother-in-law.

Willie come home for his dinner every day and Bob was cultivating his place round our house. One time I asked Willie, 'Why don't you invite Bob to come in here and eat his dinner with us?' Bob had something the matter with his arm — he'd had the white swelling when he was a boy — but he was a worker. He'd get tired and the arm would begin hurting him. I thought he ought to come in and eat his dinner and lay down before he went back to work. Willie asked him, and after that he et dinner with us.

There's where Bob done wrong. He begin to brag on my housekeeping and meals to Liz and the old lady, and how clean the house was. I was sorry because I thought a lot of Liz and she started to treat me cool. I asked Willie about it, I couldn't understand it.

The old lady told Willie what ailed Liz. 'Eh,' she said, 'do you wonder at it?'

'Willie,' I said, 'I reckon I'm in a hornet's nest; I've made another enemy in the Page family.'

'Jes' do what's right,' he said, 'regardless of everything. You're married to me, you don't have to please the rest of 'em.' But Willie's big talk didn't mean much. I knew that already.

I coaxed it out of Willie. There'd been some pretty hot words between Liz and Bob that I wasn't supposed to know nothing about.

Liz said, 'Maybe you're sorry you didn't meet Linney before you met me?'

'If I'd seen her before Bid I might have got there first!' That's how Bob answered Liz.

Now that was uncalled for. It was a hard thing for her to stand, him coming in and saying such like, bragging on another woman.

But Liz got over it and got to liking me again, the same as ever.

And as time went on the changes come. I'd been married the first day of April and next year, come the twenty-fifth of May, we had our baby. It made quite a difference with the old lady; she begin to mellow on me.

Willie had been staying pretty close at home and looking for this. On Monday morning he asked me, 'How do you feel?' and I said, 'Fine.' I did, I told the truth.

The corn was planted and Willie hadn't nothing to do. 'How about my goin' fishin', Linney, for two or three hours down the Eel?'

It was only a little ways off and I was glad to have him go. But he wasn't gone an hour until I was about as sick a woman as anyone'd ever want to see — and all alone.

We had a pen of unshucked corn, say a couple of hundred

foot off from the house, that Willie had sold to Mahoney, our nearest neighbor. Mahoney wanted to get a load of it; he sent his wife, old Katy, up to shuck it, to have it ready when he drove over.

She was outside there working but I hadn't seen her. I was feeling so bad I commenced striding up and down. I didn't know what to do. I went to crying out loud and she heard me. In she come and I was certainly glad to see her.

She asked me, 'Do you know what's the matter with you, Mrs. Page?'

'I think I do, I reckon I'm goin' to have my baby.'

That dear old lady trotted nearly all the three miles to my doctor-sister Betty's. They come back riding double.

Betty put me to bed and about two in the afternoon Willie come and him and Betty stuck their heads together. Betty thought I'd better have a man doctor so Willie went over to New Maysville, across Eel River, for old Doc Long that attended to papa and the family as far back as I could remember.

A woman that was expecting had to take good care that she had plenty fixed to eat for her neighbors when they got there. There was no telling how long they was in for. There wasn't no paying these friends so you had to treat them good.

Them days there wasn't no twilight sleep. We had children natural and stood our misery. Doc Long told Betty, 'I think everything is goin' to be all right but I don't like her bein' so long.' That was Wednesday night.

He give me something that eased me entirely. Maybe, it was chloroform. I went to sleep and after a while when the pains commenced again I hollered for more of that stuff. I was talking silly and off my head. Finally he give me another whiff but that was all.

About three o'clock, Thursday morning, Ollie was born; he weighed more than nine pounds.... When my papa heard as I'd had a young 'un, he cried. I was only eighteen, he didn't like that part of it. 'A child has a child,' was what he said.

Mama Page showed up when the baby come and took care

of me like one of her own. Being a granny makes a lot of difference....

I was young and healthy and everything went fine. Only for one thing: I give too much milk. Ollie couldn't take it all and my breasts got sore. Lumps come in them. The old lady was scared and sent for the doctor. He wouldn't use turpentine — it takes the soreness out but it dries up the milk. He tried camphor but it didn't help none.

One day he asked mama Page did she know any place where she could get hold of a puppy. I heard him. 'What!' I said, 'do you want me to raise a dog with my boy?'

'It's the best way, with no one to come here and draw off your milk.' And by crikey! If he didn't start out to find one, and come back with a female fox terrier — a little thing, a right young puppy! I put it to the breast and it sucked just as easy as the baby.

Ollie, when he begin to get a little old, would reach over and get hold of the pup's ear and pull it; I had to take Ollie and hold his hands. When the baby went to growing and the dog, too, it's the truth, I had an armful!

I was worried about Willie, he was dawdling the whole day through. It wasn't account of myself. I was happy enough, only I knew it would be his ruination there with the Pages. I aimed to make a man out of him and I never could around there. He was living in a nest of them, like a young bird too lazy to step out for itself.

And besides, I was tired of trying to make mama Page like me. It was something you had to keep at, and I didn't think nobody was that important. She wasn't the praising kind. I thought I'd win her through work but I couldn't hold a candle to that dried-up old lady. Didn't weigh a hundred pounds, but she made me feel like three cents when it come to getting things done.

Ollie was about a year and a half old when we had a chance to sell out to this same Mahoney, the Irishman, adjoining our place, and we let him take it. We didn't know where we was

going but I was glad to move. Willie's sister, that he thought
so much of, lived in Boone County about four hours by wagon.
Her name was Demarias Gardener. We went to visit her and
I liked it, and as we was going to buy somewheres she said
we'd better settle there where land was cheap.

Demarias wanted to know if I remembered seeing a big log
house over to the right, about a mile before we come to her
place. It was high-raised on a knoll.

I started Willie out to look it up and we had it boughten
three days after we got there. Demarias said it was the only
place she knew of in the whole country round about that was
any good and for sale. I reckon we paid about twenty-five
hundred dollars. Sixty acres, I'm sure of that; forty acres was
in cultivation and twenty was in timber. The house had four
big rooms; once it had been a country church. The logs wasn't
hewed, they was sawed nice and smooth. The cracks was
filled with chinks and lime until they come out even. The
ceiling was level and I whitewashed it with lime. Oh, I was
going ahead!

They have heavy winters in Indiana, I couldn't do nothing
out of doors but milk my two cows. Coming on spring I was
fixing to plant the garden. We had a fine space all paled in,
and a strawberry bed from one end of it to the other.

It was my duty to do like every other woman. I made the
family jeans, my husband's the same as for the children when
they come. I had patterns that you could lay out and chalk off
where the joinings was to be. There was nothing boughten of
a store before Ollie was ten years old. I knitted and made the
clothes and stockings and mittens. I even knitted Willie's
suspenders out of yarn, with the buttonholes in them and
everything. Every stitch of wool clothes that the men folks
wore in the winter the women made. The summer clothes we
made out of flax.

So that's the difference between country people then and
now. There wasn't no idle women and mighty few divorces.
Men and women married to spend their time together as long
as they lived. They worked, both of them. That's probably

the trouble now, they don't work enough. But it's not for me to say. All I know is that it was different then.

People round there seen me selling chickens and ducks, and their eggs and feathers, and butter and milk. They used to look at me and say that I was right smart. I was hard working, but when it come to brains I didn't have none. God, that's the truth, and here's why I say it. I couldn't spare the time so I used to send Willie to Lebanon, five miles away, with all this stuff, and if we had any kind of vegetables that would sell, I'd fix them up, too. He'd have a list of what I wanted him to bring in exchange.

And many times Willie come back staggering sick with a blinding headache. I'd put him to bed and I didn't know — or ever dreamt of such a thing — that he was drunk. For five long years. That don't sound much like brains. Smell it? I never thought of such a thing, and I wouldn't have known the smell of it if I had. I used to set by his bedside crying, and thinking I was going to lose him! He'd lay there mumbling, and talking jumbled up, and me believing he was out of his head with pain. Can anyone imagine a woman that much of a fool? Plain ignorant. I never thought of looking in his pockets or asking him about his money. I didn't know what a saloon was.

The Pages was Black Republicans. The whole bunch of them was staunch for the Union, and patriotic. Willie had been in the Civil War on the side of the North and was discharged for disability. He volunteered for three years when the first call come out, and he served two of them. He was very much lauded for it.

Willie drawed a good pension from the government so he had his own money to spend. The Page family was wealthy and Willie was going to have plenty and I never thought no further than that. I was happy. Ignorance made me happy. Good thing I was a young fool.

I found out later. Not the old man, but everybody else in the Page family loved liquor, even mama Page herself. So it was inborn in Willie. Mama Page kept a bottle of cherry

bounce to take for her cough. She'd go to coughing but I
don't know whether the drink was the cause or the cure. I'd
see her cover up the fire, leaving some live coals for next day;
such a thing as matches wasn't known. She would rise up in
the middle of the night and light her pipe with a coal — start
it to burning and inhale that smoke down her windpipe. First
the cherry bounce and then her smoke. And she'd stop coughing right off. I just mention this because I mind what she
done.

The first year at the new place I hadn't but the one baby
but I found out I was going to have another. It meant I had
to work harder than ever to get ready for it.

I had to take Ollie out in the fields while I was working; a
two-year-old ain't so very independent. I dropped every hill
of corn in a twenty-acre field. And where it didn't come up
good I done it over — an apron full of corn around my waist,
and a baby in my belly. At eleven o'clock I walked home to
fix dinner. I went right back again after the dishes was washed.
When there was a little spare time I'd hoe in the garden. The
garden was my job; Willie had his'n in the fields. We hadn't
no farm-hand the first year, but later on Willie hired one.

When fall come and there wasn't nothing much to do outside
I worked indoors — stripped cane and sent it off to the mill to
make our syrup out of. Everybody had molasses them days,
a barrel full to a family. And the beans had to be dried —
they was piled on the floor two foot deep. I used a shillaly to
beat them out of the pods. The whole place was covered with
beans, but I done it in a day and had the room spick and span
before supper. We aimed to have a bushel of dried beans over
the winter. I strung them with a darning needle; my winter-
dried beans, soaked and cooked, tasted just as good as beans
off the vine.

The apples I dried and put away; then come up the making
of apple butter and preserves. And the pumpkins. Some
people say dried pumpkins ain't any good, but they make
good pie.

Baby May was born the first day of November, on a blue sky Monday morning. Old Aunt Mary McCloud come to help out. I didn't have a hard time at all, and when they put her in my arms and I looked down into that little baby's face, I told her, 'You won't have to work like mama if she can help it.' And I said to Willie, 'The boy's your'n but the girl's mine!' A feeling come over me that May was going to be with me always, much closer than anybody else. That turned out to be true.

Aunt Mary didn't know how to take care of the baby, loving and playing with her, but not keeping her clean. I told Willie I didn't want her around. 'If you can't go after your mother account of the bad roads, you watch Ollie and fix your meals, and I'll tend to May.'

I washed her good with castile soap, and I put a little starch on her skin — that's all I had — to soothe her sore spots. I took some soot off the fireplace and dusted her with it. Inside twenty-four hours she was healing up. It's as good as anything I know to cure inflammation. But it's mighty hard to get now. Soot ain't so common as it was.

When May was six weeks old we took her down for Willie's people to see her — thirty miles distant. Called on them all. Mama Page fell for her. She liked her black hair and blue eyes— I got on to that right away. They was all crazy over her, swore that she looked just like the Pages — and she did, she was the spit image of them. They all had the same hair and eyes. And I didn't mind, I wanted May to look like Willie; he was a handsome man.

It was that visit I seen Andy Page's white house, trimmed in green. Andy was the richest of all the Pages, a big dealer in mules. ... We stayed the night — they put us in the parlor. And honest, I just lay in bed and studied it out, how wonderful it all was. I wanted a house like that, a big two story white house trimmed in green. I wondered if I would ever get one like it.

I liked to go to the Campbellite church that was about a mile and a half from us. We had a mighty nice house with

plenty of room and such like, and every Sunday dinner nearly
I had a minister or two to cook for, eating up my chickens —
all the good it ever done me!

But I didn't have the things to wear like some of the other
women that went over to the store and bought them. It set
me to thinking. During the summer I'd been trading with
the huckster — his stuff for my chickens and eggs. And now,
when he got to carrying drygoods, that just tickled me. I
could pay him for what I wanted without putting up real
money.

I needed thin white lawn to make the baby some clothes
out of and I bought about three yards of it. I seen in his
wagon a remnant of pretty blue percale with white polka dots.
I made up my mind to have that and make me a dress. There
was seven yards that cost me six cents a yard. I got some
lace, four yards for baby and one for myself — at four cents
a yard. And some pink ribbon. If I'd known the trouble I
was heading for I never would have bought it.

When I got through making May her little outfit there was
some of the white lawn left over. I bought a yard of dotted
white swiss, I forgot to mention that, to make her a bonnet.
There was also some of that left, it fell to me, too.

I went at it with my fingers — no sewing machine yet —
and made me a skirt, and a basque. It was the habit then to
make sleeves long with a ruffle around the wrist. In the place
of that I made elbow sleeves. And I left off the ruffles around
the hips and put them, very scant though, at the bottom of
the skirt. It fit me just as tight and pretty as could be. I
weighed about a hundred and twenty-five pounds, I never
weighed more than that for years.

I had nice stockings that I'd knit out of fine linen thread. I
couldn't wear my farm shoes but I had an old pair of gaiters
that I made do.

I was up against it for a hat. I dug out a frame that I
thought would be easy to cover. I covered it with a piece of
white satin off an old dress. I took and made a big black sun-
flower out of some ribbon off the same dress. I tried it on but

it didn't look good. If I only had a feather, I thought, a nice long ostrich plume like women was wearing. Well, I made up my mind I was going to get me a feather. I went out in the yard and picked up a great long gander quill. I took and shaved all the feathers off — it was about fourteen inches long.

We had some white turkeys — something new in that country. I called Willie — I have to laugh when I think of it now — and I asked him to catch a couple of gobblers and pull out some of the big feathers under the tail. Of course Willie wanted to know what was up. But it was all right, he done it.

I took a darning needle and run it into the quill and the gobbler feathers after it, all around wherever there was room. It took time punching holes in that thing.

The hat was black and white but I wanted a little pink to go with the pink ribbons on my dress. Outside in front of the house was a hollow stump with pokeweed berries growing out. They're dark red, about as big as a shoe button, and the juice is the color of blood. I squeezed some out and weakened it down until it was just a pink color. Now this was a very delicate thing I was undertaking — that's what I was thinking. I got me a hen's wing for a paint brush and tried it out. It worked fine and I speckled my feather all over.

I looked in the glass and I never seen a prettier hat. That's so, and I've paid fifty dollars for a hat at Marshall Fields, from Paris! To think how I worked and how proud I was of that rigging and what a row it led up to.

I'd been cleaning house, just as happy as I could be, and getting ready to go to church. In my new get-up, of course. Ollie all scrubbed, and May looking pretty as a peach. At church I went and talked to everyone. I didn't see no difference in the people; they shook hands with me the same as ever and said all sorts of things about how nice the baby looked. Only I noticed they didn't mention my clothes.

About ten days later than this, Willie's mother arrived and I was mighty pleased to see her. I liked her by now, she wasn't the torment she had been. But she acted funny, she acted cool. She made a fuss about May the same as ever but she sort of passed me over. I went ahead and fixed a fine dinner and along about three o'clock, when she was setting there knitting — she hadn't hardly talked to me all day — she up and speaks:

'Linney, are you busy now? I want to talk to you.' I gathered up my knitting and set down. 'Maybe it'll hurt your feelings but I got something that has to be said. Demarias was down last Sunday and told me you was the talk of the whole county.'

'I ain't done nothin' in the world to be ashamed for. I been home takin' care of my house and my children.'

'You go to church Sundays, don't you?' I said I did. 'Well, I'm a-goin' to tell you what Demarias told me. You come to church the last two times dressed like a New York millionaire!' (So that was it.) 'You know that Willie can't stand that kind of pressure against him; he can't afford it. You come walkin' into church, with Ollie on one side of you in his white waist and black panties, and the little girl lookin' like a doll in place of a baby. She says you was dressed in the most gorGEEous clothes that she ever seen in her life, or anybody else, and that every eye in the church was turned to you.'

I asked her, 'What else did she say, about what people said to her about me?'

'That they was goin' to have you brought up in church, to know why you come like you was goin' to a party.'

She meant that they would bring charges against me. I busted out crying, I couldn't hold it. 'Mother,' I said, 'do you believe that?'

'I don't see how I can dispute it when my own daughter told me.'

'But you don't know how Demarias treats me. She hates me!'

'Why, I thought you was the best of friends.'

'I treat her right because she's Willie's sister, and I'd like her if she'd let me.'

She asked me why Demarias hated me. 'I don't know,' I

said, 'unless it's account of the time her Tom come in and seen her abusin' me about my white hands. Tom said, "Linney, don't you pay no attention to her, she's jealous, that's all!"' I told her some more Tom said: '"Demarias thinks as how I like you better'n I like her!"'

For about a minute the old lady set there thinking and not saying a word. Then: 'Well, I never thought of that.' No, she hadn't.

Demarias hated me from the beginning, for no better reason than I had married her baby brother. Sisters is that way sometimes; they will hate any woman that marries into the family. Why she wanted us to settle down near her I don't know.

'Stop cryin',' the old lady said, 'and tell me all about this. I want to see them things that you wore. Put 'em on jes' like you was dressin' yourself and let me look at you.' I dressed even to the shoes.

'Where did you get that outfit anyhow?' She didn't give me no chance to answer. 'Honey' — that was the first time she ever used the word to me — 'don't you know that people, when they see you dressed like that, knowin' your husbands' a country man and ain't able to afford it, they'll talk.... Now you tell me where you got it, won't you?'

I told her how I come by it. Every lace and ribbon, and every cent that they cost. She made me go over it all again and took it down on paper. I never seen a look like that in a woman's eyes. 'Do you know what that cost?'

'I know about,' I said.

'I'll tell you to the cent. The whole shootin'-match cost ninety-eight cents!'

'That was my money, too,' I said. 'I traded it off the huckster. Willie ain't spent a dollar on me since our weddin' day.'

Believe me, here was something coming from that old lady who never praised nobody. 'I ain't much of a hand to pay compliments but that dress and hat beats anything I ever seen. I'm only afeared what they'll say that don't know the truth.' She was woken up all of a sudden that here I'd been trying to put my best foot forward; yes, she finally understood.

And if she didn't give Demarias a tongue-lashing and make her acknowledge her lies! The old lady never said so, but Willie told me. She made Demarias admit she hated me.

Chapter VII

I DIDN'T want no more children. I had my home, my work and everything that a woman raised like me could wish for. Two children was enough.

There wasn't no quarrel with Willie, no words. I was his good wife in every respect — but I wasn't going to have no more babies. And when I said that it meant something because I was posted. The many times I lived with my sister Betty, the doctor, I was poking my nose in medical books. I knowed more about how things was than the girls around me.

Then we went to visit Mary Lindren, my niece, over Saturday night. I didn't carry no paraphernalia because Willie promised to behave hisself. He didn't, and that's where our troubles commenced.

When I found out I was having another baby I wasn't only unhappy, I had an awful bad feeling towards Willie, too. I had one thought all the time, I wanted to run for it, get clear away from everybody, to live among strangers.... It ain't to be wondered at the way my second boy turned out. How can I blame him, though he's been a tramp and a wanderer all his life? He's lived everything I wished for and thought and wanted for myself while I was carrying him.

Sudden like I lost my father. Alfred come and told me papa was very sick. 'Will he get well?' I asked him. 'No,' he said, 'and if you want to see him you will have to come now.'

I was expecting in six weeks. This was February. They fixed a feather bed in the sleigh and put me in the middle of it. It was twenty-five miles in a bad storm. We got there four o'clock in the afternoon, and the next morning papa passed away. He'd been asking for me, saying 'Sinney' over and over. Betty took me in to him but he didn't know me. How sad I was! Part of my world was gone forever.

When a man died and the estate was settled, the widow

was supposed to get one-third of everything. My stepmother said she didn't want her share when papa died. 'I don't need it. I never earned it and all I'll take is a child's share. There's six of you, and with me there's seven. I want a seventh like the rest.

'I'll tell you what I'd like,' she said, 'jes' all of you chip in and buy me Susan's feather bed.' Sister Susan had finished one from her own geese. There was forty pounds of feathers in it and we paid Susan fifty cents a pound. We give my stepmother that and she was happier with it than all the other things.

She had five or six children of her own. They was all married. Her oldest, Jim Staton, went to Iowa in the early days and done good. Later he turned minister. The others was living in Iowa, too. My stepmother hadn't seen them hardly at all so she went there after papa died. We heard from her but never seen her again.

It was nigh on four years after I had May that my second boy come. I named him William — not after my husband, but after my youngest brother that died. Will was as pretty and fat a little thing as I ever looked at but he didn't fill my heart like May done.

Carrying the child and working so hard, from that moment my health begun to fail. Will was born the eleventh day of March. In the fall and winter before, I spun and wove four blankets. And made up all the clothes, the jeans and flannels for the whole family, knitted all the stockings and everything.

I had been cutting rags for two or three years. I must have been a glutton for punishment. I set at the loom — just four weeks before my time — and wove a rag carpet. With the breastpiece of the loom rubbing against me, and a grease cloth tied around my stomach to keep it from hurting, I finished the carpet and tacked it down. Sunday I cleaned house and got ready. Monday, after dinner, I had an eleven pound baby.

I want to say something here about my boy Will. He never

would have no education; he wouldn't go to school and I had to force him to learn to write his name. I learned him to read by paying him a nickel a line. I paid him, for I had money enough; he was thirteen when I commenced to bribe him that way. He would study like everything, until he got together twenty-five or thirty dollars and away he'd go.

Everybody likes him — until he gets mad, then he smashes things. Thank goodness he ain't never done nothing to put him in jail. I don't think he ever will. He sounds like a fool, but he ain't. He's smart in his way; he's got the best memory of anybody I ever seen. His trouble's a craving for travel — he has a mania for moving. He'll work at a place to make enough money to leave it. Hasn't no trade. Farming is what he likes, and best of all he loves horses. He can drive an eight horse team as good as the ordinary man can lead a cow.

I got an awful temper when it's roused but it takes lots to do that, and there's the difference between me and Will. He gets mad pretty fast. It's lucky he never married although he come mighty close to it once. He was in love with a gal but hadn't nothing to keep her on. She was only sixteen. I wouldn't stand for it, though her mother was agreeable. I told her: 'He ain't no account. He won't stay in a place long enough to hang his hat up!' Nothing come of it, and Will never looked at another woman since — not twice anyhow.

He's just a bum. He's been here with me in Chula Vista four or five times but I don't let him stay. I buy him some nice clothes and then I shoo him off. I make him take care of hisself.

Will's never been sick but once — when he had the smallpox out to Mary's house on the Boise ranch, and by gosh, they had a terrible time keeping him in bed. Wanting to leave the house with the smallpox!

He chews tobacco. That ain't nothing, but he's the first I ever knew to swallow the juice! I ain't joking, that boy of mine eats it and likes it. Listen here, I seen him set in one room for four hours and never get off the chair, with a quid of tobacco in his jaw.

I asked him, 'Will, what are you doin' with the juice in your mouth?'

'I swallow it,' he said, 'there ain't much.'

'No you don't!' I couldn't believe it.

'I don't swallow the tobacco but I swallow the juice, and I like it.'

He looks young though he's near sixty — I reckon tobacco juice is preserving him.... The last time I heard of him he was in Texas; he'll be showing up here one of these days.

We settled up papa's estate. Then I had money. But I didn't keep it. I give it to my husband. I kept a little, one or two hundred dollars — but the rest, about three thousand dollars, I give to him. I hadn't no sense about money matters and I was raised that the man was the head of the family. I'd have turned it over to him if it had been a million.

We had the money to go West now, and that is what Willie Page had always wanted. The government promised all army men a hundred and sixty acres of land, anywhere that there was territory open. Willie, since we was married and before, too, picked out Kansas and was aiming to go there.

We went and visited the folks first. We stayed a night at brother Alfred's. He told me I looked awful bad to start out: 'I don't think you ought to go, Linney. You're so weak you can't hardly walk across the floor.' It's a fact, it was all I could do to lift my baby to nurse him.

Alfred went over to New Maysville, where Doc Long lived, to ask him about my taking the trip. And when the old fellow found out who it was, that it was Plunkett's Linney that was sick, he come right over.

He never expected to see me in that fix. I was full of life when he knew me before. He set and talked to me, an old, old man, talked so sweet and kind: 'You're in a mighty bad condition to travel to Kansas, and carin' for three kids. You'll have to bring all your bravery to the front, and keep thinkin' of them and forget yourself.' He told Alfred he didn't expect as he'd ever see me again. I noticed how he squeezed my hand. 'Remember what I told you!' he said the last thing.

We rented our Boone County place. Then away we went, three wagons of us — the Charlie McCoombs, the Terhune family, and us. Willie bought him the best outfit there was. He had plenty of money — my money. New harness and a fine span of mares — not mules. And a covered wagon, with wagon-bows and canvas.

We started out late one morning, knowing as how we had to get through Sugar Creek bottom, an awful heavy-timbered piece alongside the creek. Sugar Creek was almost a river. That's where I seen the first bridge large enough to have a sign on it:

KEEP TO THE RIGHT

THE LAW DIRECTS

The horse-thieves was pretty thick around there. They'd nose in from another county, looking around, pretending they had something to sell. And come back at night after horses. The settlers hung a horse-thief them days without much palaver.

It was drizzle-wet our first night down in the creek bottom and black as pitch. There was three dogs along, each wagon had a dog. Willie had three horses — an extra one, a black stallion we called Coaley. And the other two parties had three horses apiece, so there was nine good horses all together.

By gum, the dogs commenced to bark and run up to the wagons like something was fretting them. (The dogs wasn't the only ones!) Willie had the wagon loaded, the boxes level so we could put a feather bed on top. We all turned in. I was the last one, I never did really get undressed.

Here commenced the barking again, just as dark as it could be, no moon, and no stars account of the timber. Directly a horse started neighing and one of the other crowd hollered, 'Page!'

'Yes, what's the matter?'

'I think we better put on our clothes and have a look around. Sounds to me like somebody's after stealin' a horse!'

I must say this, I was an awful coward. Even after I was a mother I kept on being afraid of the dark. Sometimes I would go outdoors just before dark, and when night come on I'd be afraid to go back in the house. There I'd stand, outside, with the baby in my arms waiting for Willie to come home.

I'll never forget that night down there in the swamp. Nothing happened to me that ever touched it. Dogs barking, horses neighing, and me crying. Good Lord yes, I set up most of the night and whimpered.... Baby begun to cough croupy, too. I was near dead with fright.

Next morning was beautiful and sunshiny. I was feeling better and the baby was nothing serious, just a little cough. There was fried meat and bacon and eggs for breakfast, and coffee; and I baked biscuits. For the children I had some bottles of milk along and special food. We bought milk the same as now. But I didn't know what bread was that wasn't baked at home — never had seen a loaf of baker's bread until we was about four days out on this trip. We could buy a loaf as big around as one of them today and about eight inches long. For three cents. I went crazy over it, I thought it was the best thing I ever tasted. I got so I could eat half of one of them loaves at a setting. I mended over it. Every day I got better.

We traveled like that for thirty days, stopping and going. When we got to Topeka I asked the others: 'Where are you people goin' anyhow?'

They didn't know; they was in Kansas, like us, to get cheap land. I told them, 'I got Willie talked into rentin' a house for the winter.' Right then it was mighty cold. 'I'll stay here with the children and let him inquire around.' They stayed three or four days and that was the last we seen of them until we got back to Indiana.

We rented a house, and bought a cheap stove and a bedstead and such like. Just what we could barely do with. Willie took a horse and rode about and asked questions, but he wouldn't budge outside the town account of the cold.

We stayed in Topeka three weeks. Then we loaded up again and moved on for ten days more. That made forty days living in a wagon by the time we got to Beloit, Kansas.

We camped there a couple of days, while Willie was riding around on his black horse, looking at the country. He got acquainted with some people, Uncle Sammy Moore and his family, and had dinner with them in their big rock house. They give him antelope to eat. He come back and said as how they wanted me and the children over. Nothing would do but we had to sleep there. They treated us like they knew us always. They was hungry for company. For downright decent people they beat anything I ever met.

We lived with them two weeks while Willie and the men went hunting and had a grand time. At last the Moores heard of a homestead that sounded good.

'There's a dugout on it,' Willie told me, 'and a good well, and ten acres of ground broke. I get everything, and the benefit of the six months the man's stayed on it. But I will have to pay him twenty-five dollars to buy him out, and it's only one hundred and twenty acres.' Willie thought he ought to have the hundred and sixty acres that was coming to him from the government.

'You take it,' I told him. And I said, 'It's more'n you'll ever plow!' There wasn't a piece of timber on the place; all he had to do was to stick the plow in and go to work.

Well, we moved in. Willie unloaded. I had my carpet along so I walked out on the prairie and gathered a lot of grass. It was dry, just like straw. I spread that over the dugout floor about six inches thick and nailed the carpet down.... The dugout was fifteen foot one way and twelve the other. It went into the ground four foot. The walls was slabs of solid slate. It was sort of like a cellar.

The Solomon River was close to us, all sycamore and cottonwood trees along the banks. The man that built our dugout cut cottonwood poles for the roof. He covered them with thick layers of prairie grass and weighted it down with dirt. It made a fine roof, only that the dirt would trickle through. I took our canvas wagon top and used it for an inside loft to catch the dirt.

I set up my bed over in the back corner. There was two windows in the dugout, one on either side of the door. Opposite the bed, in the other corner, I set my stove to keep the babies warm. There was a lot of cottonwood trees, chopped up and left outside. 'Gee,' I said, 'there's plenty there to last all winter.' It lasted longer than we stayed....

When I got the place tidied up I was happy as anybody could be. Anyhow, it was home. There wasn't no farm work now, Willie hadn't been doing nothing. It suited him but it didn't suit me. 'You ask Uncle Sammy Moore,' I said, 'if there ain't such a thing as haulin' goods from Solomon down here.' Solomon was the end of the railroad, everything had to come that way. Willie rode over to Beloit, a couple of miles, and he found a storekeeper that wanted a load brought down from Solomon. Willie went over with the team — it took him three days to make the trip but it paid good.

I was looking for Willie home in the afternoon. There sprung up a little breeze but I didn't pay no attention to it. It begun to blow harder and harder and I went to looking around to see the cause of this. Well, if there was one, I seen a thousand head of antelope coming my way, backjumping and frisking!

There wasn't a soul but me and the children in sight, and I hadn't nobody to ask. I seen a great long streak of dark blue on the edge of the horizon — that, and this whole drove of antelope. I was wondering what it all meant, and marveling. It was all so pretty, but mighty strange out there on the open prairie.

The blue on the horizon turned black. It was cold, too. I commenced collecting up the chopped cottonwood and the chips, all that I could pile down in the corner of the dugout. Cottonwood kindles like a candle nearly. It ain't much good for throwing out heat, but it was all there was.

Coming out to Kansas it blowed so hard the horses tails stood right out to one side. Twice it blowed the canvas off the side of the wagon; both times I put the children on the ground and covered them up. It almost blowed their breath away. But this was worse, much worse. Outside I couldn't hardly stand up to it. 'A real norther,' I told Ollie, 'the kind your ma's heard tell about.'

By then I seen Willie coming on a trot, setting bareheaded, and no load except some cottonwood limbs he'd throwed in as he passed along the creek bottom. He wasn't loafing now, he was coming fast!

'Well, we got it, ain't we?' he hollered.

It was getting late and I told him, 'Don't waste no time gabbin'; chop wood, as much as you can!' We went to bed early. It never stopped blowing all night. I could hear the soft dirt from the roof trickling down; we'd have had a bad time without our canvas.

I just liked to never got nothing cooked for breakfast — the wind drawed the fire out of the stove and out the stovepipe. It was nine o'clock before I had the children fed. Just as fast as Willie chopped wood and brought it in, it was burned up. Willie was all in: 'I can't do it,' he said; 'I give out.' He had to chop the logs in two and split them or they wouldn't go in the stove. His axe wasn't sharp, and cottonwood it's soft. It's like hitting a sponge.

'Well,' I said, 'what's the consequence of that, for me and the children to freeze to death?... I'll carry in the chips, you jes' chop!'

The children was playing and didn't know there was any trouble at all. No snow, just wind that cut to the bone. Every time I run out, the door slammed and held so's I couldn't hardly pull it open. This kept up until noon time, with Willie chopping and me fetching logs.

Then I happened to look our across the prairie and coming from over the Moore way I seen a team of mules galloping! Uncle Sammy Moore sure enough, standing up and waving his black snake whip! In a jiffy he was ordering me around, saying what to take and how to wrap the babies up.

And when he got us over to his place he kept us a week.

The wind blowed two days and nights more and he was afraid it was fixing to repeat, he'd seen it do it many times. I was scared just setting there and watching. It blowed so hard I thought in my soul the windows couldn't stand against it.

Willie'd had enough. No other wind-storm was going to catch him in Kansas. Uncle Sammy argued but Willie stuck by his guns. He was going home! 'I'm jes' makin' a brief visit like John Brown done. I'm a-clearin' out,' was what he said.

Uncle Sammy, the old darling, the best man I ever met in my life, he asked Willie, 'Are you intendin' to take them babies off and leave us all alone?' Willie said: 'I hate to do it but it can't be helped.'

'Well, maybe I can talk him outen it,' I said, 'I'm willin' to stay.'

And I was. I wanted to stay right bad when it neared the time for leaving. But Willie was scared to death; he was for a fact. Perhaps he wasn't to blame but I thought he was. He'd got hisself a homestead in Kansas, spent money and time getting there, and he was quitting like any yaller thing. That's what he was doing and I said so. 'Look at Uncle Sammy Moore with a fine house, a nice well, and a rock barn stuffed with provisions.' It was great country with wonderful crops, but it took nerve and Willie didn't have it.

I cried all the way, driving back to Beloit — wild prairie chickens running through the brush and crowing, and the sun shining so beautiful. There'd been a dew freeze on the grass and it sure was sparkling. 'Willie, look what a place we're leavin'! As far as you can see there ain't a tree to grub out. And the land all fenced in with rocks that nature has provided a-purpose.' I see it all now, there never was nothing prettier than the Solomon River valley....

Willie didn't argue; just drove ahead. It made me mad that he wouldn't stand up and fight back. Willie would have been a more profitable man if he hadn't been like that.

Willie didn't have much business sense, anyway. Listen to

what he done. Horses was very valuable in Kansas and we had three. Our outfit was worth a thousand dollars easy. But Willie paid out three hundred dollars for a freight car to ship them horses and the wagon back to Indiana.

Willie took us to the train and bought me a ticket to Lebanon, the babies was too young to have to pay for. I don't think there was any such thing as berths, anyhow there wasn't on this train. I could put the children on the seats and they slept good, but I done my sleeping setting up. Willie give me twenty dollars, thinking, with the nice lunch I packed, there wasn't nothing to buy but a little extra food going through. Willie got his fare free riding with the horses; he was two weeks getting home.

My ticket was good for a free transfer in St. Louis from one station to the other. But when we come to St. Louis there wasn't a transfer in sight and we missed the train. I set and waited in the depot. I asked the man in the station what the trouble was. There was something wrong that I couldn't get at, something in the air. I set and set, with the babies fretting and having no supper.

Then the train master come along. 'Where did y'all come from?' he asked.

I told him, from Beloit, Kansas.

'Don't you know what's happened here? Things is in an uproar, the epizootic has killed nearly all the horses in Missouri!' No, that was news to me. 'You will be well off if I get you away from here tonight,' he said. He went bustling off.

Everybody around there was trying to get a carriage for us. About eleven o'clock a man that owned a hack, not a bus, come in and asked me, 'Where do you aim to go, lady?'

'Any place where I can get a room to sleep.' I didn't say nothing to this party, for fear he wouldn't take us if I asked him how much he was going to charge.

Over to the hotel I asked him, 'Will you come back in the mornin' to get us to the train?' On the other side of town, East St. Louis. He promised. 'Pay me then,' he said, 'then you'll know I won't forget to come back!'

I thought that was mighty decent. You run across lots of kind people in this world and you run across lots of hateful people. I met both kinds in ten minutes. I told the hotel man I wanted a room. 'How much is it?'

'Ten dollars,' was his answer. I looked at him but I kept still. I knowed I had it to do. But when he seen I was going to take the room, he said, 'You can't sleep in one bed with all them kids.'

'Why not, I'm payin' for it? Ain't it up to me how we sleep in it?'

'Three dollars extra that way,' he said. Thirteen dollars for my night's lodging! Wasn't that a scrubby thing?

Next morning my friend, the hack driver, took us across town and was very pleasant. At the station he carried out the luggage. 'Now lady,' he said, 'I'll help see you on, though every moment of my time is worth money. There ain't many of us left to carry things across and the Lord knows how long my horses will keep goin'.'

I just felt so bad. I didn't know what to do because I didn't have money enough to pay him.

'How much are you chargin' me?'

'Five dollars.' The way he said it, I guess it would have been ten if he hadn't been sorry for me.

The tears come to my eyes. I asked him, 'How much do you suppose the hotel charged me?'

'About four or five dollars, in these times when everybody's tryin' to make money offen everybody else.'

'Thirteen dollars!'

He moved up closer and looked me in the face. 'How come?' he asked. Then I told him. 'I can't do but one thing,' I said, 'and that's give you every cent I got and that's jes' two dollars. You give me your address and name and I'll send the rest so soon as I get home. I'll start it in two days.' I'd be with brother Alfred by that time.

'No,' he said, 'give me the two dollars. You had enough trouble already. I reckon I'm doin' wrong in takin' that.'

It's pretty hard to realize what traveling with three children and no money is like. How was I going to feed them, and still two nights and a day to travel? May and Ollie played and had a grand time and was nibbling at the lunch box all the way. Little Will was nursing. I didn't have sense enough to know that if I was starving myself I'd be starving my baby. During the whole trip I never touched a morsel of food. The little fellow, laying in my lap, commenced to whimper and beg, and I couldn't understand it. When I made out the trouble I moistened crackers and let him suck them.

There was a man that set right in front of me, very nice appearing. I took him to be about forty years old. After a while he said, 'It's kind of lonesome to be travelin' alone, ain't it? I mean, without a person to talk to. Where are you goin', and where are you from?'

I told him all about it; he was very much interested. And he did pass the time and helped me to forget my troubles. He kept going out at stations, buying crackers and fruit. The children took some of everything but I refused. To tell the truth I wasn't a particle hungry.

Coming into Indianapolis he said, 'Mrs. Page, forgive me if I should say something to hurt your feelings, but ain't you travelin' without means?' I hated to tell him that I didn't have a cent. 'You set here,' he said, 'without a meal of vittles, and nobody's brought nothin' to you. I was wonderin' if there wasn't cause for it.'

I wouldn't lie about it but I was ashamed to tell him the truth. I was wondering what to say when he spoke again: 'You're goin' to have supper with me when we get in! There's a fine restaurant in the depot.'

I couldn't eat a mouthful. I tried but I couldn't. I asked for a glass of milk but he made me take coffee, the first I ever tasted in my life. I reckon it was the best thing. The children couldn't eat much. 'All of you ain't et enough for one person,' he said.

He got us seats in the waiting room and said goodbye. Then he went over talking to some people setting there — a whole row of them, wearing bonnets. He talked to one and then to another. I couldn't make out if he knew them or was just getting acquainted. Directly I seen one of the women get up and come toddling across the station to me.

'Art thou travelin' alone?' she said. 'Where is thy husband?'

Then I knew what she was. A Quaker. And them was Quaker bonnets on their heads. They'd been to a conference and was going home. About the time she went back to join the others I seen the men standing up and putting their hands in their pockets.

God! I thought, is that for me? No one that hasn't had it happen knows what it feels like. I begun crying; I couldn't hold back.

'Thou must take it,' she said, 'thy children need food.' She just piled it down in my lap and walked off. Twenty-five dollars! More than Willie give me at the start; and now there wasn't only them few miles left, a night's ride from home.

Everybody in the world at some time or other has been up against it somehow, and it ain't sense to let pride get the best of you, but I felt a beggar....

At Lebanon I went to a hotel and got us a room. That was the first real sleep I'd had since I left Beloit, Kansas. I was just natural wore out, with a big baby in my lap the whole trip, and taking care of two other children. Old Doc Long was wrong; I had the constitution of an ox.

Chapter VIII

WHAT a stretch of bad luck struck us when we got back to Indiana! We could have sold our outfit in Kansas, but nothing would suit Willie except to ship everything back. And we wasn't at Alfred's a week when all three of our horses died of the epizootic.

Bad times followed everything that Willie done. Willie bought Alfred's best cow and she laid down and died. I asked Willie, 'Is there a curse on you or what is the matter?'

We had to commence again in our Boone County house — the tenant left, he give it up to us. We stayed on two years more. We started out hopeful, trying not to think about Kansas, and working to make ends meet. But we didn't make no money. To think that Willie was offered four thousand dollars for our place before we left for Beloit and refused it. We didn't owe nothing then; now we was in debt to the bank.

Somebody had to do the thinking for Willie. 'Let's clear out,' I said, 'we won't get nowhere here; let's rent the place.' He was offered two hundred dollars a year, which he could use for taxes and interest. 'You got to do something to pay off the bank or you're goin' to lose the whole shebang. Move away and start fresh,' I told him.

I wanted to go to the Wabash River country, it was the most fertile valley anywhere near us. My sister Nancy was there, she'd rented a piece out Black Rock way and was doing fine. Willie was sure he could do good, too. The plan was to rent a farm, pay the rent with part of our crop, and maybe put something by.

A horse and a cow was all we moved. We could buy pigs at Black Rock. We come across two empty log cabins about twenty foot square, that belonged to a widow man by the name of Delaney. He said we was welcome to them and didn't have to pay no rent. They wasn't much to crow over. We cooked and et in one; the other we used for our setting and bedroom.

We rented ground from Delaney down by the river, the best black soil I ever seen, about a mile from where we was living on the uplands. It was a fine prospect to make good and pull us out of debt; we could have made five hundred dollars the first year.

But no — there come along a flood, the most heart-breaking thing; it side-swiped the whole valley. It took Willie's crop with it. I set on a hill and seen everything he'd planted being washed away. It was awful; it made you feel so mightless. I think a flood is worse than fires and cyclones.

Old man Delaney lost over two thousand dollars in the wink of an eye. Willie said: 'I ain't goin' to worry over it. Delaney don't say a word and look what he lost!' The water come up to Delaney's back door and drowned about twenty head of hogs he couldn't get out from the pen. If it had come any closer he'd have had a terrible time.

'No, we won't give up. We'll try another year,' Willie said.

Near us a man by the name of Burroughs lived, with his wife Judy and their twelve year old boy. Nobody liked the woman, they said she was cracked. She got sick about this time. 'There ain't nothin' wrong with her in the world,' said my sister Nancy, 'only her doctor is watchin' over her.' She was expecting — but if the neighbor women knew it they didn't care; they thought there was something going on between her and the doctor.

I didn't know Judy Burroughs. I asked Nancy to go with me to visit her. Trying to mix up where it wasn't my business — but I was glad I went. I found her just a sweet person. Right off she told me what was the matter with her. And she said, 'There ain't been a soul to see me or nothin'; now you know how lonesome I am.'

She had a dozen different kind of roses growing that she'd nursed herself. I didn't have no flowers at my place, only wild larkspur, and some sunflowers. When I told her, she picked me a wonderful bouquet. 'Them's the first I ever give away,' she said. 'I love my roses but I know you do, too.'

Judy had her baby. She got on fine for about ten days. Then, when she was ready to get up and out of bed, she took to feeling bad. The doctor come twice a day but he didn't know what was the matter. She just lay there in a sort of half faint. She'd brighten up and be herself for an hour or two, then go off again.

The doctor become distressed and asked about her people. He thought maybe if she sent for her sister it might help. So they got off a telegram to her. There wasn't much of that them days among country people, but they managed it. The sister come but she didn't get there in time.

Poor Burroughs didn't know what to do after Judy died. He couldn't manage without her, he didn't know which way to turn. Tom Delaney rented the place off him or we'd have took it. Tom was the bachelor son of old man Delaney. Burroughs had eighty acres of the finest land, up and away from the river, and Tom leased it all. Burroughs stayed there with his half-growed boy, and the sister took the baby off with her. Tom moved his bed up and the three of them lived there together, until Burroughs and the boy left. Then Tom Delaney was there all alone. So I asked Willie, 'Why don't you talk to Tom and see if he'll let us move in with him? I'll do the cookin'.' My idea was to get where we could have a real roof over us. I wasn't feeling none too good, with back hurts and pains, and I wanted a warmer place. I hadn't forgot them nice roses, neither.

Willie went and seen Tom. 'I don't know but as I might take you in on this,' Tom said. 'There's enough ground here for both of us.'... Believe me, I was happy to get into a real house.

We had some friends back home, some young girls, and Lidy Weaver, one of them, wrote out to me could she visit us. She come, and of course Tom Delaney was there. Gosh sakes, they was married in my house, all in no time. Borrowed a dress of mine to get married in!

They moved out and we had the place to ourselves. But hold on. There was another girl back near Lebanon that wrote me, while Lidy was visiting us, before her and Tom was married, wanting to come on. That was Burpee Priddle. There wasn't no room for her then. But after Tom went off with Lidy I wrote her to come along.

Burpee hadn't never been married and she wasn't so young, neither. Old man Delaney — that was Tom's father — come up to visit us and got introduced. He come again the next night, and stayed and talked long after me and Willie turned in. Then he come every night to see Burpee for a week. I seen her walking around one morning, picking flowers and pulling them to pieces. She seemed sort of nervous. I asked her what was up.

'Ducky,' she said, 'have you got time to tell me something? What kind of man this Mr. Delaney is?' I said as I thought he was a mighty fine man.

She said to me, 'You know, I ain't never been acquainted much with men.'

'Well,' I said, 'you can't get acquainted with them no better than to marry one.'

Delaney had already proposed to her. 'He wants to get married right away but I said as I couldn't do that, I'd have to go home and make the weddin' clothes.'

The old man was surprised at the idea of having to get something to be married in. 'Weddin' clothes!' he said. ''Tain't weddin' clothes they marry with in these here parts!'

'What will I do?' she asked me.

'Marry him. If you wait he might find somebody else he liked better'n you.' Burpee was married in the same dress that I loaned Lidy when she married Tom.

Tom took over his dad's lands down in the Wabash Valley. The old man moved away with Burpee, mighty glad to leave because he'd lost so much with the floods. And Tom was willing to risk it. So all this moving around give us the Burroughs place, and there we made a little money. Enough to go back to Boone County after the second year. The first year all went to waste account of the flood, but the second year we done better.

I want to finish up with Judy Burroughs. I went to cutting her roses and putting them in water, and I will take an oath, I never found one of them bunches the next morning that it wasn't wilted down, like it was dead. I ain't easy gulled but I stopped cutting them! Maybe she knew it and didn't like it and that was her way of asking me not to.

Burroughs had a big lamp, the finest in them parts. We didn't have nothing but coal-oil lamps — any of us. But this one held about a half a gallon and had a special kind of chimney and shade. Judy paid fifteen dollars for it. She loved that lamp, and anybody that passed by and seen it was sure to say as how it was wonderful. It truly was. When Burroughs sold out his stuff he told me he hadn't never lit the lamp hisself. Judy loved it like her roses, she told Nancy, next to her husband and her boy, and she said she never wanted no one else to use it.

Nancy's girl bought it off Burroughs. She took it back to her mother's and thought she had the grandest thing that ever was. But she never put a chimney on it and lit it that the chimney didn't crack in no time. They went to visit somewhere and Sammy, Nancy's boy, come home sleepy and lit the lamp. He laid down alongside of it. He must have dozed off. The next thing something jostled him and woke him up. The lamp was on its side and everything ablaze. He got out of there with nothing but his pants. The house burned up and everything in it — from that lamp.

That ain't all. Judy had dishes that she treasured the same way. Nobody bought them, so Burroughs left them with Delaney. They was too pretty to use, I set them up on the sideboard as a decoration. Night after night I'd hear them rattling. I used to say, 'There's a durn rat in there goin' to bust one of them plates!' But next morning every dish was setting just like I put them.

One of the neighbor women told me a story. I didn't believe it, and I don't believe it yet. She claimed she fixed the slippers on Judy when they put her in the coffin, and when they come back from burying her, there was one of the slippers in the house!

My Aunt Sally was living with us now. Her and May slept together, we had three beds in the one room. She called me in the middle of the night. 'I jes' seen Judy Burroughs!' She whispered it to me.

'Oh, you must be mistook,' I said.

'No, I seen her plain. I seen her there' — Aunt Sally pointed to the middle of the floor — 'and she walked all around and looked over everything. I thought it was you till she turned her face. She was smilin', as much as to say how everything was trim and tidy.'

We had been away from Boone County two dry years; two years of terrible crops. As lean as they was in the Wabash Valley we fared better than our Boone County tenant. He hadn't nothing to show for his toil and owed us two years' rent. He done the only thing the poor man could. 'Page,' he said to Willie, 'move in now 'stead of next March and take the crop for what it's worth. It's the only way I can pay you at all.'

It felt good to be back home and I thought maybe everything was going to go all right — even though we didn't have a dollar, only from what we gathered up and sold on the Burroughs place.

In March, following that fall, I fell sick with pneumonia. We'd been doing middling good, what I called blundering through. I know how I caught it — going out milking the cow in the cold. I didn't take care of myself — never had no time, the way Willie dawdled and loafed and left things undone.

The doctor's name was Tinkler, watching over me through this spell. I had five blisters that et into my flesh until there was sores like holes. We didn't have no cabbage like he ordered, but Annie Shepard, my sister-in-law, bless her, had it growing and she come and showed them how to manage it, drawing the corruption out with wilted, green cabbage leaves.

I couldn't stand a man that would let me suffer while he toasted his feet in front of the fire. I suffered terrible. I'd be

crying, and asking Willie to put on some fresh cabbage. 'I will,'
he'd say, 'jes' so soon as I finish my pipe.' Put-offs like that.

The God I believe in today is the power that's in us to do good.
But them days I believed like the rest of them. I prayed to God
to please to let me get out of that bed. I lay there crazy with worry.
I seen how it was. I thought: Everything that he's ever had in life
was give him. He ain't the sort to go to the bottom and climb up.
It's up to yourself, or the Lord help you and your little ones!

I kept thinking what Willie should have done and hadn't. I
had the time to study it out. I made up my mind it was sink or
swim, and saddled to Willie we'd all sink. Leave him! Staying
there meant hardship and want for the rest of my life. I was
praying for the chance to find something else for my children. I
promised God I would, if only I'd get well.

I cured up awful slow. On Ollie's birthday, the twenty-fifth
of May — I couldn't much more than drag myself around the
house — I made the children as nice a birthday party as I was
able. I knowed it was the last meal of vittles I'd be fixing them.

Mind you, I never had been away from them a day. I
washed their little feet and cleaned them up like always, before
I put them to bed and kissed them goodnight. Next morning
I said as how I was going to see their Aunt Mary down in
Texas. Then I was coming back to fetch them....

Ollie was standing, leaning up against the mantel piece.
May asked him, 'What are you doin', are you cryin'?' She
was about five years old, she couldn't understand.

'Well, don't YOU feel bad,' he said; 'don't you know that
mama's a-leavin' us and a-goin' away? Ain't I got plenty to
make me feel bad?' Ollie was nine.

'She'll come back after us,' May said, 'she told me so, and
Aunt Sally's a-goin' to care for us meantime.'

Chapter IX

I COULDN'T stand Willie's laziness another day. I wanted to get away from him bad enough to do anything.... I hoped and expected to gather up the children later on. I didn't know how, but I'd find a way.

Willie broke up the whole household after I left. He sent May with Aunt Sally, over to his sister, Annie Shepard; the two boys went with him to that hellcat Demarias that hated me. But he kept his promise by letting Annie have May, and if there ever was a good woman it was Annie.

Soon Annie picked up and moved off. It seemed like the family all moved to different places. Annie's husband was dead in the Civil War and she was drawing a pension. She went to Kansas and took May with her. Well now, Willie — that was one good thing about him — he didn't want the children scattered about, so he packed up with the two boys and went along.

When I started for Texas I was down and out, with nothing but a ticket and seventy-five dollars left from my inheritance. The train went to Fort Worth. My sister Mary lived out of Stephenville, over in Erath County. The rest of the way from Fort Worth, about sixty miles, I was fixing to make by wagon.

But at Fort Worth I was too sick and weak to go further. I found a cheap boarding house and got me a room and rested. I decided to stay there until I felt better.

Sister Mary was a money-maker. Her and Wesley Cunningham, her husband, went out to Texas and got a section of homestead land off the government. Later they bought another hundred and sixty acres close up. They had five children. Johnnie was their baby; I'm coming to him.

I wrote to Mary and give her my address at Fort Worth. I asked her to come for me in about a month, that I wasn't ready to stand the trip.

Then I seen that they didn't want me there at the boarding
house. Mrs. Swenson that was running it, she come in one day
and told me. 'Excuse me, for askin',' she said, 'but what's
the matter with you anyhow? I know you're decent by your
way of actin', but you ain't left your room, and all of us
a-hearin' you cryin' your eyes out?'

I looked her in the face. 'Are you a mother?' She said she
was. 'So am I, but through circumstances that I don't feel
like mentioning, I left a little girl behind that I never was
away from a night in my life. I was obliged to leave her;
I'm a-tryin' to gain my health to keep from leavin' her always.'

I said that I was very satisfied at her house and that I would
try to bear up. When she heard my story, she got real friendly.
'It's all right, now that I know how it is. I don't blame you
at all. Forget what I said, and if the others don't like it they
can move out.'

I thanked her, and I done my best. When I cried it was
under the covers. But I seen that I had to make a fight, or
what would I ever amount to? I asked Mrs. Swenson if she
didn't have something for me to do. I went around with her
and helped dust the rooms and fix the beds. I picked up, being
with her.

No letter come from Mary. They got their mail at Stephenville; I'd wrote to her there from Indiana and never had no
trouble reaching her. It made me wonder, maybe she didn't
want me now. And that was a godsend, the best thing that
ever happened; it begun to rouse up something in me that I
had to fight this battle alone. So I just opened up and told
Mrs. Swenson that I didn't have much money and had to go
to work. I dunno; all I can remember I didn't have enough to
keep on paying board, and later to hire somebody to drive me
to Stephenville.

She wanted to know what I could do. 'Anything under the
shinin' sun,' I said.

'There's an awful nice place here for a house girl. Mrs.
Leonard, that I went to school with, she's the banker's wife —
she wants a cook.'

Leonard & Adams was a private bank in Fort Worth. We went over to Mrs. Leonard's on the corner; the Adams place was right opposite. They was beautiful homes, both of them. Mrs. Leonard took me over the downstairs and showed me everything. They was swell. They was banker's wives; they was high-toned just the same, a class of people I hadn't never mixed with.

Mrs. Leonard told me I didn't have to do nothing but cook. I knew I could do it. 'We have a table waiter, all you need do is get it ready,' she said.

As I remember it, she paid me four dollars a week. She had a young darky named Adora to look after her two-year old baby. Adora come in and talked to me and that was all the company I had while I was there.

The first night I give them quail pie, and Adora said how Mr. Leonard told the missus, 'She's a good cook!'

Two weeks after I'd been there the coachman said that him and a friend of his was going over to Stephenville. Right then I told him, 'I want to go — not charity; I'll pay my way.' I heard from Mary, too. They was busy planting corn and hadn't been down to the post office for the mail. In her letter Mary set the time when she would come for me but that was still three weeks off.

We got to Stephenville, eleven miles away from Mary's ranch. I told them where I wanted to go, as near as I could. Both of these men was wide awake. The one that owned the rig said he'd ride me out but he'd have to rustle around to find my sister's place. He was going to see a man by the name of Jeff Cox. I never thought nothing about that, but the way it turned out it was the same Jeff Cox I was born and raised with, and him living neighbor to my sister in Texas!

After I got done hugging and kissing, all I said was: 'This looks like a family gatherin'. I thought it was a big world when I come out in it, but now it seems to me like an awful small one, seein' you people all neighbors.'

I begun to write Willie and tell him about everything. I thought I was through with him, but I forgot my animosity when I seen them homesteads. With the help of my brother-in-law I pictured it all out, and I done my best to wake Willie up. I wrote how I could borrow the money from Wesley to bring the children. Oh, he wrote me that he would come, but he didn't. I stayed there at Mary's all summer and the next winter waiting.

Come April, Mary decided she wanted to take her boy, Johnnie, to a place she heard of called Thorp Spring, about forty miles from Fort Worth. Mary had a fine span of mules and a brand new wagon, a covered wagon, of course. Johnnie had scrofula in the eyes. He was ten years old and I don't think he'd ever been able to look up at all, for the light. It did help him so that he could see the birds fly, and it liked to tickle him to pieces. It was the spring water done it. Johnnie got over that eye trouble and made a fine man.

We wasn't able to get into the hotel or any of the boarding houses at Thorp Spring — people come from all over in the summer for the water — but somebody that had jurisdiction over it told us about the schoolhouse that was empty in vacation time. We got permission to stay there; we bought cots and a stove and went to housekeeping.

At Thorp Spring I met Johnnie Ellis that had the grocery store. He wanted to call on me but I wouldn't let him. He didn't know that I was married — everybody called me Miss Jenny, or Miss Page. It wasn't none of his business and I didn't tell him. I said I hadn't no place to entertain in, living in a schoolhouse.

I was feeling that I was a wife and didn't want no company. But Johnnie kept on. You're dang right! He said, 'Why can't I come down Sunday afternoons? Your sister's there; you ain't alone?'... Well, I let him come. I thought it wasn't no harm, so I said all right.

Johnnie was a fine fellow and good looking. He was sure attentive and nice, it looked like every thought of his was to do something for me. He come Sunday afternoons; he got coming nights, too. One day, setting out in the shade under a big oak by the schoolhouse, I thought that I ought to tell

him how it was with me, a married woman with three children — and I did. I told him all about it.

And one thing more, too. 'Even if I was a widow tomorrow,'
I said, 'I never would marry again. One husband is plenty.'
I felt it, and I thought it was the truth.

'Still, even at that,' he said, 'let's go right on and be friends.
I'm awful sorry — I think a great deal of you, but I'm glad
that you told me.'

One day a man turned up from Ladoga, Indiana. Jonah
Small; he'd worked for Willie and lived with us for many
months. Back in Indiana I helped him take care of his two
little girls when his wife was sick and dying. We got to be
very good friends, and in that way he knew that I had a
sister down in Texas. So when he come down to Stephenville
the first thing he done was to hunt up Mary. Wesley Cunningham told him that we was at Thorp Spring and here he was
to see me.

With news, too! Jonah Small asked me, 'When did you
hear last from Willie?'

I told him not for a few months, that the one I'd been hearing from regular was my sister-in-law Annie. 'I know about
the children,' I said, 'they're fine. I'm fixin' so's I can go after
them or send for them this fall.'

Jonah give me a look. 'Don't you know,' he said, 'that
Willie's divorced you?'

'Why, my God no!' Not that I was so in love with Willie
but I never counted on nothing like that.'

Jonah Small told me why Willie wanted to be free. He
got going with a woman that wouldn't stand for him being a
married man. He didn't marry her though.

I didn't tell Johnnie Ellis for nearly a month. I let him
keep calling on me and I begun liking him. I wasn't in love,
I just liked him. One night I up and told him. I didn't intend
to be mealy-mouthed about it, I put it to him plain: 'I ain't
married no more,' I said, 'I'm divorced.'

'All right, what about you and me pairin' off?' It come so
fast the breath went out of me. Johnnie sure had a mind
of his own and a quick one.

'How do you know that I care for you enough?'

'Well,' he said, 'if you don't, I calculate there's time to get that way. I'll make you care for me!'

I did, I got to caring for him plenty.

Just then Mary, in place of going back to her home as we was aiming to do, decided she'd drive the forty miles to Fort Worth. 'Linnie,' she said, 'do you know what I've a mind to do? Load up' — and she could drive them mules like a man — 'and head for Fort Worth. I'm a-goin' to buy me some property maybe.' We was reading how it was growing there and she had the real estate bug.

So the next time Johnnie come, that nailed the thing. 'Let's be married first,' he said.

'No,' I told him, 'I want to go with my sister, but after I get there we can talk about it some more.'

Johnnie aimed to sell out and move to Fort Worth; he liked the idea of a bigger place. But he seen he couldn't rush me. Besides he knew he didn't come first, as much as I liked him. He told me, 'Jes' as soon as we're married, or before if you want it, I'll give you money to go after your kids.' We pulled out in about three days, us two women and Mary's boy Johnnie. We had eggs, bacon and ham, and we camped just like men.

Mary bought a big, fifteen-room boarding and lodging house at Fort Worth. But she only bought the house, the land that it stood on was leased. There's where she made a mistake, because when they went to work on the Fort Worth end of the railroad, building a branch through to Weatherford on the way to El Paso, land jumped sky-high.

We was there and settled, but I wanted to do something to forget myself. I was grieving for the babies, but I done my bawling in my room. Mary had turned the upstairs into furnished rooms and rented them out. But she didn't like to cook. She was very fleshy, weighed nigh onto two hundred pounds. I was the skinny one.

'Listen here, Mary,' I told her, 'I want to make a little money. I studied out a scheme to do it. If you'll let me have your dining room and kitchen, I'll take in day boarders and I'll board you and the boy free.'

'Sure I will,' she agreed.

I knew I could make some money at it. There was a compress, a cotton gin, over across the block from us. I went there and got six day boarders, at five dollars and a half each week. I bought dishes, tablecloths, towels and such things as I needed. And them men went crazy over my baking-biscuits — they was used to sour dough all their lives and they thought my biscuits was wonderful.

But Mary took another one of her notions. Wesley wrote her about all the work at home — it was branding time, they was gathering in the cattle — so she thought she was needed there. And good Lord, she sold out the rooming house right over my head.

I had to make up my mind quick. After buying and paying for them dishes and things I didn't want to give in. I had seven dollars and a half to my name but I wasn't going to ask Mary for nothing. Maybe she would have loaned me a hundred or two hundred dollars — I'm sure she would at that — but I was too proud to ask it. The boys all come to me in a bunch. They felt so bad when I said I'd have to break up. They wanted to know why I didn't open up a vacant house, standing over there by the cotton gin.

The day before Mary left I went over to look at the empty place they told me about. It was a double house and a Mr. Bronson owned it. He lived right across the street from it. I asked him if he would rent me half.

Yes, he said he would.

'Listen, I'm fixin' to open a day boarding-house and I ain't got but seven dollars and a half. I can't pay you nothin' in advance.' I think the rent was twenty dollars or twenty-five a month. 'But I have a brand new Wheeler & Wilson sewing machine I'll put up till you get paid.'

I couldn't have said nothing he would have liked better. They hadn't none and his girls wanted to do some sewing.

Next I had to have a stove. Mary took hers back. I was

starting out alone, without nothing except the sewing machine, a feather bed, and my dishes, towels and tablecloths. I went to the hardware store and told the man what I wanted. I had a long talk with him. I wanted a second-hand stove, see. He had one but, no sir, he wouldn't let me have it. 'You want a good stove,' he said, 'I'll sell you a new one, the best I got in the store.'

Wasn't that the funniest thing? It sure was. I asked him why he wanted to take a chance on a ninety-dollar stove.

'Because you'll make good and pay me for it.'

Then he piled that stove with enough stuff to start house-keeping with! 'You'll need 'em all,' he said, 'to feed that hungry bunch, and a stove ain't no good without cookin' utensils.'

This was a Saturday. 'I'll come in and pay you something on it Monday,' I said, 'and after that as fast as I can.'

I hadn't touched my seven and a half!

I went off to buy some lumber, enough for tables and benches for the men. And I needed some boards for legs; I got them for nothing by paying for one piece, twenty foot long and one foot wide. I bought ten cents worth of nails; and I borrowed a hatchet and a saw from Mr. Bronson. Also he give me a plank for a bench, to set along the outside of the house to put the basins on for the men to wash up.

When I opened my place for dinner Monday noon, after buying the meat and vegetables, I still had two dollars and a half left. The six men I had over to Mary's come, and four more they brought with them. They all paid me for a week in advance.

Next day there was ten more and I had twenty to feed; of course I had to have help. I sent for Emma McLaughlin, a widow woman that was glad to get the work. I done the cooking, and didn't they punish them baking-powder biscuits!

When Saturday night come I had to put on another ten foot of table and benches, and there was money enough to pay for my stove and my house rent.

As hard as I was working, every other day I went to the

post office for Johnnie Ellis' letters. Me and Johnnie had arranged our plans; he could sell out his business any time for cash but until I wrote him to come he wouldn't do nothing. The last time I was with him he told me, 'I want to be honest with you, and you be honest with me the same way. If you find anybody you like better, you jes' write and say so; I'll take it standin' up!'

After a little while Johnnie's letters stopped coming. Well, he proposed the arrangements and it was him left off. I wasn't going to let it break my heart.... Besides, I was seeing Jonah Small. He drifted in to town and got him a job. I went out with Jonah Saturday nights; I hadn't no time for gallivanting week days.

Then I took down sick — just when my business was so wonderful. I went to aching all over, every joint in me; I was just reeling. Emma made me take some pills. 'You'll be back on the job in the morning,' she said. I took four of them; two would have been enough but I took four. In the morning I wasn't no better, so I took three more.

I just collapsed; the pills done it. Emma got me into bed and sent for Dr. Bell. He looked at me, felt my pulse and shook his head. He didn't say nothing to me — I couldn't have answered him back if he had. Emma asked him what he thought about them seven pills I swallowed. 'Seven bullets through her head wouldn't have been no worse!' And the thought come to me: I ain't got one of them encouragin' doctors, that's sure!

I lay there forty-four days with typhoid fever, and Emma setting with me and watching over me. Thank God I had money enough to see me through.

Jonah Small was around asking how I was getting along and trying to help out every way he could. And after a few months we was engaged to be married and I had his ring on. I was mighty happy. He knowed Willie and the babies; he was the only one around there that did. He was good and kind, promising how we was going back for the children. He meant

all he promised. It was that more than love; I was grateful
to him for his understanding ways.

As soon as I was strong enough I opened in the same place
but I had to change my business. The compress was closed.
I had a big sign hung up, DRESSMAKING, and I got lots
of sewing — enough to keep going. Then I moved just across
the street and opened up a millinery business, along with my
dressmaking. I had all I could do. The hat part was hard
work, specially the bleaching with sulphur.

How is it that so many things comes up in one person's life?
It was probably six months after me and Jonah was engaged —
I just don't know how long it was — when I went over to the
post-office, and my land, if there wasn't a letter from Johnnie
Ellis! He wanted to know what had happened, why I hadn't
answered his letters. Asked me to tell him didn't I care no
more.

Well, the way things had turned out, that's so, I didn't
care no more. Not hearing from Johnnie I'd kind of forgot
him and I'd stopped going to the post-office regular.... But
here was something else. I was sure now, somehow it come to
me, that Jonah Small had been stealing my letters. He knew
about Johnnie for I'd told him everything....

When Jonah come to see me in the evening I asked him,
'Where's my letters?'

'What letters... I don't know what you mean.'

'I mean this; I want them letters from Johnnie Ellis that
you stole out of the post-office. I got one here saying as how
he was writin' right along!'

Jonah was dumfounded. He thought there wouldn't be no
more letters, after Johnnie got disgusted and quit writing for
a while.

I told him, 'Do you know I could send you to the penitentiary? The only thing you have to do is tell me why you done
it.'

Yes, he owned up; what else could he do? 'I done it because
I wanted you to marry me. I knew the kind of woman you
was ever since I lived at your house. I made up my mind to

court you, and marry you, and help you take care of the children, for the good way you treated me and my little girls. I seen that Ellis stood betwixt us and that's why I done it.'

There was a little ravine close by where we was setting. I throwed Jonah's ring down there in the bushes. 'Now you jes' follow it!' I said. 'I never want to see your face again.'

Chapter X

I RUN up my business to the best millinery store in Fort Worth. I had three salesladies working for me: big Alice, and little Alice about four foot high, and Emma McLaughlin. I done most of the making of the hats myself — except the frames; I bought them of course. I done the covers and the trimming.

If I wanted to buy anything I could go to Bennett's store and several others. There was times when I was short of cash but they give me credit; I never got turned down by no one, not even by Turk, the tall Jew with the little black mustache, that wouldn't give nobody credit.

Right then I took the typhoid again — in the glory of all my success. For the second time. The doctors couldn't understand it, only a little more than a year after the first time. I was just as bad but I was laid up ten days less. Dr. Bell brought in his partner, Dr. Fields, that become my good friend.

And another partner, Dr. Birch — he come in too. I told them, 'You look worried. Three doctors means something! Jes' cut out thinkin' I'm a goner cause I ain't!' I firmly believed I'd get well when I said it.

Emma McLaughlin was nursing me. Little Alice run the business and done it good. I went back to work as soon as I could. During that time I got in the habit of reading medical books that Dr. Fields give me. He said as I was calculated to make a good midwife. I didn't take that serious, but I went on studying for many years, knowing one kind of study was as good as another for a body's brain.

Willie Page begun writing me to come to Kansas. He had his divorce, but now that he got it he didn't want it. I actually packed a box with my sewing machine and my saddle that was my mother's, and some other things I had, and shipped them to Annie in southern Kansas where Willie had the children. That's how close I come to going back to him.

I was making good in Fort Worth and I thought that I could start my children off right in Kansas, even if my husband hadn't. Dr. Fields was the cause of me not going there. I got one of my bilious fever attacks and I told Dr. Fields I'd have to give up and go home if I kept on that way. I was ashamed to tell him I had weakened and was going back to Willie Page.

'Well now,' he said drawly and quiet like, 'I don't think we're beat yet.' He started to joke. 'What am I goin' to do without you?'

'I ain't foolin' about this,' I went on, 'I sent my feather bed and a lot of things to Kansas.'

He boiled up — 'What's that you say? Are you tryin' to make me think you're jes' an ordinary quitter? You ain't goin' back to that no-account and spoil your life!'

I told him I didn't figure Willie would ever amount to nothing; I wasn't fooling myself.

He answered me: 'Jenny' — that's the name they used to call me by, down in Texas — 'why can't you do for your own children and take them away from him?'

More than once I had told Dr. Fields I couldn't force Willie. No court would let me have my children, thinking I wasn't worthy after leaving them. I said something like that now.

'Let me ask you,' he said, 'are you goin' back for your children, or is there something else?' I told him true — 'There ain't nothing else, it's only that. I'd give up everything to get them.'

'You ain't crazy about lovin' a man if you was to go to marryin' him?'

I didn't know what he meant.

'I know a man that's got plenty of money,' said Dr. Fields, 'and I believe he'd marry you twenty-four hours after he talked to you. Marry him and you'll have the money to go back and fight for your children! Get 'em here in Texas and you won't have no more trouble.'

I was willing to do anything Dr. Fields told me, I had so much confidence in him.

He knew that my sister Mary was coming back to Fort Worth with her two daughters and little Johnnie. Dr. Fields had been doctoring the boy. He said, 'I'll stop in to say howdy when they get here. I'll have a gentleman with me and I'll introduce him. Then you can do the rest.' But he wouldn't tell me nothing about him, who he was or what he looked like.

Mary moved into town and one day, sure enough, along comes the doctor in his buggy. 'I jes' dropped in to see how the family is gettin' along and I brought a friend of mine with me.' He turned around and said, 'Come in, Mr. Chase, I want to introduce you to my friends here.' Dr. Fields introduced him all around. I knowed it was the man and I felt mighty peculiar.

First off I noticed his brown eyes, and his rosy cheeks and fair complexion. He had white whiskers, cut round and covering his necktie about two or three inches under the chin. His hair was brown, nearly gray and parted in the middle — on the sides it was curly. He was a handsome man, close on to fifty years old; medium size, perhaps a little too short.

'I feel like we're goin' to be good friends and I am awfully pleased to meet you, Mr. Chase.' Them was my words.

They stayed half an hour — it was about eleven thirty in the forenoon. Dr. Fields got up to leave. 'I'm a-goin' to eat dinner with the family and Mr. Chase is comin' with me,' he said.

Mary walked out of the kitchen with a fresh baked cake and wanted them all to have a piece. The doctor said as he was going straight to his dinner he wouldn't have none. Mr. Chase seemed to see that Mary was embarrassed. 'Doctor,' he said, 'I don't have no home to eat at; I will be pleased to get a piece of that home-baked cake.'

He was the grandest man in that respect; he was a gentleman. He was just being polite. But inside it made me smile, wondering if the old darling wasn't hinting already!

About two evenings after Mr. Chase stopped in to call.

He brought us nuts and candy, and he had his pockets full for the boy Johnnie. He said as he was out walking and got feeling lonesome. He smiled and it went to my heart. We just set around and talked. He asked me if I cared for driving.

'Yes,' I told him, 'I am very fond of it, and I love best to drive after sundown.'

Fort Worth was beautiful to drive through at dusk. It was level and there wasn't no trees, and the horizon seemed so far off, with nothing in sight but maybe a slice of moon. In the day the wind was hot and heavy but at night there was a balmy zephyr breeze blowing. Them summer nights was the finest I ever seen anywhere. I have always been a great one for setting out in the evening. Texas nights is beautiful.

Dr. Fields come along after a bit. 'How do you like my friend?'

'I like him wonderful, ain't he a gentleman!'

'Never was a greater one,' he said. 'He's your'n if you want him, the way I size it up. But don't take him for his money and give him the go-by. No, you ain't that sort of woman.'

Some people is inclined, it's their way, to take all they can get. But I like the give side better than the take. 'No, I ain't,' I said, 'when I bargain, I pay. Even if I knew he wouldn't be good to me I'd risk it to get the children. And I'll do my best to make him happy.'

Mr. Chase come around for me one afternoon about four o'clock. 'There's a lot of country I want to show you,' he said. 'We'll head down Weatherford way and drive home by moonlight.'

We didn't do much talking; we was still strange. Every little while I sighed. I was in heaven. I was sure I was going to get my May back. Then I'd quail. Maybe he'd think I was a flip of a girl and wouldn't like me. Did he know about my being married? Most everybody called me Miss Page. I found out later that Dr. Fields hadn't said nothing.

I told Mr. Chase how I enjoyed the ride so much.

'If you have enjoyed it as much as that you won't mind comin' out again.'

'That sure will be grand!' I replied.

I made it strong! And I made it easier for him by saying again how I liked driving in the dusk best — seeing as how he was a business man.

But I done a mean thing to him about three weeks after that, on a Sunday afternoon. Another one of my beaux drove up in a brand new rig and I couldn't resist the temptation of taking a ride. I said to Mr. Chase, 'Stay here and keep house till I get back, I won't be gone long.'

We drove out about three miles; then this fellow thought as he'd get smart and try to hug me. I told him to keep his hands to hisself but he didn't. I reached out for a rein and give it a tug that brought the wagon around sharp. And I jumped out.

I started to walk home, him driving alongside and begging me to get in. It was taking me so long to walk them miles. And I was thinking about Mr. Chase setting there. So I climbed back.

'But don't you start pawin' me!'

'No,' he said, 'I have learnt my lesson.'

When I got home and peered in Mr. Chase looked terrible. Oh, he was scorching mad! He'd been playing with Trixie, the little dog he give me the week before.

'I'll be goin' now,' was all he said. He raised up with Trixie under his arm and started out.

I grabbed Trixie — 'No you don't,' I cried, 'you can't have her!'

'Goldingit!' he said, 'you think more of that whelp than you do me!' That made us both laugh. It broke the ice.

'Come on,' I begged, taking his hand and leading him over to the sofa; 'you can hear all about it, then maybe you won't be so mad with me.' And I told him what happened. And a lot more. All about my being married, and about the children.... My voice was cracking and I had to stop to keep the tears back.

Mr. Chase set still as a mouse. After a bit he said, 'I have been married, too. I have been married twice. My first wife,

Arvilla Bunn, was an orphan. We was boarding the same place. She hadn't a living soul on earth that meant a thing to her. I lost her when the baby come — and the baby.'

He told me everything. 'I grieved a long time over losin' her,' he said. 'You see this ring on my finger; it ain't got no set, it's very unsightly. There was a diamond in it. But I wouldn't let no one touch it when the points needed fixin' because Arvilla wished it on.'

He told me then about his second wife. He lost her in three years. There was two step-children, Milton and Katy, and he was supporting them, he said, though they did not live with him.

Bless his old soul, he was looking at me so serious. Then he said, 'I'm glad this has come up and we could talk it over. I'm a-goin' to make a proposition to you, too. I ain't askin' you to love me. I think it's impossible for a young woman like you to love a man as old as me....'

I told him, 'I ain't no sucklin'. There ain't such a difference between us. Don't say that word again — hearts never grow old!'

'Ain't them sweet words!' he said. And then, 'I'm a-goin' to ask you to let me kiss you on the cheek.'

'Let's change that to the mouth! Cheek-kissin' don't mean nothin',' I told him.

After a time he said, 'I have a little property, I ain't never used a dollar from the estate of my first wife. There's a five hundred acre ranch in Tyler County rented out that pays me two hundred dollars a year. It's for you as a weddin' present.'

We understood each other before we ever tied up. We was married eight weeks from the day we met — by the Justice of the Peace at Waxahachie. In his parlour; the man's two daughters was the witnesses.

The first night Mr. Chase slept like a baby. I laid there and thought: So I am Mrs. Chase. Well, the honor of bein' a rich man's wife ain't goin' to bother me none!

We went next day to Fort Worth, to Mr. Chase's rooms where he lived above his office. He had a small private office up there. 'I'm a-goin' to rent a house,' he told me. 'We may be movin' along some day; I don't want to buy if it's all the same to you.' He had been out looking at some houses and he took me to see the one he liked best. It was on 'Quality Hill' where all the upstarts lived; that's what I called them. A nice six-room house, very high up and well-built, although it wasn't the finest house; there was others finer.

Mr. Chase moved all his stuff over and told me to buy what I pleased. I loved nice window curtains and I did get fine ones — and everything else in keeping.

'It's up to you when you want to go after your children.'

'I'll be goin' next week,' I said.

Chapter XI

I DON'T remember the name of the town in southern Kansas I was heading for. It don't matter. But honest, the train just crawled along. Stopping and backing, stopping and backing....

My three children was at my sister-in-law's, Annie Shepard. She was keeping May; and the two boys — Ollie and Will — was there, too, with their father, Willie Page. Annie seemed best pleased to see me, but I guess that was natural because children forget. Ollie and May knew me; but the boy Will was only three years old when I left, he wasn't quite sure.

I ain't able to say how I felt when I got my May in my arms. I told her, 'Honey, mama's been a long time a-comin', ain't she? She'll be a long time a-leavin' you now!' Annie said whenever she licked May, she'd be answering her back, 'Never mind, when my mama gets here I'll be sayin what you done to me!'

I wrote Annie, before I met Mr. Chase, that if I did come back and marry Willie again I was going to keep boarders. Annie took the idea. She found a house and went to doing that herself. I was glad to know the babies had plenty to eat. They looked fine, only they didn't have much to wear — at least the boys didn't. May wasn't so bad off. Annie cut up some of my old stuff for her after writing me to see if I minded.

Willie Page was man enough to say that it served him right, my being married again. 'You done a sight better for yourself than if you had stuck to me.'

We set down and had one big talk, just like I done with Mr. Chase. I told him everything that had happened to me, sickness and hardships, and how at last I come to marry. 'I was always good to you,' I said, 'but I was an innocent fool and let you flummox me.... The only time I plagued you was tryin' to make you work.'

We talked on like that for a long time. 'Willie, I got a fine house and a wonderful husband, and I invite you to come and see us. So I ain't bitter; that proves it. I come here to plead with you to let me have my children. I don't want to make no trouble, I don't want it to come out in life that I had to take them away because you couldn't raise them right.' I asked him to let me have them peaceable.

He set there, shook his head, and said he wouldn't do it.

'Maybe I can't force them away from you. But I'm takin' May back with me or I'll do something desperate.' I was at the end of my rope, I felt it as I was talking, I never would have left there alive without May.

Willie knew I meant business. Sure, he knew me by now. He said, 'I don't want to go through that ordeal. But I love 'em too.'

I put it to him straight out: 'You think you do but you won't even work for them; that ain't love!'

'All right,' he said, 'I'll tell you what let's do. You take May, and I will give you my word of honor that I'll bring the boys soon.'

'When's soon?' I asked him. He said 'in a few months.' Then I said, 'What's to keep you from comin' along now, you and them, I got the money to pay for the tickets?'

'No thanks, I don't want to travel on no woman's money.'

I was glad to hear him say that. 'I got one horse,' he told me, 'and I'll get me another and a wagon, and drive through. The boys'll like campin' along the way.' It was arranged like that.

I felt happy about everything when I started back with May. I was thinking all the time how Mr. Chase would receive her; I told her how he looked and what to expect. 'I want you to love him for what he's done for mama and what he's fixin' to do for you. Mama is goin' to buy you a doll and pretty things, and send you to school so's you can write letters to your papa.' I didn't want her to get homesick.

We arrived in Fort Worth and everything went along beautiful. One afternoon, maybe six months later, I was setting by the window looking out and I seen Willie Page coming along. I knew him by his walk. If I hadn't, I'd have thought it was a tramp come for something to eat.

He was alone. And so was I; May was at school. 'Hullo,' I said. 'Where's the boys?' What's happened?'

'Nothin',' he answered, 'they're with Annie.'

'Willie, what have you done? You vowed you would bring them, why ain't you?'

'I didn't have the money.' He said his conscience wouldn't let him write and ask me. He beat his way through like an ordinary bum.

I asked him, 'Then what have you come here for?'

'To ask you, if I would make a home for you, would you come back?' He really meant it. He expected me to try to get some money off Mr. Chase and to go back with him.

(I was thinking, he ain't worth killing!)

'Why can't you work like other people?' I wanted to know. 'Why don't you think things over before you plunges into them? Did Annie know where you was goin'?'

No, she didn't. 'I used to do the thinkin' for you,' I told him, 'and before me, when you was growin' up, your mother done it — but you're alone now.... Look at your hat, look at your clothes. Ain't you got a lick of pride in you? Comin' here, and the neighbors my friends. They'll all know that you are May's father.'

I said just what I was thinking: 'I ain't cruel nor hard-hearted and I don't want May to think bad of you neither, but that child ain't goin' to call you papa; I won't allow it!'

He didn't seem a bit upset about that; thought it was a good joke. I bought him a new outfit and he was mighty pleased. He stayed in our house and Mr. Chase welcomed him.

Everything was fine for about a week until Willie took sick. Mr. Chase told me to send for Doctor Fields. 'I don't know if he's sick enough for that, but you better get him in and we'll quick find out.'

He was sick all right; he didn't get up the next morning

neither. I got to worrying and wondering. I said to myself, 'He ain't all bad; maybe it's humiliation, the way I been actin'.'

I went up to Willie's room and I told him, 'I been worried enough by you in the past. You better tell me right out what's the matter. The doctor's comin' and whatever it is he'll find it out, for he's a good doctor.'

'I don't know what's the matter with me, only that I'm sick.'

'All right then, Dr. Fields will soon pull you outen it. You'll have every care,' I said, 'and you can order what you want to eat and I'll bring it up to you.'

He said he was much obliged.

'May can come in and set with you but there's no need till the doctor comes; I don't want her catchin' nothin'. She's outside playin'; if he says it's all right I'll send her up.' I told Willie before, that I didn't want him pawing around May and spoiling her.

Dr. Fields come and I said to him, 'You will be very much surprised when you see who it is.' I introduced him: 'This is May's father, this is my ex-husband; he's sick and I want you to do everything you can for him.'

I waited for Dr. Fields to come downstairs. 'What's the matter with him?' was my first question.

He kind of grinned. 'I had a hard time findin' out. It's something that won't bother his lady friends if they stay away from him. But if they don't, it'll bother them a lot. It ain't the mumps!'

So that was it. Willie was around there almost a month, and Mr. Chase as nice to him as he could be.

Then Willie said to me one night after supper, 'Well, I'm leavin' tomorrow.'

'Oh,' I said, 'so sudden?'

'I been a long time imposin' on you and I'm much beholden.'

'I know you ain't got no money,' I said. That was the only thing that made me feel a little good to him. I already give him some money to go down town with and get a shave and a bath, and some underclothes, and now I told him I'd buy him his ticket to Kansas.

'Why, what's the matter with my goin' back the same way I come? It will be all right if you want to give me some money, but I don't need no ticket.' I give him ten dollars but I begun to get suspicious.

May was leaving for school next morning and she come to kiss me goodbye like always. Willie was with her. I asked him if he was leaving then, and he acted kind of uncertain.

'I'll walk to school with May,' he said, 'and go down town a spell. I'll be pullin' out this afternoon.'

I got to worrying so, of what he might be planning to do with May, I decided I'd better go to the station. This was two hours later. I didn't see him nor her. The train was coming along and I was chasing around in a frenzy trying to catch a glimpse of Willie. I looked up and down the platform to see if he was there. I started to go back through the waiting-room and here May come in at the door! I grabbed her and made a streak to get out and put some buildings or something betwixt us and the station so's Willie couldn't see us. I didn't ask her nothing until we got to Mr. Chase's office — I was scared to take her home.

I was all blowed. 'Darlin',' I said to May, 'I am near dead with fright. You're as white as a ghost, too. Set down and tell mama what happened.... Did papa tell you to come down to the train to see him off?'

'No, I come down to go with him.'

'Would you rather go home with him than be with me, honey?'

'No, I wouldn't, mama; but he begged me so, and he cried when he went with me to school, and told me how bad the boys was fixed without me and needin' me, and if I'd go with him he would send me right back in a month.'

I asked her, 'Would you rather stay with me if I can get the boys here?'

'Why mama, I don't want to leave you, but you know I would love to see my little brothers, too.'

Mr. Chase wasn't at the office, but when he come home that night he asked me what happened. 'Bah!' he said, 'I knew he was a cad but I didn't think he was a scoundrel. He ought to be horsewhipped to treat any woman like that, let alone her that's been his wife.... He's a Christian, in the way that he was learnt, but he was learnt wrong! Don't you worry, Jenny, it ain't got nothin' to do with us. We treated him good; next time I'll know where I stand.'

I wrote Willie's sister, Annie, and told her what Willie tried to do; I wrote her the whole thing....

About two years later, in September, I seen a covered wagon come up and stop at the door. Willie Page was driving it. A little boy jumped out of the hind part. That was my son Will, but I didn't know him. When Ollie got out I screamed and run outside.

I shook hands with Willie Page. Think of him coming back after all that had passed. I never mentioned nothing about that, but I didn't invite him in. I was honest and open with him: 'I want you to let me take the children and keep them a while. Whenever you like you can come back. Let me have them to myself and you go on away. It's better if you ain't around here when Mr. Chase gets home.... Ain't you got no money?' I said.

'A little,' he replied.

'Jes' wait here, I got my house money and I'll go in and get you some.' I give him twenty dollars. 'Tell the boys good-bye, and to stay with me till you come back.'

He told me where he was going. He knew some Kansas people that had moved outside Fort Worth, in the country. He was expecting to visit them.

Little Will was old enough to go to school; I recollect that. I dressed them both up and they was the happiest youngsters. And if Mr. Chase wasn't surprised! The raggediest, dirtiest boys you ever seen, but I had them in new outfits before Mr. Chase come home to supper. Ollie was sure proud with his first store clothes.

Everything was serene and beautiful and Mr. Chase was kindness itself. He had a soft, sweet voice, and his way of talking sounded like he was always pleading for something. He had only one fault — drinking. Every now and then — periodic. Once he said to me, 'Now dear, don't let what I do hurt you when I'm drinkin' because it don't mean nothin'. I never intend to get so lushy I can't get home to you.'

I asked him, 'Why don't you, when you get that way, go to your bedroom over the office and sleep it off?'

No sir, he didn't want to do that. He told them down at the office, 'So soon as you see that I'm gettin' too much, take me home to my wife.'

'Why do you want to bring me all your burdens?'

'I bring you my love,' he said; 'I reckon the good and the bad goes together!'

One time he come home pretty full.

'Say,' I told him, 'it appears like you got more'n you can carry.' He couldn't talk quite plain. He said something that sounded like 'Don't give me no more.'

I ordered his whiskey by the gallon, at the same time that I ordered my tea and coffee from the grocer. He had a trick of throwing that big demijohn around his wrist, laying it over to his shoulder, and taking it down that easy you wouldn't have thought it weighed an ounce. But never did he drink too much at home nor nothing like it.

Well now, about this special time. He felt sick. 'Let's go walkin' before we eat,' he said. It was time for the evening meal and we used to take a walk afterwards.

He didn't feel like eating. 'Oh, come on,' I said, 'have a bite of supper first.' He set down but he couldn't eat.

So I said, 'I'm goin' to make you up a drink that will do you good, then we'll walk.' I took, I guess, about a third of a glass of strong hot tea, and I put something of everything on the table into it: salt and pepper, tabasco sauce and sugar, anything that poured! He was too full to know much what I was doing, but I didn't leave the room and I guess he figured there wasn't nothing there to hurt him.

'Now toss this off like a man!' I told him. He drank about half of it, and he said to me, thick like, 'Dear, this tastes awful, you ain't tryin' to poison me, are you?'

I answered him, 'Drink it down, you'll feel better right away.' I didn't ask him to eat no more. 'Come on now,' I said, 'we'll take our walk. Where do you want to go — to "Quality Hill" the same as usual?'

We went for a way but he balked. 'I don't think I can go no further,' he said, 'I'm gettin' pretty sick. Maybe I better be goin' back.'

'Oh no, give me your arm. You come along with Jenny, we'll walk fast and it'll make you feel better.' We didn't get to the top quite. He stopped, poor darling — he looked at me and he said, 'Jenny, I sure believe you poisoned me!' He set down and commenced to vomit.

'My legs is drunk, but I ain't drunk here,' he said, putting his hand to his head. 'I want to tell you something before I die' — he just kind of crumpled over with his head in his hand. 'But I want to tell you first, if you poisoned me, I don't blame you.' Then he said, 'I have always been jealous of you. I don't mean that you ever done nothin', or ever will, that's wrong. But I lay awake at night, thinkin' how can I ever be happy when I die, away from her and knowin' that she's layin' in some other man's arms? I ain't jealous of you in this world but I know that I will be in the next.'

'Well now, I do believe you are drunk, talkin' like that.'

'Drunk? No,' he said, 'I ain't drunk, I'm a killed man!'

I made him rest his head in my lap. Right there by the side of the road. I got him relaxed and told him to be quiet. And he went off to sleep in my arms for two hours. I knew that he was awful sick, but there wasn't nothing I give him that could hurt and I didn't worry.

He come to. He straightened up and asked, 'Where are we, anyway?'

'Darlin',' I whispered, 'we are in heaven!'

'Didn't I tell you, Jenny, I was dyin'!'... Pretty soon he begun to laugh. 'I been awful drunk. Jenny, I humbly beg your pardon... but God, I was sick!'

Mr. Chase got home one afternoon and tried to slip in the back way without being seen. Will come running in to me and he said, 'Mama, you better come out, there's a man fell in the slop can and he's a-goin' to drown!'

That's right. Good gracious, he'd fell in head first! But he never remembered it and I never told him. He didn't want the children to see him, and somebody, from the office, brought him to the back figuring he could navigate the rest of the way — but he couldn't.

Mr. Chase was a commission merchant. He was what they called a cotton broker but his firm handled most everything. He was sure smart — a wizard at untangling figures and straightening out books that no one else could manage; I heard that more than once.

He got to studying over this drinking of his and he used to say to me, 'Dearie, I'm goin' to quit it.'

And I'd say, 'That's good, for how long?'

'Jes' so long as I can stand it.'

'How long's that?'

'Let's swear off for thirty days!'

'All right, how about writin' it down?'

'No, my promise is enough,' he said. I got him as far as sixty days but that was the best I could do with him.

Willie Page come back again in a year; it might have been a little more. He had his covered wagon with him. He'd got hold of some money picking cotton, then he come for the boys. I thought they was with me for good but I never said a word; they was old enough to remember things and I wasn't bothered they'd forget me. I let them go but I had a talk with them first. I said to go to school and be good sons to their father. 'I don't need nothin' but to know that you're happy,' I told them.

I didn't allow Willie Page to sleep in the house. He only stayed but a day and a half anyway. It was the only time I locked my house while I was living in Texas. I didn't let May out of my sight. I didn't even send her to school for three days after he was gone as I was afraid he might be hanging around on the outside of town.

That was the last time I seen either of my boys for eight years — until Ollie come to me up to Revenna Park, outside Seattle. I got a letter from him asking if he could visit me. I wrote back and sent him some money. I didn't hear nothing for a long time. Then one day the bell rung and there was a young man standing at the door when I opened it. 'Don't you know me?' he said. He took off his hat and smoothed down his hair. The buzzard! It was Ollie sure enough.

I'll have to explain that. Back in Indiana, more than twenty years before when I was carrying that boy, a sick buzzard lit on the gate post in front of the house. Its wings had drooped and it was about half crouched down in a squat. I said out loud, 'I'm a-goin' to kill that bird!' I could shoot good. I shot at the thing; I thought I shot him sure. But Mr. Buzzard just turned his head around like to take a good look at me, and flew off.

I don't know why I done it but I clamped my hand to my head. I was scared I reckon; the bird acted so human. And when the baby come there was a patch of black hair, shaped like a buzzard, on the right side of his little tow-head scalp.

That simple act of mine, putting my hand to my head, made a big difference in my life. I kept thinking, if I marked my child with my brain for the bad, what's to prevent children being marked in the same way for the good? I knew they could be marked on the flesh. Why not their reason, too? Couldn't a woman produce a better child, thinking right?

That was verified later when I seen an eight-year-old boy, standing on the rostrum, and there wasn't, I don't think, many questions in history you could ask him he couldn't answer. He was a fine musician too, but he hadn't went to school a day in his life. His name was Samuel Lawrence Harrison; they called him the 'Infant Encyclopedia.'

He knew more than his teachers. They wanted to know how it was possible. The mother said, 'I had one thought while I was a-carryin' — that a woman could bear a better child by thinkin' better things. I done nothin' the whole time but read history and played my music and went to concerts. There he is to prove it.'

I become so interested in Sammy I sought his mother out. We found we was living four blocks apart; this was in Seattle. We got to be very close friends and I had plenty of chance to study Sammy.

I was thinking all the time about my theory. 'I would to God,' Mrs. Harrison said, 'that the whole world knew what I done and would do the same thing!' I read everything on the subject I could get my hands on. I was determined some day to preach that theory when I had studied it out better.

And then I had a dream that changed everything and set me on the right road to learning. I dreamed I went into a theater that was crowded. I seen the rostrum up there where I was going to speak; and here come a nice-looking man that stepped out of the crowd and tapped me on the shoulder. He said, ' You can't speak on your subject — you or nobody else knows enough about it.'

'Why, I don't know nothing else,' I said. 'What can I speak on? I've studied hard and know jes' what to say.'

'We have chose your subject. You go on and speak on " KNOW THYSELF."' I woke up then.

Why had I dreamt that when I had never thought it or heard it in my waking hours? How wonderful that I should dream something I never knew.

Now if I hadn't studied that out nothing would have come of it. But thinking about my dream I realized I didn't understand the subject I wanted to preach and I was being warned.

My task was to analyze myself; the message was plain. Know Thyself! I begin thinking backward, watching my actions, and I found out I had a big job on my hands. Before that I was a stranger to myself. I tried hard. I set to getting myself straightened out. I begun to look around, too. And pretty soon I seen that life wasn't at all what I thought. Here I'd been all this time, seeing all the faults of others, all the unpleasantness; how about my own bad ways?

It was almost like being born again. And it seemed so queer that I owed it to a dream. I made up my mind to remember my dreams, not to let them slip away from me. I forced myself to it until after a few months it become a very easy habit. And my thoughts I clung to and puzzled over.

Dreams. That's the wrong word for it. Messages that come to me when I am wide awake, too....

Chapter XII

MR. CHASE'S partner, Captain Simmons, took sick. He made a proposition to break up the business. He put it up to Mr. Chase and the third partner, Cy Harris.

I was good friends with the Harrises that lived near us on 'Quality Hill.' But I wasn't never in Captain Simmons' home and I wasn't well acquainted with his wife. She was delicate and never went out in society. Oh yes, I had to go into society. That broke me of it. I won't say nothing against it or its women — more than that I didn't like them. They would say nice things to your face and belt you one when you wasn't looking!

Mr. Chase talked it over with me. 'What do you think?' he said. I didn't know. What did he want to do, and what else did he feel he could do?

About three months later there was a great hubbub over gold being discovered in the Wichita Mountains, almost in sight of Wichita Falls. It was mica, but it don't take much to start a rush. Mr. Chase thought it was going to be a big town; he figured he'd maybe open a grocery business there; once he kept books for a grocery store in Dallas. But he didn't want to start in alone, without a partner. I thought I knew how that could be managed. Ever since I come to Fort Worth I traded with the Tucker Grocery — I went to Mr. Tucker and had a long talk with him.

'I'm in a good business here,' he said, 'and I can't pick up and go, but you tell Mr. Chase if he wants to come and talk it over I'll be glad to see him. I'll make this proposition to you now if you want to tell him. You know my head clerk, Mr. Daggett?'

'Yes,' I said, 'I know him well. I always want him to wait on me. He's the one that fills my demijohn!' He laughed, and I laughed too.

'He's a very reliable man,' said Mr. Tucker, 'and he's got some money of his own. I'll stand back of him, tell Mr. Chase, and if they want to go in together and open up in Wichita Falls, I'm for it.'

I talked it over with Mr. Chase that night. 'Jenny,' he said, 'listen, I'm a better bookkeeper than a higgler. You done the talkin' so far; you go right ahead, and when the papers is ready to be signed I'll put my name down. Tell Daggett to order his groceries and I'll be ready with my half of the money.'

So that's the way it was. Daggett attended to everything, and when he wanted to ask something of the Chase family he come to me.

We left Fort Worth for Wichita Falls about the first of April, me and May. The men folks went ahead. It took a long time to get there, though it was only a hundred miles. It was ten o'clock in the morning when the train pulled up. They had a platform built but it was a very ornery place to step off. No depot yet.

I told May, 'Let's go out and view the town.'

'Where is it?' she said, as she looked around. Bless her, she was right, I wanted to know the same thing.

I remember it well. I seen a house and a barn. 'There it is,' I said, 'and here we are!' The child looked scared. 'It's goin' to be lots of fun,' I told her. Well, it wasn't that exactly, but it was a great experience. We brought tents with us on the train and there was some men there looking for work, ready to help out. And teams to haul anything you had. By four o'clock our tents was up, we was moved in and at home.

Mr. Chase opened his grocery — him and Mr. Daggett — in a big store tent. There wasn't no buildings except a few farm lay-outs. This was the first big tent put up for business. Our double tent was about twenty foot from it. We lived like that for three months until we got us a house.

There was some few there ahead of us, a hatful. Just the farms and a few tents. It was new and raw and wonderful.... And one morning about ten days later, when I looked out, there was a city! Smoke was curling up from a hundred tents!

They just made one of them rushes. They was coming in droves.

How happy we was and business so good — until the curse of sickness come along. Typhoid broke out from not having proper sanitary conditions. There was only one doctor; he was a good one too, but just up against it, poor fellow. He didn't know what to do for nurses or nothing.

Yes, I felt sorry for him — he come over to my tent and told me: 'I understand you're a good nurse, Mrs. Chase, and a benevolent woman. Will you undertake to care for a family that's in terrible straits? You go up the street till you come to this number' — the tents all had numbers — 'and you'll find a pitiful state of things. The woman's layin' in bed and don't know nothin'. Her baby is by her side. A widow woman, and only a seven-year old daughter to take care of her and the baby. I ain't easy affected but I sure took it home to myself — it's enough to break your heart to see it.'

I said, 'I'll see to it right off.' I went to three or four women that I was acquainted with. Two was willing to go with me and that was enough for once.

I never, never will forget how I felt when I got there. The little girl was standing at the flap of the tent; she was very polite, a smart little girl. 'Good mornin',' I said, 'are you alone?'

'No, mama is in bed.' I asked how her mama was.

'I don't know, she ain't spoke to me.'

'Where's the baby?'

'Abed with mama.'

I walked in and turned the cover down from off the child. The light hurt his eyes and it made him blink. But pretty soon he begun to coo and laugh and maybe them little baby smiles didn't go to my heart! And them big blue eyes!

He was wrapped up in what they used to call a breakfast shawl, just little colored affairs that women wore around their shoulders, very common of that day. I picked him up. I asked the women with me, would they be willing to tend the mother. 'If you'll look after the sick woman, I'll take the

baby home and send a basket of groceries over from my
husband's store.' I said, 'Don't give her one thing in the
world to eat. No matter how much she begs, give her nothing
but water.' I knew enough about typhoid and how feeding
could kill people.

Well now, about this child. I fed him on condensed milk
and he done good. May was a sleepy head, a young girl then
not twelve, but believe me she'd get up at night to warm milk
for the baby and glad to do it. It wasn't hard to love little
Frankie.

When his mother was almost well she told me she wanted
me to keep him. She'd had a terrible time. They come out to
Wichita Falls when her brother wrote for them, but by the
time they got there he'd sold out his cattle ranch and moved
off and she hadn't no idea where he was. Then her husband
died two months after little Frankie was born. She was plain
stranded: took in washing for a living for her and the two
children.

I kept that child a year and three months.

One day his mother come to me. 'Mrs. Chase,' she said, 'I
know it will hurt you awful but I'm a-goin' to leave it to you
to answer. You was one of the causes of savin' my life, and
I ain't forgettin' what you done for Frankie.' She was afeared
to come out with it. 'Some people I was washin' for here,
went to Kansas City and run into my brother. Here's his
letter that jes' come.'

He wrote her, 'Following this letter will be some money on
the way, and you and your children can come to us. Bring
the baby even if you have to ask the people to give him back
to you.' Him and his wife had no youngsters of their own and
it was plain to me they wanted the woman most for her children. 'It's up to you,' she said; 'you ain't adopted him but I
said you might.' Of course, I let her take the child.

Frankie thought I was his mother. He was crazy about
May, too — and she over him. He was beginning to crawl
around and walk now. And here was the cutest thing about
him. He'd set in the middle of my lap at table, hungry as a

wild cat, and wanting to get started. Set there panting, with his mouth open and his small hands fanning the air, but I'd learned him not to put them on the plate. God, the first dinner we set down to after he was gone, I thought it was all over with me. I couldn't swallow a mouthful; I looked over and seen my May. She hadn't et and the tears was rolling down her cheeks. I jumped up and left the table....

Mr. Chase said, 'I know how you feel; I feel that way myself.'

I got two letters. The brother wrote me the most beautiful letter, thanking me and saying how I would be repaid a thousand times. And I have been. The other was from the mother. I never heard from them but that once; I don't know what become of little Frankie.

The first time we seen the frame of a house going up in Wichita Falls, the first new house, Mr. Chase rented it for me. The man that built it put up twenty houses and this was the first. They was all rented before they was up.

We stayed in Wichita Falls through the fall and winter, over a year to the next spring. In that country it didn't snow much but they had northers — hard, cold blows — that was worse than any snow-storm. It must have been Christmas, I ain't sure no more — only that we was having a big turkey dinner and May was outside picking the gobbler.

I baked the cakes and cooked everything ahead of time. We washed our clothes and had them hanging out on the line. Then I heard May outside calling me. I run out and I seen the same nearly as that time back in Kansas, a blue streak across the horizon — everything but the antelopes. I hollered to Miss Kincaid next door, 'There's comin' a big norther!' Then I run into the house with May after me. I slammed the windows closed and run out again fixing things as best I could. I had to hustle, too.

May hollered, 'What will I do with the turkey?' It was about half unpicked.

'Fetch it in, and run and gather in the clothes!' But before

that child could get to do it I run to the door and called her
back. I never since I was born seen nothing like it. The air
was gray with dust and dirt; clothes, blankets, and something
that looked like a sail that must have ripped off a tent —
everything that wasn't nailed down, passing overhead and
sweeping by.

May was jumping up and down, yowling at the top of her
lungs. I grabbed her in my arms. 'If the house starts to go,
you follow me out and we'll lay down on the ground, face
foremost.'

It blowed for ten minutes. When it was gone, all I can say
is, it was gone.

May wanted to go out for the clothes. 'They must be
blowed dry,' she said. When she come back her eyes was
sticking out of her head. 'There ain't one single piece on the
line!' Some of them clothes was picked up two miles off.

That's what took us away from Wichita Falls; them blows
didn't do Mr. Chase no good. I didn't know at all that he was
afflicted in any way; he was always rasping his throat but he
didn't cough nor spit up. Now he got to coughing quite a
little and feeling bad all the time. Mr. Chase was a cheerful
man but he wasn't hisself at all. 'I got a chance to sell out,'
he told me; 'what do you think about it? I don't think the
climate agrees with me here, I don't feel none too spry.'

'All right, I'll go with you wherever you say.' I would have;
I learned to love him, so would any woman. He was that kind
of man.

For the time being we was going back to Fort Worth. Mr.
Chase sold out the grocery. They was about a month straightening things out. Mr. Daggett and him had it all talked over.
He confessed to Mr. Daggett what he wasn't telling me about
his health and that he had to get away from Wichita Falls.

We sold our house fixings right easy, prices was good. We
went to the Waverly Hotel in Fort Worth and it was a fine
place to stop. But I told Mr. Chase, 'May can't stay like this,
she's got to start back to school.' Mr. Chase thought as we'd
better put her in the convent; the schools didn't amount to
much.

'Will they take her in there; are they takin' children that ain't Catholic?'

'You needn't worry about that, the sisters will be pleased to have May. We ain't goin' to housekeepin' for a while,' he said.

'Am I to live here and be a lady — with nothin' to do?'

That's how he come to mention something that night I wasn't expecting. 'I'll tell you what I have been wishin' for,' he said. 'You don't want to leave May?'

'I should say not.'

'Well,' he went on, 'you wouldn't think hard of me if I was to take a vacation and go down to see Milton and Katy?'

'Why, I sure wouldn't. You go and stay as long as you please and get your visit out.'

'But that's why I'd like for you to put May to boardin', so's to be free to come to me in Galveston if I sent for you. That way there wouldn't be nothin' to hinder. We might want to make a trip.' He put it like that.

Mr. Chase was a brave man — elegant, the most I ever met in my life. I am eighty-three years old, and tomorrow, if I would meet a man like Mr. Chase and he asked me to have him, I'd say, 'Yes, and thank you!'... No woman can say more about a man than that.

He packed up his little trunk, the first leather trunk I ever seen, and he went to Galveston to see his step-children where they was living with their grandmother. He wrote me a letter every day that he was away — as long as he had the strength.

The landlady at the Waverly had a beautiful phaeton and a fine horse. We went driving, shopping, visiting, and went to parties. I kept pretty busy and had a nice time.... I owned twenty-five dresses, every one of them silks, satins and velvets; there wasn't one I could put on to do an hour's work in. Seeing me them days you'd have said I was a fine lady. But I knowed better. I wasn't so fine. I had fine clothes; and that's all I had, unless you'd count common sense. I was getting some of that knocked into me....

Dr. Fields called one day. I was feeling so good. 'You old

rascal,' I said, 'I been in town six weeks and you ain't been in
to see me.'

I noticed he looked pale. 'What's the matter with you,
you ain't the same?' Always when he called in the old days
he'd put both his hands out and give me a hug. That meant
nothing except friendliness; he must have been twenty years
older than me; he was older than Mr. Chase.

I seen there was something on his mind. 'Set down,' I said;
'you are in trouble, something's wrong. Is your wife sick?'

'No, not that, but there is trouble.' He looked at me hard
when he said it.

'Dr. Fields, you got some awful bad news for me!' I felt
just like there was a pair of hands pressing on my shoulders
from behind.

'Tell me,' I asked, 'is it Mr. Chase? Is he sick?'

He set there just so still. 'William ain't sick' — he was
talking very slow — 'that's not what I want to say. William
was an awful good man, the best. I have learned that; you
can't tell me nothin' I don't already know about him, but I
don't want you to think he is sick or sufferin' because he
ain't.'

So it was his hands giving me the strength to stand the
blow. I set there and he was behind me, I felt it.... My husband was dead.

Not long after that I went to see a woman medium, the best
that I could find, and I thought to myself, if there is anything
to it that a person can come back I'll find it out now. I set
down and she commenced rasping her throat. 'Lady,' she
said, 'there's someone here that died with an affliction of the
throat. Do you realize who it is?'

I wouldn't open my mouth. 'It's a man, he wants you to
know him so bad,' she said. She waited, trying to draw me out;
but I was stubborn, I wouldn't talk.

'Well, here's how you will recognize him: his hand's restin'
on your shoulder, and there's a ring on his little finger without
a set in it.' Then I burst out crying.

Nearly a year later I went to a second medium. I went, and I was stubborn again. This one didn't cough or rasp her throat. She said, 'I see a grey-haired man,' and she described Mr. Chase as plain as plain. 'He is caressin' your hair, don't you feel his hands on you?'

I said, 'No, I don't feel nothin'.' I didn't. 'What is it he wants to say?'

'He wants you to tell him if you know who it is?' I shook my head and said I didn't know.

'Well, he will make you know, he will write his name out.... Over the top of your head is the letters now, made of ropes of cotton — "W. W. Chase"!'

'Yes,' I said, 'I know.'

Then there was a message: 'She is thinking of marrying a man but she won't. Tell her I am perfectly willing that she should marry when she wants to but she won't marry this one.'

I lived in Fort Worth over a year. Me and Emma McLaughlin had a four-room flat together. I've mentioned her before. And in that time comes up something though it don't amount to much.

Emma was a widow woman and she had for her sweetheart an iron moulder and blacksmith by the name of Alec Garrison. Emma told me he was coming to see her that night. He was taking her to a show — a dramatic play with real actors, a stock company.

Alec brought a friend, a railroad conductor. When I come in the setting room I seen this young man standing by the other door, with his hand behind him holding on the knob, and it flashed through my mind how he looked just like a picture in a frame. He was a tall, neat-looking blond with cheeks like roses.... I felt a quickening of my heart.

'Will you have a seat?' I said politely. Alec was walking around the room, paying no attention, waiting for Emma to get her hat. Alec introduced us then; Charlie Hanks was his name.

Alec said, 'Do you folks want to go with us?' I said I didn't, I hadn't been prepared and I wasn't dressed for it.

Charlie Hanks turned to me and said, 'If you haven't no objections I would like to set here and chat with you.'

'Not the least bit in the world,' I answered, 'you are perfectly welcome.' He talked, and he kept on setting, and that wasn't the last talk. He come like that every time he was in town — his run on the railroad was some place in Mexico right across from El Paso, and his lay-off at this end was Fort Worth.

Of course he told me of his life. Men are like that, when they get a woman to listen. There was two in the family, him and his brother. Their grandmother died and left them each twenty thousand dollars — in dollars, not real estate or nothing else. And she wasn't passed on more than two months until the brother died leaving everything to Charlie.

He said he was very lonely and he wanted me to marry him. He said that before he'd known me a month. He was only twenty-nine years old and I reckon I was about thirty-three.

I told him, 'I ain't been a widow yet a year and for the respect I hold for Mr. Chase, even if I thought ever so much of you, I wouldn't marry now. And I ain't goin' to say as I'm crazy in love with you neither.'

I went ahead and told him more about myself and my children and how I was a widow twice, once by the court, and now again by God's will. I didn't keep back nothing that I thought he ought to know.

'You ain't scared me none,' he said, 'I'm still askin' you to be my wife!'

'I'll give you an answer the next time you come to town,' I told him. And when the next time come I said as I would marry him — but I didn't feel good about it. Good Lord, I said to myself, this will be the third one. There's an end to everything, but there don't seem to be no end to this marrying business. . . .

Yes, it was Charlie Hanks the medium meant — that Mr. Chase was saying I wouldn't marry.

I ain't said nothing yet about my friend Ida O'Connell that had left Fort Worth and was living in Hot Springs, Arkansas, and writing me all the time to come there. I told Charlie I thought of visiting Ida. I never said nothing about going into business, but in the back of my head I had that idea.

Charlie said it was all right with him, my going, provided I didn't keep him waiting too long. Could I give him any idea when I would be willing to marry him?

'What's the matter with the Fourth of July,' I said, 'when everybody will be celebratin' with us?' So it was settled that way.

Charlie Hanks meant business, and I reckon I did too. And so did a twenty-three year old, card-dealing whipper-snapper, by the name of William Graham Jenkins. You ain't heard of him yet, this Jenkins, but you will....

W. W. Chase left me a five-hundred-acre ranch and sixteen thousand dollars — Jenkins got it all. And Charlie Hanks and his forty thousand dollars — I give them up, too. I wasn't no more able to resist Jenkins and his handsome face than you could expect a bulldog to smile at a cat.... I was crazy and I knew it and I didn't care. I tried to forget Jenkins but my heart wasn't in the trying. I was in love for the first time in my life and I give up.

I went to Hot Springs wearing Charlie Hanks' ring. I left May in the convent, I didn't want to break off her schooling. If I wanted to see her too bad I could always hop a train. And Mr. Daggett — he was back there again in Forth Worth — promised to see May every ten days and write me.

When I got to Hot Springs I went to the Jordan Cottage. Ida O'Connell married the landlady's son, Ike Jordan. Ida was sick in bed but she nearly jumped out of it when she seen me. 'Jinny!' was all she could say; she was so excited. She always called me Jinny — she shunned the name Malinda for years, like I done. But I took it on long after and I learned to love it as my mother's.

There was nothing much at Hot Springs but the stores, hotels and hot baths. Nobody was living in the town steady, only them that was making money off the sick people that come there for the cure.

I was at the Jordan Cottage visiting with my friend Ida and looking for a place to get into business. Ida was telling me about the Mountain House that was standing idle. At last I rented it for a hundred dollars a month.

Ida told me to take it although it was right across from the Jordan Cottage. Ida's husband Ike owned a stage that run to the train. He made Ida a present of it; he couldn't bother with no stage, having his hands full running the Jordan Cottage for his mother. And Ida knew if I opened up, my guests would travel by her stage and leave the same way; she knew what she was about.

You know there's such a thing as Fate. Deny it all you want, but it's there just the same. Everybody that's had anything happen to them knows what I mean. I had been running the Mountain House a month or so when Jim, the stage driver, told Ida that he had picked up a fine-looking, well-dressed man at the station. Just off the train. This man wanted a good place to board.

Jim said, 'I been taking some people over yonder to the Mountain House and they seem well content. It belongs to a young widow from Texas.'

It was Jenkins. He answered Jim back, 'Take me to the widow from Texas; she's my meat!'

But I didn't find that out for a week. The night that Jim was telling about, the clerk come to my room to say as there was two men downstairs asking for a front room.

'Tell 'em to wait,' I said. I put on a black velvet dress that had a red silk, pleated ruffle under the skirt. Then I put on a gold colored polonaise and took a good look in the glass before I went down.

A strange feeling come over me when I seen him. I could have painted his picture; but the other man setting beside him, I'll never know what he looked like. Something said to me, 'You have met your fate but fight it!'

Jenky was there three days when he paid me a month's bill in advance. I couldn't figure that out, what he aimed to do at Hot Springs for a month.

The next night he tried hard to get thick, and after a time
he asked me to go to the park with him. But I couldn't stop for
no nonsense. Then come up that thing that Ida was telling me
and it riled me so bad I wouldn't speak to him — I passed him
in the hall without even saying howdy.

Behaving like that made me blue though; I was acting
against my feelings. I wasn't happy. Could it be that I had
fallen for this youngster? I couldn't make it out at all — still
I wouldn't give in.

Then Jenky made believe he was sick, and in the morning
someone wanted to know would I look after him until the
doctor come. I said as he was living in my place I'd have to do
anything I could for him. I went up to Jenky's room and he
asked me to put cold towels on his head. Pretty soon he confessed he wasn't sick at all and before I could tell him all the
cutting things that come into my head, before I could get a
word out, he'd proposed to me.

'I can't stand your bein' so near me and not havin' you....
Seein' how you won't take me no other way, maybe you'll
marry me?'

'No!' I said, and I rushed out of the room.

He asked me three times more, once across the office desk!
He said he knew I had a little girl and he'd care for her as if
she was his own.

'No, I ain't goin' to marry you, I don't want to have nothin'
to do with you.'

'Well then, I ain't stayin' on where I can see you, I'm a-
goin' over to Texarkana.' And that was the smartest thing
Jenky ever done in his life.

Before he left he asked me would I call for his watch where
he left it to be fixed, and hold it until he let me know where to
send it. I said I would if there wasn't no other way.

I was trying to fight my fate and it got me into bed. I lay
there three days thinking my head would split open. Then the
feeling come over me that I must get out of town and run away
from everything that reminded me of Jenky.

I settled my affairs and bought me a ticket to Fort Worth.

I sent Jenky a telegram to Texarkana to meet me at the station when the train went through and I would give him his watch. Back come a telegram from him saying, 'Buy a ticket to Texarkana instead of Fort Worth.'

But my mind was made up and I didn't do it. I traveled all that night. The next day, about fifty miles outside of Texarkana, Jenky boarded the train. He come in the car and set down and my heart sunk inside me.

'I'm goin' to ask a favor of you,' he begun. 'It won't put you out none. I want you to stay over until eight o'clock tonight and take the late train to Fort Worth. I have engaged a nice room for you where you can rest and clean up and my landlady is goin' to cook your dinner.'

Well, I thought, I can gratify him that far. So I said all right, I would.

He must have told the woman where he boarded about me for she praised him up to the skies, what a fine fellow he was. And Jenky talked and talked until it was six o'clock in the evening. 'It's all up to you,' he said. 'I've told you everything there's to tell. You know I am a gambler; I ain't got a dollar in my pocket this minute. But that don't signify nothin'; I'll have money again.' He was a loser then; but he was a money-maker, too. He never stopped, he never quit, he knew that he would make it some time....

Something said to me, Why don't you risk it? Against that I kept saying to myself: Fight it! Fight it!

One thing I couldn't deny. I was in love with him; it was all I could do to keep from throwing myself in his arms.

Suddenly it come to me: Try it even if it only lasts a year, and the worst that can happen, if it comes to the worst, you can divorce him. Divorcing was more than a sneeze them days. I was scared at myself for thinking of it, but I was crazy for the man and there wasn't nothing I didn't think of, trying not to give him up.

Jenky was a handsome scamp but I often thought about it since — maybe I was more in love with love than with the man. God knows, I'd gone all my life without it. And all the other things I thought of, along with love. A fine home and children around me, no end of children. That was the picture that was framed in my heart, but Jenky no more give it to me than the other two I married before him. I was obliged to change the frame but the picture was always there. It still is. I long for the same things today as when I was Willie Page's bride. But now my life's behind me.

Chapter XIII

I LEARNED more from Jenky than all the others put together. I oughtn't have married him but he was the man
I wanted and I had to. I was horrified at his gambling. I had
the big head; I thought I was better than some people. But I
couldn't get away from Jenky, he was too slick. His way of
making love was different. There was no lovey-dovey. He
was artful; he dug hisself into my heart.

Even after I promised Jenky to marry him it was hard for
me to go through with it. I was that narrow, if I'd seen a fast
woman coming towards me I'd have crossed the street, afeared
of tainture. And gamblers belonged to the same breed.

Jenky loved me as much as a gambler could love anything
outside of four aces. Down deep though I wouldn't call it
love; he wanted me, and I expect he admired me. And out of
it all come the suffering and the laughter....

I knowed what I was doing; my eyes was wide open and I
bunched into it. I wanted one year of love that I'd been afire
for — even if it meant fifty years of hell. Well now, I done
better than that.

When Jenky walked off from the Mountain House at Hot
Springs he left behind a month's rent that was due him. I
couldn't make him take it. But when he goes to marry me a
few days later, in Texarkana, at the office of the Justice of the
Peace, my money bought the marriage license. 'I'm short of
money, dear,' was what he said.

Back that time at the Mountain House, when Jenky paid
his month in advance, I had my purse in my bosom. The stairway come down into a kind of social hall, and I walked over to
the stairs with my back to him and counted out the change.
Years after, you see, when some people was talking to Jenky
about love and such like, and they asked him, 'How come you,
a young man, to marry a woman with three children?' here's

the answer he give them, just to show you how cute he was.
'Hell,' he said, 'what did I care? When I went to pay her the
room rent she set her foot on the stairway and under the red
ruffles, round the bottom of her skirt, I seen her leg. Nothin'
could have stopped me askin' her!'

He never told me for all them years, until he sputtered it
out in front of a lot of people.

We was married June 14, 1883. At seven o'clock at night in
Texarkana. Eight o'clock next morning we went on to Fort
Worth. Jenky was a stranger there and his idea was to go
West but I wanted to go home to May.

The first thing I done wrong, I asked Jenky for his overcoat
that was rolled up in the train rack; I was cold. I spread it
over me to keep me warm and when we got off the train we
was in such a rush I forgot it. A beautiful black overcoat, too.
He never got it back; it just made me have to buy him a new
one.

We stayed in Fort Worth three or four weeks. We went and
got May and took her out riding. She didn't like it, she kept
looking at Jenky and sizing him up.

'Listen here,' I whispered to her on the side, 'don't you like
your new papa?'

'How many papas am I goin' to have?'

I told her, 'Honey, you know what's happened. Your last
papa has gone to a better place than this. You don't blame
me, do you?'

May was very happy at the convent. Before I left Fort
Worth for Hot Springs the Mother Superior asked me if they
could make a Catholic out of her.

'Why,' I said, 'you can if May wants it.'

'We are all very fond of her,' said the Mother Superior.
May was an open-hearted child and loved the Mother Superior
and wanted to do whatever was right. She was young and took
it all in, but when she come out and was older, she left off.
Not that she ever changed back, but she don't belong to
nothing. No church. She's just a good woman.

The third or fourth day we was in Fort Worth I told Jenky I was going out to see my friend Melissa Knuckles in the country. She was from Georgia. She kept May out to her place one time and had been awful kind to her. I was dying to show her Jenky's picture and tell her how I had found the man I loved.

Melissa hugged and kissed me and was so glad to see me. 'So you're married,' she said; 'why didn't you fetch him out and let me look him over?'

I said, 'I brought his picture.' I held it out to her, she stood there looking at it.

'There's the prettiest man you ever seen,' I told her, 'and it's me that's got him.' I was so proud, and waiting for her sentence.... I felt like a pea-fowl with his fine tail all spread out. He struts so swagger when the wind blows it back over his head. But when the wind blows the other way and he sees his ugly feet — that's what people say — he folds up, he's done with strutting.

When Mrs. Knuckles turned round and told me what she thought I folded up like that pea-fowl!

'Linney, do you know what you went and done? You married a sport!'

'What's a sport?' Imagine a woman falling dead in love with someone ten years younger than her, and marrying him without asking nobody — and then going to a good friend to have her talk like that.

'Set down and let me talk to you.' She didn't know but what she'd stunned me. 'Don't look so pale,' she said; 'honest, don't you know what a sport is?' I said no, I didn't.

'You never mixed with 'em and you wouldn't know. The first time you married a farmer, and next it was a business man. Now you're married to a man that makes his livin' by his wits.'

And I reckon she put it just right to open my eyes, as near as a body could.

She asked me, 'What are you aimin' to do with him?'

'I'm a-goin' to live with him as long as I live, if he treats me right; that's all I have in mind.'

'Yes, but on what?'

'If he don't know nothin' I will try to learn it to him if I can. If I can't, maybe I'll travel along the same road as him — and love him.'

'But say, dear, you can't live on love. I wish I knew him a little because perhaps I could tell you better. I'm much older than you and I've knocked about more. I don't believe you will ever make a farmer outen the man on this picture. By the looks of him he's too swell.'

That was my first knock and it made me ready for the next one, after Dr. Fields seen Jenky.

'In the first place, Jenny, you married as fine a lookin' specimen of a man as I've seen round these parts. So he's from North Carolina?'

I said, 'Yes sir.'

'Well, you have married a Southern gentleman. I'm from Macon, Georgia, myself, and I think I know one when I see him. But,' he went on, shaking his head, 'them hands won't never work. What's his trade, what's he ever done?'

'A gambler.'

Up went his hands. 'I want to know! Then I pity you. I know his whole story. He's a Southern gentleman, no doubt, and he is tryin' to live it by gamblin'. He wears the clothes — but will he be able to support you and your daughter?

'I'll give you a little fatherly advice, Jenny. I know you better'n you know yourself. I know your strength. With a man like that it's entirely up to you — you can't never drive him; you got to lead him mighty gentle.'

We stayed at Fort Worth a couple or three weeks. Jenky was getting restless and we talked it over. 'There's nothin' for me here,' he said.

I told him about Wichita Falls where I thought there was lots of opportunity. 'We done a good business there — if you aim to go into business let's give it a try. But it ain't no gamblin' town,' I said, 'if you're fixin' for that.'

He bucked at first; it wasn't far enough west to suit Jenky. He come around though. 'I'll quit gamblin',' he told me. 'We'll go there and see what's doin'.'

We rented a house in Wichita Falls — three rooms, just for him and me. And right off I took sick. I expect it was the change of climate and the water. But I was worried, too. What Dr. Fields said to me and Melissa Knuckles, I'd took it to heart.

A doctor come but couldn't find nothing wrong with me. 'I reckon you have jes' collapsed; you've had too much excitement. I expect you're upset about something?'

I told him no, but maybe that was it. I asked Jenky to hunt up a woman to come and stay with me. 'Try Mr. Hall's place and tell him I'll pay his little Ellie to look after me.' I nursed this little girl through typhoid fever a year and a half before.

Jenky come back alone. 'He wouldn't hardly talk to me,' he said. '"If it was Mrs. Chase that sent for Ellie and Mr. Chase was her husband, she could go, but she can't go with you."' That's what Mr. Hall told Jenky.

I didn't sleep much that night; I was already good and sick and couldn't stand much of that. Jenky went to sleep and snored. It didn't phase him. Good thing.

The next day Hall called. He come in and shook hands and was mighty pleased to see me. He drawed up a chair by my bed and he said, 'Do you know what kind of man your husband is?' I told him I thought I knew.

Hall said, 'I had some business next door to my place and when I walked in your husband got up from a card table to tell me you wanted Ellie to nurse you. There was three big stacks of poker chips piled up in front of him. I don't let Ellie associate with his sort!'

I said, 'I knowed he was a gambler when I married him.'

I'll allow I didn't care much what Hall said. I mind though one thing. 'You told me three or four times,' I said, 'that it was me saved Ellie's life; but now, when a body's needin', you say, "No! Ellie can't help!" You married your wife for the same reason I married Jenkins, because you loved her. You told me some of your back experiences in life about bein' a good Christian and I ain't forgot them. Are you fulfillin' the rôle of the good Samaritan?

'I'm goin' to stick to Jenkins if he gambles all his life....
You ain't found yourself, Mr. Hall. You don't know what true
religion is. Pride is your trouble. You dasen't let Ellie help a
sick friend that's the wife of a gambler.'

He set there and drooped his head. He wasn't a bad man,
he just hadn't been awoke.... 'She can come if you want.'

'No,' I told him, 'I'll do without her. I'll send for May over
to Fort Worth.'

Ellie found out about it and come to see me but I don't
think Hall ever knew it.

Jenky made me love him and there's where I suffered many
years — most of it, I guess, because he was a gambler. I didn't
understand nothing about it, I was a praying woman and
belonged to the church — I hadn't been educated to gambling.
The way I was raised I thought there was just a God and a
devil. I was afeared of both and praying on my knees whenever I got the chance. That was the woman that married
Jenkins.

Later on in life, after I learned more, I found out that
Jenky had as good a right to gamble as I had to pray. Now
why do I say that? Because life is a gamble; everything we
take hold of is a gamble — everything we go into. Jenky was
a square gambler that gambled to make a living, that paid
when he lost and if he won expected to be paid. I've a sight
more respect today for the right gambler than I have for the
wrong preacher. How many preachers is making a living
preaching something that down deep they don't believe?
Plenty! You get an even break from the honest gambler and
a chance to beat him at his own game. But the preacher talks
a lot about the hereafter that you can't prove against him and
he knows it.

One thing I found out too late. No woman ever need be
jealous of her husband if he is a gambler; cards look better to
him than any strutting blonde. I only had to worry about
Jenky when he got hisself a job!

Jenky attracted me because he always stayed a stranger.

People is interesting while you're getting to know them, and when that's done you're three-quarters through. But there wasn't no getting through with Jenky, he kept me guessing and going over the jumps for forty-three years. There was too much to know about that man....

Chapter XIV

MAY come to Wichita Falls. She had growed so much, God bless her, she growed up like a weed. All in three months.

I went out after a bit, but I was a very weak woman. I knew I had to go to a doctor. I decided to go to Dr. Fields in Fort Worth and tell him what was the matter with me, as much as I knew. I was trying to get some strength back for the trip, and at the same time I was doing my best to get May acquainted with her new daddy.

Jenky was gambling. But I didn't say nothing and I wasn't going to. He come home with his cuffs off and his collar open. It was hot weather, but that wasn't no excuse. I asked him why he done that; remember Jenky was a dresser.

'Oh,' he said, 'we had a pretty tough crowd, and so many of us in a small room, and everybody a-smokin'. It was hot in there.'

A few nights after that he come in without his watch and chain that I give him for a present. He had put it up to be repaired. That's what he said.

Jenky had four or five suits of clothes and every day he would change to a fresh one. This time when I was brushing out his things before putting them away, something dropped at my feet, out of the vest pocket. A pawn ticket! Jenky'd pawned his watch. Didn't I hit the ceiling!

When he got home for lunch I was ready for him. He always kissed me when he come in. He started for me but I put my hand up.

'What's the matter with you, Linney?'

'There's nothin' the matter with me but there's plenty wrong with you!'

Poor man, he turned white, he hadn't never seen me mad.

'Look at me all you want to,' I said. 'I'm disgusted and

humbled into the dust. I always was proud of what I was so long as I earned it, but now I am the wife of a liar and everything else that is contemptible.' Them was terrible words for a woman to use to her husband.

But I felt it. I said, 'I'm quittin', I'm a-goin'! I could forgive you the pawning of my gift — all of it except the bald-faced lie at the end.'

And it come to pass — I left Jenky.

Any other man in his position would have said something — either begged and pleaded, or walked out hisself right then and there. But not him. He said, 'I don't blame you a damn!' His actions was the same as his words and that went further than anything because it made me feel that I had been too harsh.

'Don't you figure you will look at this a little different after a while?' he asked me. 'I had a terrible feelin' when I pawned the watch but I thought you'd never know it and I'd get it back in a day or two.'

'Have you any of the money left?'

He said he still had most of it.

'Keep it, I don't want none of it. I'm goin' back to Fort Worth to get operated on but under the conditions, as this thing is, I don't want you there.'

Jenky wasn't feeling too good; he was sick hisself, and down deep I was worried about him. He begun to look awful yellow.

Knowing he was out gambling and that we was leaving the next morning I made May sleep with me so's Jenky could have a bed by hisself and sleep late. I had all our things out to slip away quiet.... I was trying to reason with myself, and thinking what everybody had told me about the mistake I made marrying Jenky, but all the time knowing I loved him.

When we was ready to go and standing outside waiting for the wagon Jenky come walking out. 'I got to tell you goodbye, I ain't been asleep yet. I'll sleep after you're gone. You're quick tempered,' he said, 'but I don't blame you for gettin' sore. I know you love me and I'm a-goin' to try to be worthy of it. I'll write you wherever I go, so soon as I land there.'

He didn't ask me for a kiss but I walked up and throwed my arms around him.

Back to Fort Worth. I took May out to Mrs. Knuckles in the country and left her there. Then I went to Dr. Fields. He said I was in bad shape and had to be operated on.

'Listen here, I'll have something to say about this too,' I told Dr. Fields. 'You can cut me up all you like, but I won't take no anaesthetic, and I won't go to no hospital!'

He said, 'Are you crazy, Jenny? Don't you know no better'n that?' We talked it back and forth but neither one of us would give in. 'I absolutely refuse to operate,' he said. 'as much as I don't like no other doctor to touch you.'

'Well then, it's got to be somebody else.'

'You couldn't go through with it, if there was a doctor in town would do it your way.' He meant all he said.

I told him, 'You don't know me as well as you think.' I believed that I had gone through worse things and I wasn't going to have no hospitals and chloroform.

Dr. Fields insisted. 'You can go on a while like this but I don't guarantee nothin' if you ain't operated on; you can't go on for long.'

His partners was Dr. Bell and Dr. Birch. I asked him did he think one of them would do it.

'I don't know but Bell might be ass enough to try it!' Bell was always killing everybody with his talk, he'd scare you to death if you wasn't on to him. He was the one that told Emma McLaughlin the first time I had typhoid, 'She'd be better fixed with seven bullets in her head.'

I went first to two other doctors. It looked like there wasn't none of them would agree to it. So then I had a talk with Dr. Bell. He said as he would be down to my room the next morning; he wanted to think it over.

The old fellow come; he was tall and stately, about seventy years old. 'Let's see,' he said, 'didn't I doctor you first under some other name?'

'Page was my name then. Now I am Mrs. Jenkins.'

'Where did he come from?'

I said, 'The South.'

'He must be somebody!' he remarked.

'No, he ain't nobody but a gambler.'

'We is all that. If I do what you're askin' me we'll both be gamblers.'

So he didn't condemn Jenky and it made me happy; you bet it did. It done me more good than the best medicine; it give me hope at a time when I was all broke up over what people was saying.

'Tell me, doctor, I'm in pretty good shape, don't you think?' He thumped me all over and went through the whole proposition, felt my pulse, and tested my heart with his ear-globes.

Then he said, 'Can't I persuade you to go to a hospital and have an anæsthetic?'

'No; I'll prove it to you, I can go through with it.'

'You rest today,' he said, and he told me what to eat. 'If there ain't no inflammation sets in you can get up and go where you please after three days. If it does set in they'll be readin' your will day after tomorrow, so you'd better write one.'

That was pretty straight, wasn't it?

I set down and wrote a letter to Jenky and told him what I was doing. I wrote out everything. 'I'll be all right when you get this,' I said, 'or I'll be passed on.'

I hadn't heard from Jenky up to then, only that he was going to Tennessee. Jenky was awful sick too, with yellow jaundice that turned into the black jaundice. He come pretty near dying in Knoxville. His doctor told me, out of his own mouth, he thought Jenky was a goner.

Mrs. Knuckles come in to be with me during the operation. And I got Emma McLaughlin in, and the landlady. The doctor was there at ten o'clock, like he said. I wasn't nervous, not a bit — though I can't understand it, setting here and thinking about it years later.

'Well,' he said, 'what are we goin' to do? I want a table.' They took the one in my room. They prepared everything and laid it out, hot water and this and that — whiskey, and everything he needed.... I went through with it. It was an ordeal. No anaesthetic. I jumped around plenty but I never cheeped once.

Afterwards Dr. Bell took my pulse. Then he put his hand on my head and said, 'You're a wonder!' He told the other women, 'I'm proud of your sex!'

What a horrible fool thing I said to him: 'Doctor, you ain't never had a baby, have you?'

I tried to recoup up; I went out to Mrs. Knuckles and stayed with her and May. But I come to town every other day for Jenky's letters.

After three weeks in the country we packed up and started for Knoxville. On the way down when the train rolled into Memphis May pointed out the window — 'Look there on the street!' Well, they just turned the gas lights up and it seemed, to her and me both, like the streets was full of walking corpses, they was just that pale looking.

'Mama,' she asked me, 'is that their color or are we in the city of the dead?'

'It certainly ain't one or the other,' I told her, 'but more'n that I don't know.'

When the conductor come along he told us where we was. May asked him, 'What makes everything look so funny and white?'

He said, 'Why it's the lights that throws that color.' That was the first time we seen a city litten up with a system. It's been a long time ago.

I sent a telegram ahead to Jenky in Knoxville and he was there when the train pulled in. He was wanting us to come all right. He was always crazy about May. He wasn't never gusty over me, but he come close to it the way he acted now.

We drove to the boarding house of Grandma Childress where Jenky was putting up. You wasn't risking nothing leaving it to him to find a good eating-place and this was the best. There was two beautiful rooms, one for us, and another for May. Jenky was a fine dresser and handsome; Grandma Childress said there wasn't nothing too good for his wife and daughter — she didn't know but that May was his'n.

Jenky wasn't doing nothing, he'd been too sick — but he was gambling. He paid Grandma Childress three months in advance before we got there, scared he'd begin to lose.

Now he asked me was I willing to stay in Knoxville. 'I ain't never done nothin' in my life but gamble,' he said, 'save once when I tended bar. I was give up to be the best there was in Raleigh.'

I asked him, 'Who did you ever work for?'

'Mr. Upchurch, and I helped him make enough to retire on!' He wanted me to write him over to North Carolina. 'As a favor to me,' he said, 'and ask him what my abilities is a-runnin' a saloon.'

I planned to put up the money for Jenky to go into the saloon business and that's why he talked like that.

'No, I'll take your word for it. Go ahead and hunt your place, the best in town; it's the location that will make the money for you.... I don't know nothin' at all about the saloon business, that's up to you. But there's one thing I do know,' I said, 'you got to promise me you'll be runnin' a saloon and not a gamblin' house.'

Jenky got a location in the Hattie House, the biggest hotel there was in Knoxville. It had three hundred rooms and they figured on the best part of the downstairs for his bar. When they was fixing it up I got Jenky to set down and have a heart to heart talk and that was an awful hard thing to make him do. I told him that he should give me a pledge, with his hand on his heart, that he would not gamble while he was in the saloon business. I told him, 'Let somebody else gamble and you get the money!'

He done it, he promised to quit. And I believed him — I reckon he believed it hisself.

As soon as the fixtures was in, the night before the saloon was ready for business, Jenky took me down to see it. I thought it was the finest place, all mirrors in back of the bar, and oil paintings that Jenky found. He'd been around and bought some of them from saloons that had closed up and some from second hand places. I knowed they must have been painted for saloons a-purpose.

'My God, you got your courage, hangin' them naked women!'

'Why, it's the whole life of the place.'

'They ain't decent to look at.'

'Shucks, ladies don't visit here.'

I said, 'Tell me what you do.'

He stepped behind the bar and he put on an apron, a clean white apron. 'Now,' he said, 'they come in and stand where you are in front of the bar. If I know 'em I call 'em by name; if I don't, I say, "Gentlemen, what'll it be?"' He turned around and pointing to the rows of bottles he took a glass and set a bottle up on the bar and poured out some whiskey. Then he put another glass on the bar and put some water in it, down along side of the whiskey. 'Mrs. Jenkins, have a drink on the house!'

'Nothin' doin', not for Linney!'

He picked up the glass and drunk it hisself. 'There you are; now you know what bartendin' is!'

I said, 'I want you to put one small thought in your heart before the door is open, because I will probably never be in here again. Remember you got my all in here — and remember it was give me by Mr. Chase. I didn't work for this money. You come by it through a man's regard for me; now you prove to me that you care as much as he did, and some day we will be rich. But if you ever break your oath and get to gamblin', it's all off between us.'

A few days later he opened up and was going full tilt.

When we was at Grandma Childress' three months we left and rented a house on Fifth Street, from people by the name of Elsey. They was very well off — this had been their home until they moved to their new place, a big brick house. I never seen people like that. They built a special room, with little pigeon holes and cupboards on one wall from the floor to the ceiling. Everything stowed away. Figamarees and gimcracks, tied up and labeled. They just couldn't throw way nothing. To prove it, when we went to leave Knoxville, I had some ordinary paper dress patterns that I cut out for May. I didn't want to bother taking them along, and would you believe it, the old grandmother Elsey, she come over and seen them and picked them up.

'Grandma,' I said, 'what do you calculate them old patterns is good for?'

'Old patterns can make new dresses for my grandchild.'

She told me the secret of her life: 'Never waste nothin'!' She'd been poor, see, and she'd made that her rule. When she got her hands on money she could hang on. But she wasn't close with the poor. When people was collecting for anything, the Elseys was good givers.

They was all as friendly and nice; nothing stuck-up about them, but my, how saving! It seems like I got the habit from them, I can't throw nothing away neither....

Jenky fitted out the Fifth Street house with new furniture — with money he was taking out of the saloon. He paid five hundred dollars for my bedroom set. All mahogany, that was counted the best. The money was rolling in like marbles but Jenky was spending it the same way. The whole town was buying drinks at Jenky's bar. Why shouldn't he have made money? It was the best in the land, real Kentucky bourbon, and there wasn't nothing against drinking.

Jenky wouldn't stay home nights. He'd go back to the saloon after supper and it was midnight or worse before he'd show up home. It made me unhappy; I was worried he was gambling but I wouldn't let on. May seen me pray so much, on my knees by the bed, it made a heathen out of her and an unbeliever. She said that if the Lord didn't answer my kind of prayers he never would hers.

There was a young man bartender working for Jenky, living upstairs with us in the spare room. This Spicky Harper was supposed to take Jenky's place over to the saloon at nights. Before leaving I always give Spicky a hot cup of coffee and a piece of pie. I asked him why Jenky come home so late.

'Oh, he's stayin' there talkin' to customers and keepin' his accounts; sometimes we has big crowds and I can't tend 'em all and Mr. Jenkins stays to help out.' That probably did happen, but not the way they was making out.

This night I am leading up to I was reading, and to make myself more comfortable I set up against the head of the bed. I fell asleep, and I dreamed I started out to hunt Jenky. I asked for him over to the saloon; they said he wasn't there, he was upstairs talking to Mr. Hathaway, the proprietor of the Hattie House. Spicky Harper come out then — in my dream — and said he'd go upstairs to fetch Jenky. The saloon was on the ground floor of the old hotel. I heard Spicky run over to the annex and out into the street.

I decided to follow him. I climbed the stairs to a room in the annex and I seen Jenky and three other men with piles of poker chips in front of them, white, yellow and red, and Jenky's stacks was half a foot high. (Later I told Jenky what them men looked like, the color of their hair and everything.) Jenky turned around and seen me; he was shuffling the cards and he throwed them in my face! It woke me; that's what woke me.

Next, here's what I really done. I put on a dress skirt and jumped into my brown-woolen travel ulster. I grabbed a hat and the heaviest veil I had. In five minutes I was going full tilt up the street, with a six-shooter in my pocket! I don't know why I took the six-shooter but I took it. I went to the saloon, to the side door, like in my dream.

I asked for Jenky and a strange man come to the door and wanted to know was I Mrs. Jenkins. He said Jenky wasn't there but he'd fetch him. 'No you won't,' I said, 'you'll take me to him!'

He reached out as if he was going to lift my veil. 'Who are you?' he asked.

He was looking down the barrel of the six-shooter. I said, 'Take your hand down; get away from my veil if you know what's good for you!'

Spicky come out then and seen what was going on. He went

for Jenky. In a jiffy he come back with him — oh, and they was both running!

'Where was you, Jenky?'

He'd been upstairs with Mr. Hathaway. He said, 'I'm ready to go now, come on.'

We started off but neither of us spoke. We walked about two blocks, then I turned and looked at him. 'I want you to tell me the truth, was you a-gamblin' up there with Hathaway? Be careful how you answer that, because I seen you settin' and playin' cards with three men.'

'Do you mean that?' he said.

'I certainly do, Jenky. I ain't a liar.'

'All right.... Yes, I was gamblin'.'

I had my hand on this here six-shooter — it was a wonder I didn't kill Jenky, and blow my own brains out too, for I was desperate. If he'd lied to me I believe I would have done it. I wasn't what you'd call angry; I was just earnest. No, I don't know what I would have done but, inside, my heart was breaking.

'Let's be off,' I said, 'we have lots to talk over.' At home we went in, and I set down.

'How much have you got in your pocket?'

He said, 'Twenty dollars.'

'Give me it. Take off that watch that cost me two hundred and fifty dollars. I want that, too. In the mornin' you're goin' before a notary and make over the saloon and everything to me.'

He said all right. He never crossed me once. I'm laughing now but it wasn't no laughing matter that night.

'Is that all?'

In a few minutes I answered him. 'That's all for tonight, let's go to bed.'

'No,' he said, 'I'm sick. I don't reckon I can sleep.'

'Will you have a cup of coffee?' I had it setting there, all I had to do was heat it. But he wouldn't take it. He said he wanted to go to the water closet and that was outside. He went, but he didn't get more than half way before I was after him — he could see me from the doorway when he got there and turned around. The same thing happened again, and I knew in my heart that he was trying to get away. The next time I said to myself: All right, let him go! I knew there wasn't no use wanting to hold him. I kept still for a while; then I went out and looked in the water closet and sure enough it was empty.

I set at home for three days, waiting. The fourth day I sent for Frank Gibbons that was clerk of the court in Knoxville and had been boarding with us over to Grandma Childress' place. He thought a lot of me and I knew he would want to help.

'Frank,' I said, 'I got some very sad news but I can't tell nobody but you.' I told him what happened, how Jenky'd run away from Knoxville, and why.

There's no forgetting his answer. 'How come a woman like you to marry that blackleg gambler?'

'I ain't over lovin' him yet,' I said.

Frank hadn't never been married; he was mighty outspoke for a man with so little experience: 'Forget him! He ain't no account. You get a divorce and marry me and I'll take good care of you.' I told him no.

He didn't stop at that. 'I'll settle this up for you and get you a divorce, then we'll get hitched.' I said I didn't want no divorce.

'All right, have your own way. I'll send you a lawyer to-morrow — the best one in town, Sam Grabfelder.'

I told him that was what I wanted. A lawyer, but no divorce. Frank told Grabfelder to try to persuade me to get a divorce and that's what he done when he come.

'There's lots of good in Jenky,' I said to Grabfelder, 'but I reckon I'll have to wait till it gets woke up.'

He said, 'You'll never cure a gambler of gamblin'.'

And he told the truth. What happened was that Jenky made a gambler out of me....

Grabfelder wanted to know how I come to let Jenky have all this property, the saloon and money and things like that.

He asked me, 'Have you a note or a receipt or some proofs where Jenkins used your money?'

I said I'd look and see but I knowed I hadn't.

'All right,' he said, 'I'll be back tomorrow. If you have his note there won't be no trouble at all.'

I never closed my eyes that night, studying out what I would do and how I would get along. Daylight next morning it come to me: You can sign his name to a note! You can get his name offen the letter he wrote you when he come to Knoxville!

And I, well say, I believed it once I had the idea. When Grabfelder come I handed him a forged note. And he had no bother with nothing — he closed the saloon in my name, sold out and everything and got a good price, too.

Jenky come back after two months — rode up in a cab with the curtains pulled down, ashamed to be seen.

That was the time Jenky called me a witch — when we talked it all over and he found out I hadn't seen him with my natural eyes, in the card game upstairs in the Hattie House. He couldn't bring hisself to believe it.

'You told me you seen us!'

'I did,' I said, 'in a dream.'

Yes, he called me a witch, but it wasn't the last time. 'Ma's a witch!' he used to say, laughing. 'Where do you get them things, how do you come by 'em?'

Dreaming and hearing things before they happened didn't appeal to Jenky and I couldn't make him understand. 'Seein's believin'!' he'd say.

Only four or five years ago Jenky up and said to me, 'Gee, I done a better deed than I reckoned when I give you a note for the money you put up for the saloon in Knoxville, ain't that so?'

I never told him. Jenky died not knowing I forged his name.

Chapter XV

JENKY wanted to go as far west as the train would take him. He'd always been that way, and that's why I say it was Jenky educated me, instead of me him. I was narrow; it took him to open my eyes.

He decided on Oregon. That was 1884 or 1885. We left Knoxville for St. Paul. There was the cuttin'est wind blowing in St. Paul — it was so cold Jenky walked the streets with a quilt over his overcoat.

We was waiting for the emigrant train to be made up. There was berths along both sides of our car but there wasn't no bedding. You had to furnish your own. May's berth was over us. We bought calico and made curtains out of it. And provisions, what we figured would last us to Oregon. In the back of the car, in place of a heat stove, there was a big cook stove where everybody could make coffee and do the cooking. Fuel was furnished free, and the water.

I was sick for the first time after my operation, the same pains as before. Perhaps that's why I rebelled. 'Jenky, do we have to travel like this? We've got a little money left and I'm for spendin' it while it lasts.' The fact is our funds was awful low.

'Jes' let's go on without complainin',' Jenky said. 'You will find people on board that's better fixed than us. Besides, I kind of want to do it, it ought to be an eye-opener.'

We landed in Portland and went to the Portland House — not the Portland Hotel, we was mighty close on to broke. I was sick, too, good and sick.

I told Jenky he'd have to hustle. 'You got to find work, and I can't help you. What are you goin' to do?' I asked. You can bet I was worried.

Jenky didn't know. I looked at his hands; they was gambler's hands, softer than a woman's. Gamblers kept their hands soft to spot crooked marks — they could feel a pin scratch on any card in the deck.

'Well,' Jenky said, 'I'll go out and try.' He was willing enough.

So the first day — this is the story he told me and I know it's true — he found a job carrying mortar up a three-story building. The contractor told him, 'We'll go and see what's doin' up top.' Jenky followed him up the ladder to where the foreman was. 'Come around in the morning,' he said, 'and you can go to work.' When he went after the contractor to climb down Jenky found that he couldn't. He said his head was swimming. Poor Jenky, when he told me that he said, 'Linney, don't laugh at me, I felt awful cheap, but I couldn't help it to save myself. I'd 'a' broke my neck!'

Someone told Jenky about a job across the Willamette River. But he didn't get there in time. He started over on the trestle that carried the street cars, and he walked out quite a little ways before he seen the water rushing underneath. Then he couldn't walk another step. He had to crawl back. Jenky called it a-coonin' it; he was praying to Heaven he'd get back ahead of the street car.

'Well,' he said, 'another failure, honey.' Then I got an idea. 'I believe I know where you can get work. You go round to Mr. Nipplerjack's hardware store and tell him that you're the husband of the woman from Tennessee. Introduce yourself and ask him for a job.' I got acquainted with Nipplerjack and had told him that we was strangers. He seemed very much interested.

Jenky went to see him, and he put him to work over to his own place. There was two big fir tree stumps about four or five foot across, in the barnyard, way off from his house. He told Jenky how to get there, and to tear them out. Then he clean forgot about Jenky and the stumps. That was the chore he always give tramps when they come around asking for work; he knew they'd walk off when they seen what it was like.

Now this was the thing that kept me with my husband, because I would have thought we was going to starve to death otherwise. Up to then it certainly looked like Jenky wouldn't work. But he hacked for two solid weeks at them stumps; Nipplerjack never even seen what was happening. When Jenky come home nights his hands was all blistered and bloody, until I made him some half-handers to put on.

When Jenky finished up he went around for his pay. Nipplerjack scratched his head. 'Who in hell are you?' he asked Jenky. 'What do I owe you for?'

Jenky was dressed up when he come in first to see him; now he looked just like any other overall bum.

Jenky told him, 'I been rootin' them two stumps — I wouldn't do it again for Goda'mighty!'

This was the time that I was just barely able to stand up. When Jenky was out there trying to make good for me, I was setting sick in the parlor of the Portland House. Mr. Furr run the place. He had a good friend stopping there by the name of McNary, a rich cattle man from Montana. McNary's only daughter had just married and he was left alone.

I feel easier with strangers if they're old. McNary wasn't old exactly, but he was old appearing. I liked him right off. Young faces don't show much, but it's all writ out on the old ones.... McNary apologized for talking to me the way he done. 'I fell for you because you was the first woman I ever met that could entertain me by talkin' sense.'

I was heeding McNary, but telling it all to Jenky nights when he come home. McNary wanted me to leave Jenky and get a divorce. He offered to give me twenty thousand dollars the day I married him.

Do you know what Jenky said when I told him?

'Go on, honey, and do it! Then leave him and come back to me and we'll be rich!' But the next moment he held out his hands and showed them to me. 'See what I'm a-doin'?' he said.

'Ay, and you told me you couldn't work; you *are* workin', ain't you?'

I was a sick woman, and worried to death about May, if anything happened to me. I told McNary, 'It's only a business proposition, but I may be forced to do it. If you'll meet me here in a year from this time, and if Jenky ain't made good and can't take care of us, I'll get a divorce and marry you.'

We'd been down for a year near Oregon City on a ranch — I reckon it was the happiest time of my whole life. (That story's a little further on.) We come back to Portland — me and May. McNary was there, sure enough. I told him how I'd learned to adjust myself to what people was doing around me. There was times when I was too proud — that was a mistake and I always paid for it. Suffering taught me to forgive faults in others. And sorrow learned me to submit; I wouldn't cringe, but I learned to be humble. I told McNary, 'That's one thing the angels won't have to teach me.... We're still poor, but Jenky knows the feel of work and he's learned to like it.'

McNary said I was a good woman. 'I'm glad you found your happiness, even though I figured on havin' you.' I like a man like that, that takes the breaks as they come, and goes out quiet....

I was still sick and the doctors told me the only way they could save me was if I would be operated on. McNary knew this and that's why he said, 'If you get well you will make good, Mrs. Jenkins. Then some day you'll be wealthy yourself.'

Getting back to the first time I met McNary, I stayed on there with May in Portland while Jenky went down by Oregon City to look at a ranch that he read about in an ad. He rented it and come back for us. Jenky agreed to pay one hundred dollars for a year's rent but we didn't have the money. I asked him how he come to do that.

'I reckon I can go out and gamble and get the hundred....'

'You ain't a-goin' to do no gamblin', you're a-goin' to work!'

The man that we rented the ranch from was named Reinhart. The first morning we got there he come down for the money and I just up and told him the truth, that we hadn't it. We had sixty dollars left; that was all we had.

'Ain't you got no way to let my husband work this off? We'll stay on then, otherwise we're goin' back to Portland.'

He had a catch in his voice. 'Sh-sh-sure,' he said, 'all them st-st-stumps out there in the me-meadow, if he'll grub 'em out and er-er-burn 'em up, he can have the r-r-r-ranch for nothin'.'

Gosh, Reinhart didn't make no mistake in that trade; it was a heck of a job. Jenky cut hisself a fifteen foot pole for a lever — he'd dig under a stump, chop the roots off around it, and pry it out with the pole. He'd want me to come and help him, and many times I would. I'd ride the pole until the stump come loose, and more than once I got a bump that set Jenky roaring with laughter and made me so mad I'd quit and go in.

While Jenky was stumping me and May was busy with other things. We'd go over to the orchard, about a quarter of a mile off, that belonged to the Greens. They'd picked all the apples they supposed was any good. They must have been far-sighted. The trees wasn't near picked and there was plenty on the ground, too. We gathered them up, and back home we peeled them and stringed them in front of the fire for drying; the rest of the apples we buried in a hole in the ground. A big snow come on a few weeks later and kept them fine.

That was one of our assets. Another one was stopping the chicken coops I'd see going to town. I'd buy a few chickens at a time — whenever they was cheap — until I had six dozen.

Reinhart, that we rented the ranch from, had seventy-five bushels of white potatoes there in a bin, six to ten inches long and as big around as my arm. They was all froze and he give them to us. That was where we got our chicken feed.

The potatoes was full of water, and thawed out. But we used them — cooked big pots of them, first for ourselves; we'd mash the rest, throw in some cayenne pepper and feed it to the chickens. That's what they lived on, and we had as fine a lot of barnyard hens as anybody'd want to see.

Half of them had names. We didn't have but one rooster,

a big Dominique — white and gray, with yellow legs and a pink top. Jenky named him Brigham Young; he'd come and eat out of his hand when he called him. Them hens kept us in meat, and all the sugar, coffee and tea that we needed to buy. I got fifty cents a dozen for the eggs and they laid the whole winter, cold weather and all. Don't it show what people can do by nursing things along and managing right?

May and Jenky was just like two kids, catching snowbirds in home-made traps, cleaning and cooking them up with potatoes. Nights we pulled candy, and set and et roasted apples and told stories. We was never so poor before nor since — and never so contented.

Springtime Jenky went out to plow a piece of ground to put some potatoes in. He didn't know how to plow — I did but he didn't. He come in and he said, 'I can't make ol' Doll mind.' That was a horse Bob Reinhart give May to ride.

'No wonder you can't,' I answered him, 'she's afeared to death of you!' May'd go out and catch Doll anywhere. Reinhart's children could crawl under her belly. But she'd want to bust out of the pasture when Jenky come along. He didn't know how to say whoa right; he'd bark it. He used to holler at me, too — till I broke him of it.

'What am I goin' to do?' he asked.

So I told him, 'I'll go out and lead her.' But I didn't know what I undertook. I had Doll by the halter and Jenky held the plow. I had a bad time navigating over that rough ground, keeping my feet.... It was hard work, but I stuck it out until it was done. All day we plowed. May stayed at the house and cooked dinner and we went right back at it in the afternoon.

By the time we was done I thought I'd drop in my tracks. Jenky asked me, 'Do you want to ride Doll to the house?'

'No,' I said, 'you go on, I'll come when I get ready.'

Well sir, I made up my mind I wasn't never going back. I felt mean, too. I can't go on and live like this, I said to myself.

I went into a thick woods on the edge of the field. I got the notion to climb into some fallen tree and lay there in the branches. I was thinking I'd like to go to sleep and never wake up.

I laid down and this is what come to me. Back home in Indiana we had an old gray dog called Paint. I loved him very dear — all the children did. He just growed so old he couldn't chew, we had to cook his stuff and feed it to him. Poor old Paint mosied off one day. Six months after we found where he crawled into a hollow tree stump on the ground. Lay down there and died.

I thought, now old Paint done all he could until he was wore out, then he crawled away to be no more trouble to nobody. I can't go no further and here I am doing the same thing. I even forgot my May. I was just at the end, ready to give up; at least, I believed it.

I don't know how long I'd have been there or what would have happened, but while I was thinking about old dog Paint and wondering if they'd ever find me, something made me look up and I seen a coyote! A critter that can't do nothing to nobody. But I hadn't never seen one before and I didn't stop to reason. No sir! I forgot all about being tired; I rolled off that log and run!

Me and May stayed where we was on the ranch but Jenky was gone on. Got a Swede named Manuelsen in with him, and they opened a saloon in Tacoma. Meanwhile I got better acquainted with the Greens, the ones that had the apple or-chard. And with some people by the name of Myers — they was way-ups, one of them was a state senator. They all got it into their heads — how in the Lord's name I don't know — that we had money. And every Sunday some of them would come over for dinner. The young 'uns was stuck on May. She was only fourteen, but the sap was rising in her fast and she was pretty. I used to say to her, 'If they only knew we didn't hardly have enough to eat through the week, a-tryin' to give 'em a big meal on Sundays!'

They wanted to know where we come by all our apples. May told them, 'We went gleanin', where you gathered your'n.' They looked as if they couldn't believe it. They'd et up all theirs — now they come to us and et ours.

We were going back to Portland in about six weeks but we didn't wait. The nosebag was empty, we was forced to get out. Left there and run away. Just absolutely! Picked up then and there and never told a living soul goodbye.

I shipped my chickens to Portland. My idea was to find a little place in East Portland that I could rent, raise chickens and sell eggs, until Jenky got on his feet and we could join him in Tacoma. I found a house and we moved our stuff in. There's where I took sick again, just alone with May. I sent for Dr. Royal, a smart man and well experienced. May was frightened, being alone with a sick person, but the doctor soon got me out of bed.

He wrote out a prescription to have filled and he asked me if May was the only one around with me. 'I dasen't leave it with her to give it. Keep it,' he said, 'it's the best thing I know to relieve pain and make a person sleep — with no harm in it if it's give right. But don't use it without there's an adult by.'

I didn't have it filled — he give me some other medicine that helped me. But I had it made up later....

We was just doing fine there selling our eggs. There was a good woman, Mrs. Blum, that I had for a neighbor. She bought some of my eggs, and cheered me up when I was blue and worried and needed it most. Her husband was a butcher that got broke up in a town in the north. He come here and was just starting again. He was a smart man. He told me I ought to be with Jenky. 'What's the use of havin' a husband, if you can't be with him?'... I thought it over and decided that Blum was right. We stayed in East Portland to the end of the month. Then I sold my chickens and whatever else I could. The rest of my things I shipped north to Jenky.

Chapter XVI

IT WAS night when we got to Tacoma. I hadn't told Jenky we was coming. We went, I think it was, to the Cliff Hotel. It stood on a cliff, just a jump away, and right over Puget Sound.

I felt tired and weak. It was still dark next morning when I woke up. May had slept her sleep out. I seen her standing at the window, looking out.

'What made you get up so early?'

''Tain't early, it's jes' murky.' She come walking over to the bed, her eyes blazing.

'Mama,' she said, 'we can't never go no further.'

I didn't catch on to what she meant. 'You get up, and look and see,' she said.... 'You know about the jumpin' off place: this is it, we come to it!'

I didn't blame her for thinking that. There was the deepest, gloomiest fog hanging over the water; it sure looked like the edge of things.

'Mama, what do you reckon we'll see if we look over the cliff?'

'I don't know; water, I guess.'

'I reckon nothin',' she said, 'jes' like lookin' up at the sky.'

We went to Jenky's place, over the saloon he was running with the Swede. Before night I had some furniture moved in that I bought on the instalment plan — enough for three rooms. Altogether there was eight rooms. I used the rest of them to rent out. As fast as I rented a room I bought stuff to furnish the next. We didn't have none too much money, not by a lot.

Don't it seem like people spend a big part of their time getting sick and hunting cures? I was just fine for about two weeks but then I fell sick again. I begun to inquire around about a doctor. I knew what was the matter with me; up to then four doctors give me up if I wouldn't be operated on. But I made up my mind I was going on through the rest of my life all together; I'd had one scraping and cutting, what I wanted was relief from pain.

I went to see a Dr. Skanson. I told him all about my case. 'I ain't afeared to die,' I said, 'but it's the worryin' about my little girl. If she ever needs a mother she needs one now.'

He went and stood with his back to me, looking out of the window into the street. He stood there a long time, I was wondering what was the matter with him. When he turned around he was smiling. 'I reckon your girl won't have to change mothers yet!' He talked to me some more. 'I can't cure you without an operation,' he said, 'but I'll do my best to keep you goin'.'

He done more for me than any of them. He wouldn't give me no opiates, he give me herbs; there's one of them I take to this day. It's old fashioned yellowroot — what they call Golden Seal in the drug stores. It's good for that peaked look. If people knew what a wonderful thing it is there'd be more of them using it. Sometimes I go as long as three months and don't touch it, and other times I take it three times a day until I take an ounce.

Jenky's business was doing good, and we had our rooms all rented. I was curing up steady, too. I was in bed one morning — everything was still — and all at once I heard an awful ruckus downstairs, right under me. It sounded like chairs was being smashed. I hadn't nothing on but a night-gown so I went down the back stairs to the saloon.

There wasn't but two people there and one of them was on top of the other. I run up close to look; it was Jenky underneath! Just covered with blood! I know what I done but how I done it I don't know. I grabbed the other man by the neck of his shirt and jerked him off Jenky and on to his feet. He looked at me and I seen his face was a mess of blood, too.

'He's bit off my ear!' the man yelled. His ear was half gone; that was why Jenky was all blood.

Jenky was on his feet in a jiffy and after him, roaring like a bull. But this other fellow was just as quick. There was a metal box, standing on the bar, that they used to cut cigars with; he got hold of that. He lifted it to slam Jenky and I let out a scream. Jenky catched his arm and hit him a lick that sounded like a paper bag busting. I never seen a man cold-crack another before. God, he landed backwards through the swinging door, I thought he wouldn't never come to a stop!

It was exciting all right; how I had the strength to pull that man off Jenky I don't know and never will; its the kind of power comes to people when they need it.

He was one of our roomers. He owed us a bill and wouldn't pay up. This same morning he slipped his clothes out through the window. Jenky went into his room and seen that he was gone. Every morning he come down to the bar for his dram and now Jenky was laying for him. Jenky said to me, 'I'm goin' to lick hell outen him if he don't settle up!' — but I didn't think it would come to that.

Now what happened to me? I reckon it was the excitement. I kept getting worse and worse; I lay upstairs there, with the doctor coming every day and trying to ease my pain. Nothing but something strong would help me, and he wouldn't give me drugs.

Meanwhile Jenky was over at Henderson Bay, not far from Tacoma. There was a crowd of them went to look at some homestead land and they got him talked up to going with them.

I decided I'd tell Jenky to have the prescription made up that Dr. Royal give me in East Portland — the one he made me promise never to use unless there was a grown person to measure it out.

Jenky got back next day; he fetched it and give me a dose. When Dr. Skanson come about ten o'clock in the morning I felt fine, just fine, and I told him what I done.

'All right,' he said; he didn't pay much attention.

Jenky come in and asked me what the doctor thought about my taking the medicine.

'Why, he was jes' as happy as a little dog with two tails!'
One spoon of that stuff had made me daffy.

I slept good most all day. I only took but one more dose.
But I had an awful bad time coming. Jenky told me he was
up and down most of the night; whenever I'd rouse up I was
in a torment of pain. I kept asking for more of the medicine
and Jenky give it to me — nearly all, and I didn't know better
than to take it. I told him to go strict by the prescription,
no matter how much I begged. But he wasn't like that —
Jenky couldn't stand watching nobody suffer.

Next day I made Jenky go to the doctor and take the prescription with him. I was afeared.

Dr. Skanson come back with Jenky. I heard him say, 'She's
in a helluva fix — no one can help her now but herself!'

Well, it was a lucky thing I was listening because I knowed
what he meant. I decided to suffer it out and not touch another drop of it... I was conscious, that was one glorious
thing. But I was crazy, as crazy as a loon... I did fight it out,
I never took a drug knowingly since.

I begun to feel a little better. I got over that spell but I
couldn't gain my strength. I said to Jenky one day, 'How
about that place over to Henderson Bay that you could get
for twenty-five dollars?' He could buy it for that. We only
had a hundred dollars cash between us but I said, 'Let's go!'

'How can you go, layin' there sick?'

'It don't matter, I want to get away from these everlastin'
towns.' The saloon life — and now the worry of him fighting.
It seemed like he'd turned bulldog and wanted to clean up
Tacoma. Wouldn't take nothing from nobody. It was fretting over money troubles that made him grouty, I reckon,
and me being sick all the time.

Jenky said as how I couldn't walk to the steamer.

'I ain't intendin' to walk. You hire a hack. And go on and
get to packin' up. And tell me exactly what it's like, and what
we are expected to do when we get there.' I made up my mind,
if I had to die, it was going to be out in the air and under
the trees. And I didn't die.

Jenky said, 'Well, what about Manuelsen?'

'It's none of our business about him. If he wants you to keep on as his partner you can leave your money in the business.'

We went, and that was all there was to it. Manuelsen sold the saloon after we left. He was kind of stuck on May. 'Ship my rockin' chair and the stove with your things; you can have 'em to use,' he said. 'I'll be over when I get sold out.' That was agreeable.

May done up the sheets and bedding — the other stuff we sold to a second-hand man. We shipped our things to a place called Minter, where there was a small log hotel and a few houses.

The hotel was about a hundred yards from the boat-landing. Jenky and May helped me get up to my room. And mother Minter — she was only about four foot high and weighed two hundred and fifty pounds — come waddling along, the dear old soul.

Jenky told her: 'She's sick, she wants to go to bed.' She turned and started to run to the house, like a soft, plump ball bouncing along the ground. I had the first real laugh since I come to Tacoma!

For three weeks I hadn't been able to eat a mouthful of nothing but sauerkraut. I got it fully in my mind that there was a snake in my stomach — when I et kraut it seemed to stop kinking and twisting around. I'd feel perfect until I was hungry again. I wanted kraut, and as soon as they give it to me then I was all right. I heard since of people getting like that. It was the nerves of my stomach pulsating.

I went to bed and felt pretty good. Mrs. Minter brought me a lovely meal but I told her to take it away and not to waste it. I asked her, 'Have you got any sauerkraut?'

'Yes,' she said, 'the best you ever tasted, I made it myself.'

After three days I could get up and put my clothes on. I told Jenky to hire a wagon and get started. This land he'd taken up was six miles from Minter. There was five or six men in Minter knew Jenky from his saloon in Tacoma and they said as they'd see us to our journey's end. They didn't have nothing to do and they wanted to see what our lay-out was like. They made a place for me and May on top of the load; the men piled on the back part of the wagon.

We got there and got down. May said, 'Jenky, where is the house?'

He told her, 'You crawl on your hands and knees a few hundred foot along that there trail, and you'll come to it.'

She hollered out to the man that owned the team, 'You ain't goin' without us, me and my mama's goin' back to Minter!' She liked it down there. It was a pretty place and May'd been having a good time. She didn't like the looks of it here.

Nor me, neither. I thought to myself: Well, Malinda, you've been a long time on the move, and you've wound up your travels in a dog house.... Jenky, he didn't care for nothing. Come Sunday, come Monday, it was all the same to him. ... And thinking about Jenky cheered me up a little. Somehow or other, I didn't mind much. What's life without experience? Even a bad experience is better than none at all.

I went up the trail and believe me Jenky hadn't overstated it much; you had to part the brush to get through. It was a good thing that the men come along to help us. Where the cabin was you couldn't see nothing ten foot away, only a hole above with the sky showing through. And I was that weak I had to back up against a tree to look up.

Them wonderful trees! There was three big 'uns had been felled across, in front of the cabin. Their tops was off yonder, but the roots was right by the doorway. The men went to that first. They grabbed hold of a bucksaw and sawed through and pulled them logs away.

But hold on, before I come to the unloading of the wagon. May went inside the cabin and she come back with her eyes popping out. 'There's someone lives here! There's a bed, and clothes hangin' up! We can't take the bed out neither, it's nailed to the wall.'

It was a bunk. A man was camping there, cooking and eating at a fire outside.

'Never do you mind,' I said, 'wait and leave it to Jenky.'

The men carried everything up and left it by the cabin — except Manuelsen's stove; they took that in. They made a platform for it, and someone said to May, 'Go in and look, it's ready to cook.'

'Yes,' I said, 'and get something goin' on it.'

May acted sort of downcast. 'Honey,' I said to her, 'you can get a good dinner out of what we got here; they'll be wantin' it.' I was bossing everybody, but I hadn't moved from the chair that one of the men brought up for me.

Afterwards, somebody said it was the grandest meal they set down to in six months. May fried bacon and potatoes, and cooked turnips like we had them on the Reinhart ranch. And biscuits and coffee, and some canned goods. After me livin' off sauerkraut for weeks — I et it all and it never hurt me a particle.

We set round and talked for a while but the men had to be moving. They was going to foot it home, the wagon had gone already. Here then comes a man trudging up, with an axe over his shoulder. Jenky said, 'My friend, I reckon I am trespassin' on you.' Then one of the men spoke up and said, 'Hullo, Merrill! What are you doin' here?' He introduced us.

Jenky looked at me — 'What are we goin' to do, mama?'

I said, 'He can still stay in his bunk, he ain't goin' to bother me none. If he don't mind, I don't.'

We lived just a kind of every-day life there at Henderson Bay and it made a well woman out of me. Good air, plenty of good food — and enough work to make me forget what the doctors had been saying.

The first morning was elegant and sunshiny, even if all we could see of it was the glitter through the branches.

This man Merrill said, 'Use my stuff, and if the young lady wants to cook for me I'll pay for my share of the grub.'

Jenky had a lot to learn. Well now, naturally, he couldn't fell a tree; I told him to get Mr. Merrill to show him the knack of it.

Merrill spoke up. 'Day after tomorrow my job's finished and I'll help.' Which he done. They got a big place opened up where the sun could shine through.

'We ain't goin' to do much to this jerry-built place,' Jenky said, 'it ain't worth mendin'. We ought to have a log house.'

Merrill had lived around there about four years, off and on, and he knowed all the ups and downs of it. He was a big help to us, as much as he was in after life. He said, 'Jenkins, if you let me pick you out your trees, you can have the trimmest house you ever stepped your foot inside of. But you'll have to wait till the sap rises in the spring; then the bark will strip off easy, every bit.'

There was nothing to do that first summer and fall, and no money to keep going. Our funds was used up. We heard there was hop picking at McMahon's place, outside of Tacoma, and that a crowd was going. Jenky thought he'd go along.

'We'll all go!' I said.

We went in life-boats, about sixty of us. Working all day long we made a dollar a piece. It was a big job, the hops would sort of mash down.

At McMahon's I met old Judge Botsford from Boston. He was picking hops like the rest of us, though he said it was just for the vacation and camping out. Maybe.

Him and me used to have great arguments on religion. One night he asked me, did I believe in spiritualism? Well, I did and I didn't. I was afraid of it, and a little ashamed of being like that. Anyway that was my business, not his'n. I answered him, 'I don't know.'

'There's someone here,' he went on, 'that knows a lot about it, and I'd like for you to meet her.'

'No thanks,' I said; 'I ain't curious, I would rather not.'

I thought that was the end of it, but next day, when we was over by her box, the Judge introduced me to Achsah Staley. She was a gaunt woman, all of forty-five, mighty stray-looking. A six footer, with a face more like a horse than a human being. Yes sir, her jaw and teeth and underlip was horse. She had one yellow eye — kind of yellowish-green

like — and a gray one.... She was staring at me hard. Then
she started in, as if she'd been waiting for this chance a long
time: 'My dear daughter,' she said very slow, 'it's years and
years I been tryin' to get to talk to you. The family is all
together now.... Your papa was the last to join us. He ain't
fat no more, or lame.... The four boys is growed up, and we
is all very happy.' She kept right on, but I noticed her voice
was getting rough and coarse. 'You will start to climb the
ladder from now on and will continue till you have plenty.
You're goin' to have your white house trimmed in green, and
you sha'n't never want again as you have in the past. But
don't you take too much credit upon yourself; it's us will be
helpin' you.' She took her crazy eyes off me. I was scared,
and out of breath. I felt like somebody'd let go of my windpipe.

I never seen nothing like that before! Hearing things from
a stranger about people you ain't thought of in years; talk
from your mother that died when you was a youngling; telling
me my father wasn't lame; and saying things I would have
sworn there wasn't a man or woman knew this side of Heaven's
gates.

I'd done a deal of talking in my time, and for a while I
thought maybe Jenky or May put her up to it. Yet that wasn't
possible. Jenky wouldn't have took the trouble; and it wasn't
like May, neither. Anyway, they couldn't tell this Staley
woman what they didn't know themselves.

I pondered it over and twisted it inside out. How did she
do it, how did she come by it? The way she stood there looking
at me, bleary-eyed and talking hoarse, I was sure she hadn't
no more to do with the words that was spilling out of her than
I had.

I wanted to get to the bottom of this business worse than
anything I ever run up against. Only I didn't know where to
start.

About a week later it come to me, perhaps there was a way.
I set down and wrote a short letter to my brother Alfred
Plunkett, in Crawfordsville, Indiana. I didn't tell no one.
And I just asked him the one question — how many of our

family died young? There was three boys that I knew of and only three, but Achsah Staley said that there was four of them there with papa and mama. I knew I heard her right.

Alfred's answer come in about ten days. 'There was four,' he wrote. 'Abram and James and Buddy. And there was Jared that died a babe before you was born.' It's the solemn truth as I set it down. *Achsah Staley knew about a baby brother by the name of Jared that I hadn't never even heard of!*

That settled it for me. I had to know what it all meant, and I was willing to do anything to find out. I went to Mrs. Staley and I asked her what I could do to get messages like she done. I said I'd give her the few dollars I had if she would help me. 'The little I can tell you,' she said, 'you are welcome to. If the power is in you, you won't need no one but yourself. Judgin' from the eyes in your head I think you got it. But if you ain't, you ain't.... Set down at a table, and compose yourself any way that comes best. Take your shoes off — plant your feet flat on the floor and rest your hands on your knees; leastwise that's what I do. Relax, and make your mind a blank. Set down fifteen or twenty minutes every day, but don't expect nothin' quick.'

I tried hard from the beginning, but it wasn't until I was alone, after Jenky went to Alaska, that I had the quiet I needed. I worked steady for six years.... It all come gradual. First it seemed like I could see tiny lights. Then I begun to hear faint tappings on the table that didn't mean nothing to me. As my power of concentration got strong I was able to see people, very dim at the start and then very plain. So many faces begun to crowd into my vision it vexed me; it wore me down. I become so weak I knew they was using my strength. I knew I would have to get control of myself or they would suck me dry. It was the battle of my life.... Finally my voices come. Voices. To me that's what they are. But it don't matter what you call them. The air is full of what's happening; nothing is lost; things keep going on.... And then the dreams begun that was so plain, there was times I didn't know the dream-world from the real.... The voices is gone but my dreams ain't never left me.

Chapter XVII

WE GOT through with the hop-picking and was back at Henderson Bay. Merrill hadn't nothing to do over at his homestead so he give his labor free. He was sweet on May, that was it.

When spring come him and Jenky set to work felling trees and May helped. The trees was just as white, with the bark stripped — there wasn't hardly a knot on them, nor a split — though they turned a little yellow from the sun and air.

The Uttersons was our best friends — they lived about a mile off. They had the only span of horses around. Jenky used them to drag up the trees. We offered to pay Utterson but he wouldn't take a cent.

The cabin was down on what was called the bottom, close to the creek where the brush and trees was thick. Up where we was fixing to build our log house there was six hundred yards of level land with only small brush standing about — and some beautiful, big fir trees, but scattered.

We had a regular house-raising. Eight or ten men come with their axes, knowing what they was wanted for. All I had to do was give them a big dinner.

The logs was sawed off for a house twenty by twenty. The men done the fitting in and the notching. I wanted an upstairs and they give it to me.

Jenky went down to Minter to get what lumber was needed for the inside — for flooring and rafters, and the window casings and sashes.

In a few days Merrill and Jenky went to putting the roof on. They'd been at it all morning. I was busy, but I run up to see how they was getting along. I expected to see it all fixed ready for the shakes, but there wasn't a rafter in sight.

Then I seen the roof! Instead of being nice and sloping they put it on flat. I didn't cry... I howled! Merrill, he stopped hammering over in his corner and he said, 'I told Jenkins it was too level, but I ain't the boss.'

I moved over to where I could look up at Jenky. I ought to knowed better, but I couldn't hold my tongue — 'Don't you know you ruined that house?'

He had a hatchet in his hand. He raised up and throwed it; it didn't miss me by inches. Then he seen what he done and how he scared me. He climbed down, but all he said was, 'I'm through!'

I was crying when Merrill come down. 'I think it's spoilt, myself,' he said, 'it's a shame to put that kind of roof on such a fine place. I told him the pitch it ought to have, but he was figuring to save the lumber on the ends for something else.

'It can be remedied,' Merrill went on to say. 'It won't cost much for new rafters, and the horses come free. Jenky'll get his little mad off and then I'll talk to him.'

That made me feel better and I went to look for Jenky. I was thinking to tell him what Merrill said. I seen Jenky coming towards me with a grip in his hand. He never turned his head, he come and passed me by.

Merrill called down to him from the roof: 'What's up? Where you goin'?'

He said, 'I'm leavin' this goddamn place! I don't know enough to build houses, I'm a-goin' to what I can do!'

That was the last I seen of Jenky for three months.

He was gone, but we had to do something so I said to Merrill, 'I don't aim to get your work for nothin', but I expect you to finish the job. I want to get some new rafters, and I'll hire a man to help you.' Merrill set down and told me just exactly what to buy and May went off to fetch the Utterson team.

Merrill didn't want no extra man. May helped him and they got the rafters fixed in place. Then Merrill had to leave; he had something over to his homestead he wanted planted by the light of the moon.

'Listen here,' I said, 'you go ahead and do that. Meanwhile we'll clean up here.'

May stood around, looking at them shakes waiting to be put on. 'Mama,' she said, 'I can put them on jes' as good as him.'

'You can't do it.'

'I can. I'll carry them up the ladder and fix them right and proper.'

That sixteen-year-old girl done the job. Then she went to lay the floor. She done it just as good as anybody, the above and the below, upstairs and downstairs. She made a sort of stairway, too, a sloping ladder that wasn't never changed while we lived there.

Now that was as far as she could go. I told her to borrow one of the Utterson horses and ride to Minter after Chips Quill, the carpenter, to put in the door and windows.

When we was all settled and happy, along come Jenky. I didn't know if I'd ever see him again. I thought he'd go to Tacoma and start gambling. And maybe, when he got money enough, he'd come back. But I wasn't none too sure. I can't say that I bothered — I was too busy working on the house, and feeling real good for the first time.

One morning May dashed in. 'Come outside,' she said, 'I got something to show you! Run!' She pointed down the little path that come up to the house. 'Don't you see what's comin' up there?' Yes, I seen a man.

'Don't you know who it is?'

'No, I don't think I do; it ain't Merrill.'

'Why,' she said, 'it's Jenky!' He was all stooped over, dragging something.

We stood there watching. ''Tis him!' I said. 'Glory be! What's that he's got?'

He had been working in a saw-mill and was bringing his pay home. Silver dollars, in a gunny-sack!

Maybe you ain't never been broke. I have — lots of times — and, believe me, it's nothing to joke about. Things was a little better with us, but there wasn't no money for luxuries. My mind was set on a cow and a cow belonged in that class....

May'd went to help Mrs. Utterson when her baby come. I heard they needed a cook in the logging camp so I thought I'd slip away and try for the job. I went down and got it. May come along a week later and they hired her to wait table.

Mr. Winchester owned the logging camp, and a lot of others. But he wasn't there much. His top foreman, Mr. Fulton, stayed at another camp, too. Bludcross, the foreman in charge, hated me. He didn't intend that I was going to hold my job, neither. He was one of them underhanded men that hated everybody; I reckon he hated hisself.

Fulton's son come and warned me. 'He ain't goin' to let you stay if he can help it. He hates all women. He stamped on his wife's grave, crowin' that she was gone!' I was standing behind Bludcross and I had hold of one of them steel knife-sharpeners. He was talking to the men, making nasty cracks for my benefit. I declare the temptation come over me to grab him around the head and cut his throat!

The kitchen was built on a raft, out on the bay. A few days later Bludcross told old man Fulton I stole some sugar and boated it off. Then he fired us; that was after two months we'd been working there. Told me he'd got another cook — but nothing about the barrel of sugar.

It near broke my heart; it was something new for me to get fired and I couldn't swallow it.... Anyway, I got enough money to buy a cow.

Jenky got Utterson's wagon and took me down to Minter. I went from there by boat to Tacoma. That's where I run into Mr. Winchester hisself.

'What are you doin' in these parts, Mrs. Jenkins?' He was real pleased to see me.

I said, 'I come over to go to the hop fields to buy me a cow. There's good cows there.'

'Well,' he said, 'I want to go out that way; I'll get a buggy and take you with me.' Yes sir, he done it.

We found the finest big red cow. She cost fifty dollars; she was guaranteed to give three gallons of milk, and the guarantee was correct. Mr. Winchester handled everything. The next time I seen my cow they was taking her off the boat at Minter.

As we was driving back to Tacoma I said to Mr. Winchester, 'I want you to tell me something if you can.'

'Certainly,' he said.

'I had the worst humiliation in my whole life workin' for you. Do you know why I was fired? I don't, maybe you do.'

'Mrs. Jenkins, it all come as a mighty surprise to me. I know you was much wronged. They told Jake Fulton there was a half barrel of sugar carried away and they blamed you. The foreman said it disappeared in the night and to fire you two women. He said you was poor and probably took it over to your homestead. Now I'll tell you what really happened. The foreman give a boy five dollars to throw it overboard. Later on he abused him and the boy told on him.

'To show you how bad I feel about it, if you want that job back I'll put you to work in another camp, and pay you ten dollars more a month to do it. And the job's your'n as long as you please.'

'Maybe I'll take you up!' I said.

We stayed at Henderson Bay our second summer, and enjoyed life immense. I got so strong I quit praying for a tree to fall on me.

We lived on vegetables that Jenky planted down on the bottom lands — cabbages, turnips, lettuce and onions. And three gallons of milk a day. That was the main bill of fare. We figured on plenty of eggs. A man that was working there and had to go away left us a hundred beautiful chickens, but they lasted just about three weeks. Jenky started to build a coop from small saplings but before he was half done there wasn't no hens. The coyotes got them all.

Autumn I went to the lumber camp with May, the main one where Mr. Winchester hisself was staying. We didn't know what kind of place it was. We rolled our blankets and away we went. It was seven miles and we hoofed it. Jenky come along and carried our things. He left us at the boat landing, three miles across from Tacoma.

I was very much surprised when we got there. We found a

beautiful bungalow, not so very small neither, built out on the water on a boom. It had plank walks all around on the outside.

Mr. Winchester lived in the bungalow, nobody but him and his son Harry. But neither one was there much, with five other camps to watch. Many lumber people come there to buy his logs. There was a big dining room where the men et, and a kitchen and a storeroom. And an air-tight ice chest where they piled in tons of ice to keep the meat fresh. They fed them meat three times a day. I never stepped into such plenty. For the past couple of years we hadn't had too much of nothing; it looked good to Malinda!

Well now, I am going to boost ourselves a little. We cooked so good the men bragged on it. Jake Fulton told young Harry Winchester, 'Yes, it's swell grub, but you're payin' for it!' I put up a whole barrel of corned beef, off of what Fulton had brought from another camp. He come in and wanted to know where we got it. I told him that I had put it up. 'Where from?'

'From the beef that was here. It was goin' to spoil so I corned it.'

That opened Jake's eyes that we was saving, not wasting. He acknowledged up to what he had said. 'I was complainin' to the boss about you. Like as not you're savin' as much as the rest has been throwin' out, over at the other camps.' That made me feel awful good.

After working hard all day we'd go to the dances when we could. There come a masquerade at the school house and it was made a big thing out of — people even come from Tacoma.

Jenky showed up about this time. He'd been over to the homestead until it begun to turn winter. Now he figured to get a job at the camp. I asked Jake Fulton to take him on.

'What can he do?'

'Nothin'! He's tryin' to learn to be a farmer.'

'I'll have him earnin' thirty dollars a month in no time. I'll learn him, don't worry!' The second month they paid Jenky fifty dollars.

So we was getting ready for the masquerade. May dressed

as a nun — she knowed how to fix herself from the convent days. I was rigged out like a young gal, with a great long dress. 'I'll give out sure,' I said, 'but I'll go it as long as I can!'

I never went; it's just a little incident to show what them boys was like. There was an old man there, Uncle Ban, that was a hard drinker. Fulton wouldn't give him but thirty dollars wages when he was paying the other men big money. I heard it talked around and it made me sore.

'What's the matter that you don't give him the wages that's due him? Why not let him save a little for his old age?' He didn't even have an overcoat.

'Gosh,' Fulton said, 'I'm a-tryin' to save his life, let alone anything else! If I give him what's comin' to him he'd be dead next pay-day.'

Sure enough, Uncle Ban come home from Tacoma the morning of the evening of the dance. Sick as a busted snail, and it seemed like he just got worse and worse.

I could hear his moans. 'Mr. Fulton, ain't you goin' to send over to Tacoma for a doctor?'

'No, he's that way every time.' They had a camp-tender — somebody that always stayed at the camp. I heard what Fulton said to him: 'Looks like Uncle Ban's goin' to die.'

'Don't let's go,' I said to Jenky. But Jenky wanted to go to the dance. 'All right, you take May but I ain't leavin' Uncle Ban to die alone.' I looked after him, and when they come home about two o'clock in the morning I had him setting up and eating. Didn't he bless me!

It's a curious thing, this drinking business. Lots of people think a man gets drunk for the fun of it. He don't. There ain't no fun in getting drunk regular, and every drunkard knows it. Way down deep there's misery somewhere. Often it's trouble over a woman. Sometimes it's another kind of unhappiness. When a man gets drunk he has a notion for a while that he's as good as anybody, or even better. I never see a drunken man that I don't think what made him take to liquor.

Chapter XVIII

JENKY went to see how things was going over to the homestead, at Henderson Bay. The horror of it brought the tears to his eyes, to see the wreck of our cabin. The squirrels had got in and et the pictures off the walls even. The floor was covered with filth.

'That's enough for me,' I declared, 'I don't go back!'

Eighteen months altogether we put in working at the lumber camp. I got to weighing two hundred pounds — I gained seventy-five pounds since I left Tacoma. But my feet was broke down and give out. Fourteen hours a day on my pins; they couldn't stand it.

Besides, I made up my mind I wasn't going to marry May to no lumberjack. Going back to Henderson Bay meant that; they was swarming after her like bees. Moving over to Tacoma or Portland didn't appeal to me, I'd been to both places already. Seattle was a good town and commencing to boom; we was getting the advertisements. I wanted to keep going. It's a rule I've tried to follow, to keep going, never to turn back.

I left for Seattle with May. First thing, I looked up Bob Reinhart that owned the ranch we lived on, that time near Oregon City. Major Reinhart, his uncle, was a prominent man in Seattle, the head of Reinhart & Sons, the best grocery store there. Bob offered to put us up at his home. 'No,' I said, 'I want to go to a small hotel, I may be here quite a while.' I begun, the very next day, to rustle for a little piece of land and a house — something for Jenky to come to. Every minute I was more sure I wasn't going back to Henderson Bay to live.

I went to the real estate office of Turner & Dorfell, and Mr. Turner took me out to Revenna Park, about a quarter of a mile outside the city limits.

'I think we have got the exact place,' he said. It had five

rooms and was two stories high, with a pretty fair barn. A lovely garden spot with gooseberries, raspberries, currants and rhubarb — pieplant we called it back home — and cherries to beat the band. There was a nice lawn in front, and a little rippling brook within fifty foot of the house.

I looked at everything, and the more I looked each time I found something I liked better. We'll be happy here, I thought; seemed like quite a step from the backwoods of Henderson Bay.

Five hundred dollars they wanted for it, a hundred dollars an acre. We just left a hundred and sixty acres we paid twenty-five dollars for!

'Mr. Turner,' I said, 'I'll take it. It ain't cheap but it's what I want. I'll only pay you half down — the rest of my cash I need for chickens and a cow.' He agreed to everything. 'Lemme tell you something,' he went on to say, 'you're new here. I'll get you a thousand dollars for this place in a year. In good times it will be worth twice that. We have good times,' he said, 'and we have bad times. Everything goes in cycles.'

He was right, it's just like the tide, coming and going. When times are good enough you know they are coming bad. And when they are bad, the other way around. Whenever anything gets above its real value it's like counterfeiting money, someone's going to get in trouble. The high tide washes the riff-raff up on the shore, and leaves it there. That happens just so often.

I bought two growed cows and three heifers — yearlings that never cost me five cents to keep all winter. The heifers stood me twenty dollars apiece; I was offered sixty for them the next spring and turned it down. I bought a third cow on the Fourth of July, the best one I ever owned, out of the milk I was selling from the other two.

Mr. Turner paid me fifty cents a dozen for my eggs, when he could buy all he wanted in Seattle for thirty-five cents. He said mine was purely fresh and half again as large. He took all the butter we'd sell him, and three gallons of milk twice a week.

I wrote Jenky to come at once, that I'd got located.

I went and ordered what I wanted to go housekeeping with. We couldn't get nothing over from Henderson Bay for a couple of weeks so I bought what I had to have — a small stove and two white iron bedsteads, chairs and a table and things like that. When Jenky come, he got a wagon and moved us out.

I bought some brown muslin to make three bed ticks. We put shakes across the beds in place of slats. Sure, but we slept on good clean sheets, one above and one below. I hadn't forgot what civilization was, entirely.

Jenky was mighty pleased; winter was over, the sun was shining, and everything beautiful. He went to one of the neighbors and got straw to fill the ticks, and I made the beds.

The first time I drove to town in a neighbor's buggy Major Reinhart said to me, 'How are you goin' to get in from out there next time?' It was five miles. 'You can have an old daisy-kicker I got, and a buggy, if you just say the word.' He claimed he didn't have no use for them. Wasn't that nice of him?

I guess we hadn't been there a month — only really camping out — when me and May took the boat over to Henderson Bay to get our stuff. We got the cabin straightened out, but it wasn't home no more. We was there a week, maybe, when in walked Jenky! My land, I never dreamed of such a thing. He come around in a little boat on the other side of the Sound and got off at a place called Colby. Hiked through the woods and come in tired as a dog.

The daughter of one of the neighbors said to me: 'Ain't it wonderful the way that man followed you up? I hope I get one some day that thinks that much of me.' Him and May was outside, looking over the place. He hadn't said nothing yet, but I knowed it wasn't love that fetched Jenky.

He come in directly. 'Well, Linney, pack up your grip; you're goin' back sooner'n you counted on.'

'What's all the rush?' There was some real news coming.

'Listen,' he said, 'I got forty boarders! The world's turned upside down since you left. They're goin' to build the railroad right a quarter of a mile from us, and I agreed to feed a crew of men as long as they're within our reach.' Somebody fixed it with Jenky for the men to board at our place.

Going to Revenna Park, I was thinking it out. I knowed there wasn't but one thing to do. We had to set up a big tent in the yard by the kitchen. And build some benches out of lumber, like I done back there in Fort Worth. But I was fixed for money here to what I was then.

We done the cooking between us, me and May, and Jenky waited on the table. I made hot cakes for forty men on a No. 8 stove! When everything else was cooked, and the biscuits in the stove baking, I cleaned off the top of the stove with a grease rag. I had my batter ready to pour on, a tablespoonful at a time — with May turning them over and Jenky carrying them out. Besides that, I give them fried meat for breakfast. We cooked it on top of the stove, the same as the hot cakes.

Jenky took them their lunch, on planks across a wheelbarrow — in coal oil cans with the tops cut out. Time was everything. Them coal oil cans done for cooking as well as carrying. Boiled potatoes, or boiled beans that we seasoned with bacon, and sometimes fresh pork for a change. We give them light bread, sliced into great big chunks. And about ten pies, four men to a pie.

Jenky loaded it on and away he went, with a coal oil can full of good coffee to wash it down; everything just as hot as it could be.

Supper was much simpler because we had more time to get it ready. We give them soup at night, and such like.

They was there about two months. The railroad boss paid us off in one chunk. When pay-day come we thought we was rich.

I had a rest then, when that crew was gone. But Jenky went right on working, our five acres more than kept him busy. He set out an orchard, though we didn't get no benefit from it.

Anyway, it was a happy time. We liked it, and we had everything to eat a body could wish for. That fall I sold seventy-five dollars worth of blackberries, and I was doing a good business the second year in butter and eggs and milk. We never seen Henderson Bay again.

May was having all kinds of callers. She was engaged to a fellow by the name of Eben Wood, but it didn't look as if it was going to stick. She got acquainted with the people all around — they was buying five acre tracts like us, and building their homes there.

May met Arthur Castleton Labor Day at a picnic in Revenna Park. She'd been slipping it over on me, seeing him on the side, knowing I wouldn't like it because she was engaged to Eben Wood. May said Eben got smart and followed her and Castleton, and it riled her. Let it go at that, but the fact is May was going with him for a long time before I knew it.

Castleton was an iron-moulder in Seattle. I was very much impressed with him. He was a fine-looking young man — about twenty-eight, ten years older than May. I wasn't in the habit of liking the men that liked May; I was mother-jealous, I reckon. He was the first one that sized up good.

I told May to ask him to come over. The first time he was at our house he took off his collar and tie, rolled up his shirt sleeves, and went out to working with Jenky while May was fixing the dinner. That made him solid with me. I said, 'There's a worker, and a man that will go ahead!'

I bucked a while, I didn't want nobody to have her — but I give in. 'It ain't nobody's business but yours,' I told her.

My son Ollie showed up now, a fine boy six foot tall. I hadn't seen him in so many years that I'd forgot how he looked. He come to see May married. In time for both of them to take the smallpox. There was a lot of it in Seattle and I told Ollie to keep away from town. But the city life was what Ollie was looking for. Next thing, sure enough, he had it good.

I went to my Dr. Chase's recipe book and found a mixture that looked all right — sulphate of zinc, digitalis, a little

sugar and a few tablespoons of water. I sent May into town
to get it made up. Ollie broke out with eruption pits on his
face and everywhere. So thick he couldn't hardly lay his
head on the pillow. I kept him painted with sweet oil and
egg white. I was scared he'd be all pitted up, but it soothed
him and kept him from scratching. Ollie was walking around
when May come down with it. And that was more than
Jenky could stand. He wouldn't come into the house. I
cooked his meals and set them out on the porch, and he slept
in the barn in the hay! May had it worse than Ollie, but got
over it — both of them without a mark.

Then a man come from the Health Office. So mad he couldn't
hardly talk. I got mad, too — the things he said about my
not having a doctor in, and not reporting to the authorities.
When we cooled off I told him about the treatment. I seen
him putting something down, I guessed he was writing out his
report. But no, in a few days it come out in the Seattle Post
Intelligencer, the biggest paper up there, all about me and the
recipe and him; mostly about him, but that didn't keep me
from feeling mighty proud.

May and Arthur Castleton was married in Seattle, on
the twentieth of May, 1889. They had a bunch of young
friends at the wedding, but there wasn't none of the family
but Ollie. I wouldn't go; I stayed home and cried all day,
and I didn't let Jenky go neither. I don't think he wanted
to go very much.

I liked Arthur, but all I could think of was losing May.
It took their baby to come to make me content.

Jenky sold the place in Henderson Bay when we was sure
we liked it at Revenna Park. He got a chance to trade it for
a span of black horses. He had them at Revenna Park, plowing with them. He got a wagon and a plow in the trade, too.
And a hundred dollars in money that he give me.

We was getting along fine, so much so that Jenky seemed
to have more ambition than me. A neighbor of ours planted
two acres in cabbage on some rented land. But a heavy rain

come along and spoiled the crop. Jenky thought he could earn a piece of money by making it into sauerkraut, so he bought it. He went to town and got him some barrels, and him and Ollie had to gather the cabbage, and wheelbarrow it down the road about half a mile to our place. It was messy work, as all the outside leaves had rotted. Finally they got it cut and piled up out in the shed by the house. They shredded the cabbage with kraut cutters and salted it down. Pounded it tight with a heavy maul until a barrel was packed full, and set to one side to ferment. They went on until there was more than fifty barrels packed. We kept out one small fifteen-gallon keg for ourselves. It set right by the kitchen door, and nobody hardly passed it that didn't grab out a handful of kraut.

Jenky went into Seattle to sell his kraut. Poor Jenky. He got rid of four barrels! At last Major Reinhart told him to fetch it over; they'd try to sell it for him. I think they sold three barrels more. The big Seattle fire took the rest. That was the end of Jenky's sauerkraut deal.

I was contented with farm life and I didn't want to do nothing else. But when this fire come along Jenky seen a chance to make money in Seattle; and he did make it. He moved over to town with his team and was busy all the time. He rented a house in a back alley, bought a cheap stove, and set up to housekeeping for hisself. Meanwhile we stayed out to Revenna Park, me and Ollie.

That wasn't for long. Ollie got a job, and I went into town, too. I rented the Revenna house for fifty dollars a month, and moved all my stuff over to Jenky's place in the alley. Jenky was working right along — everything in the city had to be cleaned up and he was making big wages. We lived there six months, until one day Jenky sold his team and wagon; he got about three times what it was worth. Jenky was worked out, anyhow.

Then we moved down on Cherry Street into a larger house. I had several extra rooms there that I rented. Jenky took a rest.

Chapter XIX

MAY and Arthur Castleton lived in Seattle. Arthur worked in an iron foundry, about half a block from their flat.

May supposed her baby was due in about a week. She was trying to put a quilt on a frame. She wasn't feeling none too good; she'd rest, and go and lay down. Then she'd work some more on the quilt.

It went on like that until four o'clock in the afternoon. May begun to feel worse and worse. She was all alone. She went to the window to see if there wasn't somebody outside she could send after her husband. Down there below she seen the little nigger kid that Arthur got after a few days before. He'd give him a good shaking for throwing rocks on the porch.

So May called out to the boy, did he remember the man that give him a tongue-lashing? 'Yessum!' he said. She asked him would he run over to the foundry and tell her husband to come home quick — that his wife wanted him.

Arthur got there and seen how things was. He went after the doctor, and stopped in for me on the way back. May kept wanting to go to the privy — one of them outside kind. She was thinking she had a stomach ache; I couldn't make her believe it was something else. 'You stay right there in that bed,' I said, 'or you'll be droppin' your baby in the back yard!'

Billie — that was May's boy — was born about half past nine. He was a corker! I've been mid-wife to many a woman but I never seen a child that acted like this one. Dr. Terry laid him in my lap by the stove. He opened his eyes and looked around and viewed everything like a wise old man.

Jenky was standing there with me and he seen it, too. 'Mama, what do you suppose that child thinks?'

'Why,' I said, 'I guess he don't think nothin'.'

'Well, he does! He's lookin' us over, and makin' up his mind about us.... Goldam, he knows this ain't the place he come from!'

Jenky wanted to know what I thought about him trying for a job on the fire department. I wasn't for it. Firemen is chasers, they're away from home too much. And women is crazy after brass buttons.

But I wouldn't stand for Jenky's gambling, and I felt it was the fire department or that.

Captain Clark was a good friend of Jenky's — he took him on as an ordinary fireman. Jenky was very much enthused over the job — he didn't have to work near as hard as trucking with his team.

After Jenky was there a while we moved up to Pike Street to be near the engine house. And the Castletons moved up along side of us; the baby was about six months old.

Right along about this time me and Jenky come passing near to a bust-up. I was walking with a couple of lady friends; it was a warm day and we thought we'd have something to drink. The saloons had side entrances then for women to go in to get a glass of beer, or whatever they wanted.

I walked in the place, and by gum, I heard Jenky's voice! And he must have seen me just that quick. I was wearing a cape trimmed with black and white feathers — I reckon he caught a glimpse of it.

He was in the booth next to mine. He pulled the table up to the further partition and climbed out. Right over the partition. I noticed the talk stopped. When I went and opened the door to go in he'd vamoosed.

A woman was setting there alone. 'What was you doin' in here with my husband?' She said she didn't know anything about it. 'Who is your husband?'

'The man that jes' sneaked out.... If you know what's good for you you'll leave him alone!' I told her, 'This red-headed woman ain't bluffin'!'

'I didn't know he was a married man,' she said.

'Of course not! A nice innocent gal like you wouldn't think of that. He is,' I said, 'and don't you go to forgettin' it.'

When Jenky come home I said, 'Look out them brass buttons don't get you in no trouble. The next time you see your lady friend she'll explain.'

'That biscuit-shooter!' he said with a snort, like she didn't mean no more to him than one of the horses down at the engine house.

I found out where this girl worked, in a restaurant. I looked her up and I give her a lot of motherly advice. She wasn't bad looking, but awful lusty and overstuffed. She said as how she was very much in love with Jenky and that he was in love with her, too.

You can't change a woman's mind arguing with her. There was only one sensible thing to do. I told her to take him; I'd had enough, I was through. 'If you want him, as far as I am concerned, he's yours and welcome!'

I told Jenky to marry the girl, that I was leaving him.

'I can't stop you,' he answered, 'but I ain't marryin' no one else, least of all that wagtail!' She wasn't the only one I suspected. There was a raft of them hanging around Engine House Number 2, making dates. Jenky had me bothered as long as he was in brass buttons.

He kept on with the fire department, but he wasn't home much, the cool way we both felt. One day, being off duty, Jenky was playing cards in the back of a saloon, downtown, and he run into a man by the name of Max Liddicott, a miner, with a placer claim up the Fraser River in Canada. That man turned the whole world upside down for Jenky and me. I'd have lived and died in Seattle if it hadn't been for Max. Like as not.

Max persuaded Jenky to grub-stake him. He told him exciting stories that made Jenky want to see what mining was like. Got Jenky to ask for a thirty-day leave and the two of them left for British Columbia. They used canoes up the Fraser River until they struck rough water, then they packed the rest of the way in.

When Jenky come back he had a small bottle of gold dust, about four ounces. He was all fired up. His days off he visited the saloon where he first met Max, and he run into a lot more miners and prospectors. That's how he come to hear about Alaska and gold mining at Circle City — two years before George Cormack discovered the Klondike.

New Year's day, 1895, Jenky told me he was going to Alaska. He'd even talked his friend, Ace Blakey, into going along. Their real idea was to gamble. They thought they could make some money running a gambling house.

It didn't make no difference that there wasn't nobody around there knew much about Alaska. And that Jenky hadn't the money to buy a good outfit. It scared me thinking on it; I was terror-struck.... But it was better than the fire house chippies Jenky'd be leaving behind him; even the gambling part was better than that.

We patched things up and I decided to help Jenky all I could. I sold out the furniture and give him the little money I had. It meant going to work and I was glad of it. I was sick of setting on my rump.

Jenky bought mackinaw cloth, and a sled; and enough provisions to last him and Ace a year. Outfitting was quite a task, to know just how much a person is going to need. Jenky was awful green at it but he done his best.

They took the boat from Seattle to a place called Dyea. That's where they all used to land — later it was Skagway. Quite a crowd was going, but Jenky didn't know nobody but Ace Blakey. He told me down at the dock so soon as he made a strike he'd send me some money to join him.

'Whoa there!' I said. 'Don't look for me in that God-forsaken place....'

Now and then Jenky wrote me from them icy lands. I lost most of his letters, moving around, but I have the first one he wrote, and two or three more. Here's the news of his landing:

Dyea
Monday March 25 1895.

DARLING

We have had all kinds of weather and all kinds of grub that was N.G. We landed here yesterday. We are now ready to leave.

This is a small indian camp one store. Bear skins is legal tender $20.00. They give small skins for change. The camp is full of eskimo dogs. They steal anything they can put their mouth on. Ace stayed up and throwed rocks at them all night.

Darling go to Kales and tell him to let you have groceries to the amount of 10 lbs. baking powder we paid for that we never got. Up here we pay 50¢ for the same size can that cost 25¢ down there. We are ready to start out with our sleds. Me and Ace win $45. coming up on the boat from Juneau. I sent you two Juneau papers. Let the boys read them when you get through. Tell grandson Billie his cup is very much appreciated. It comes in handy.

We have a hard trip before us but I am ever confident. If any one comes down I will write you a word. Ace sweat blood while we was packing our things one mile yesterday. He won't weigh so much when we get on top of that mountain. I want you to be a brave woman. I am confident of making money and if I do we will have one continual round of pleasure the balance of our lives. For you love in hope wealth. Write to Forty Mile Creek. Goodby darling.

W. G. JENKINS

Well, that wasn't so cheerful. That Ace Blakey fellow was a fat, soft man. I knowed before they started that he'd lose his wind. Another letter I have is from a camp on Lake Lindeman, and it was wrote on April 14, 1895. This is only part of it — the most interesting part:

... We are here for a few days until we get our packs from the summit which is 9 miles back. We come near freezing coming. The wind blowed so hard you could scarcely see. The snow was drifting until we couldn't see the trail. We had to feel with a stick finding where it was packed. That indicated the trail. Three of us brought one sled with blankets and tents. It was after 9 P.M. when we struck the first camping place. The man there just pitched his tent. He told us to come in and sleep on the snow with him. We thanked him and accepted his hospitality. When we got up this morning our clothes was froze stiff as a board. We managed to put them on by leaving off some of them. We then went down to the lake and pitched camp and et pilot bread. It is Sunday and we are taking a rest before going back to the summit to get our provisions. Ace is sick. It has been 8 days

since he had a passage from his bowels. He is taking medicine today....
   My lips is cracked every way for Sunday my nose is all blistered
and I am sunburnt. I tell you it ain't no picnic to go to Alaska. Darling
I want you to have faith in me. I am sure I shall have it in you....
When you see May give her my love and tell her to be a good woman.
Tell Billie I will sure bring him a nice dog one he can work to a wagon.
By by

                                                    W. G. JENKINS

   Another letter is from Forty Mile Post, wrote on July 21,
1895. That's way up the Yukon, beyond Dawson. Maybe
you don't know it, but the big Yukon river runs north and
then turns to the west. In getting to the Klondike them
days you had to cross a mountain range, and then go down
in boats.

Mrs. W. G. Jenkins. Dear Wife.
   I received your most kind and welcome letters three in number.
Darling I have not struck a lick of work yet. I have about 5 oz. of
dust that I win. You bet I don't throw no money away.... We went
up the Hootalinqua River a piece but Ace was such a drawback we
had to come down.... I can't make much money mining this year, but
I have great faith in the winter for poker. If I make mine I shall come
home next spring.
   Darling the skeetos is awful bad. It is terrible. I see a great many
people with the rheumatism. I subscribed $5. to send one man out
today. People is very generous up here. Its tarnation few makes any
money. Not the lazy. Stores and saloons gets it all. Whiskey is 50¢
a drink....
   Ace went up Stewart River. You bet I was glad to get shut of him.
He could not tie up a sack proper. You have to look after him just as
much as you would after baby Billie. You will be my only partner
after this....
   I know you would not like to live here. All indian women nearly.
It is very quiet. The only excitement was a squaw fight this morning.
They wanted the white men to know what the trouble was so they
wrangled in American French and Chinook. It was too much for me.
You don't know how glad I would be to see May. I have dreamed so
often of her....
   I will write you again in July which you should get in the fall. I am
going to Miller Creek as soon as Forty Mile goes down. I close with
love and kisses from

                                                    W. G. JENKINS

All along I'd been scared about Jenky. Ever since he took the boat from Seattle. Alaska was another world, as far as I was concerned, a place I never expected to see. I didn't admire gambling, but I was getting around to Jenky's way of looking at things. Jenky was certainly some poker player. When he said he counted on poker that winter I felt relieved. To tell the truth about it, I stopped worrying.

Chapter XX

I HAD to get out and hustle. I went to San Francisco because it sounded like money to me—a place to get ahead.

I left May and Arthur thinking that everything was all right
with them. But it wasn't; they hadn't been hitting it off.
They separated, and later May got a divorce. Meantime
she got her a job to cook in a hotel at Vancouver, and took
Billie with her. For a while there, me and May always seemed
to be cooking for somebody....

I landed in San Francisco with fifty dollars borrowed money.
There wasn't a soul I knew in the town. But I didn't want to
go to work for strangers. I had another idea. I'd learned
something about it in Seattle — I thought I'd open a beauty
business. I seen a rooming house sign and went in. Across
from the No Percentage Drug store, on Market Street. They
wanted the rent in advance but I wouldn't give up no money.
I needed it for what I planned to do; I give them my trunk
for security.

The next day I got a printer and had a sign made and some
cards printed. I opened up for business as soon as the cards
come. I made most of the beauty preparations myself; I had
everything all fixed and ready.

Say, I got a laugh off my first customer. The bell rung, and
when I went to the door a man was standing there. Right off
I knew what he was hunting for; he was in the wrong kind of
beauty parlor, see.

'Step in,' I said, 'nobody's goin' to hurt you!' He looked
scared. I give him a seat and begun to talk to him. 'I have
some very nice things... but that ain't what you expected to
find. You thought there was some girls here.'

He owned up. 'As long as I am here,' he said, 'you go ahead
and talk to me; you're all right!'

I told him what I had. Showed him hair tonic, and things

for the face. He seemed kind of embarrassed. 'I'll tell you what, give me a treatment for my scalp.' I done it. And before he left I loaded him up. He went away with nine or ten dollars worth of tonic and face creams. All that off a man that come looking for a gal and found a woman close on to fifty.

When John Davis, the printer, come with my cards and sign, he asked me 'What are you doin' in business, a woman of your age startin' in?'

'I need the money. My husband went to Alaska and I give him all I had but a few dollars. I'm countin' on people buyin' my goods.'

'You ain't no ordinary woman.'

'If I wasn't, I wouldn't be down to borrowed money at my time of life.'

'That don't follow. Maybe your trouble is not knowin' your assets.' He waved his hands at the shelves. 'You've something more valuable to sell than lotions. I know a medium when I see one. It's your eyes,' he said. 'Why don't you use the knowledge that's give you?'

'Well, if I got the talent you speak of, it won't bring in no money.' He declared it would bring in a fortune.

'Not to me. I don't believe in sellin' it. It ain't intended for that.'

We talked on, and he told me what happened to him. 'I was a seeker. I was huntin' for someone to show me the truth, something to set me right. I heard of a woman here in San Francisco. I went to her, and before I even set down, she knew what it was I wanted. "You go down town and buy two small slates, and some colored chalk, and come to me tomorrow."

'So I went back next morning. "Wash the slates clean, and break off a piece of chalk about half an inch long. Fix your handkerchief flat on the table there and lay the slates on it, and the chalk.... Now fold it together, the four corners to the middle."

'She moved up to the table. "You are done with it," she said. "Now you set real quiet and listen."

'I heard the chalk writin' in betwixt the slates. "Them is

spirits," she told me. It sure was queer listenin' to the chalk scratchin' away.

'It stopped and she laid the slates on the table and folded her arms over her middle. "Now open it," she said; "take up the slates."

'This is what I seen with my eyes fully open; there was a letter written in yellow chalk, and my father's full name signed to the bottom.' John Davis told me what was in it. He told me once he would give me a copy of it — I wish he had.

But this is what he said when he was through with his story. 'Could I say that wasn't true — could I say she wasn't an instrument to give me my father's thoughts? Nine people out of ten would say it ain't possible. But it wouldn't be the first time nine people out of ten was wrong!'

He was a smart man, this John Davis. Many talks we had together. I thought the world of him. But little did I know, for a long time after, what it all meant.

My first Sunday in San Francisco I was setting on a bench in Golden Gate Park. There was a man close by and he moved over.

'You are a stranger, lady? The reason I say that, you are alone.'

'Yes sir, I don't really know a person in the place.' He asked me what was my object in San Francisco.

'I am in the beauty parlor business.'

'Are you open already? I am a real estate man, perhaps there is something I can do for you.' He handed me his card.

'Let me tell you,' he said, 'this is the hardest town in the West for a stranger to get started. There will be a hundred people come to you with all kind of schemes. Don't heed 'em, don't you pay no attention. Remember what I'm sayin' — it's a cruel, hard place. If you begin to make money, jes' you shun everybody.'

His name was Jimmy Reed and I ain't like to forget it. He come to me in about a week. 'How's business?'

I said I was doing fine.

'I got a proposition for you that I don't think you can afford to overlook. There's a woman, an old maid by the name of Mumble, has a lodgin' house at 1035 Market Street. I want to get her out. She's scared to death of men; as soon as ever anybody rings the doorbell, if it's a man she locks herself in instead of rentin' rooms.'

I laughed. 'It's a good story!' I said.

'Yes, and it's a true one! I'll take you to the house and you can see for yourself.'

We went up there about a week later. She come out, but the way she acted I had a feeling that Reed told the truth.

Two rooms was enough for me, they was the dirtiest I ever seen. You couldn't find the figures in the carpet for the filth. Reed went on to tell me the carpet was really good, and the red plush furniture could be cleaned and made fine.

'Let's go,' I said. 'I seen enough! I wouldn't have it if you give it to me for nothin'!'

But he kept coming, urging me to take it. He knew I was making money and he figured I could make the lodging house pay, too.

So help me but it was a dirty place! It was right stylish outside; I could stand across the street and look at it for an hour. There was two stone figures in front, holding up the second story balcony.... Still I was fully determined I wouldn't undertake a dirty place like that.

Jimmy Reed come to see me again. 'You are missin' a grand opportunity. I'll make you a new proposition, but it's my last. If you take it and don't want it, after a month I'll take it off your hands and no cost to you!'

It seems that the Mumble woman wasn't making a go of it. A man named Tittlebaum held a five hundred dollar chattel mortgage on the furniture. He was scared he'd have to take the furniture. Would I rent the place, buy the furniture and run the shebang? That was Jimmy Reed's plan.

Well, I had an idea of my own. Up in a little place near Seattle I owned eight lots that had cost me fifteen dollars apiece. I proposed a trade, the furniture for some of my lots.

Reed said he'd go see Tittlebaum and try to fix a deal. 'There's a school up there,' I told Reed, 'and a church, and quite a few people.' I give him a map and everything pertaining to it, but it was all sight unseen. I bought them lots that way and so could Tittlebaum.

He was a good horse trader, this fellow Jimmy Reed. Tittlebaum took four of my lots in exchange for his furniture. Both parties was satisfied, I had the furniture and Tittlebaum had the lots. He come to see me. 'I feel I done good,' he said. 'Up to the time you come I thought I was goin' to have to cart it away.'

To this day I wonder what was the matter with me, I was so flustered. I ordered a cab and drove over to 1035 Market Street — one block away. Mr. Reed was there and all the papers signed. 'Take the keys,' he said, 'and tell her to pack her trunk and git!'

I climbed them stairs, and I asked Miss Mumble for the keys and told her to move out. Just what Reed told me to say. The keys filled my hands full — it seemed to me like I was in a daze.... It come to me, I wasn't out nothing — them lots I didn't count. Six weeks after John Davis hung my beauty parlor sign I was landlady of a three-story lodging house!

I felt sorry for Miss Mumble; she seemed so helpless. 'Ain't you got no friends you want to go to? I'll order a cab and send you.' She shook her head and give me such a funny look. She said she didn't know a soul in San Francisco.

I'd been told to make her get out, don't forget that. 'Listen here, honey,' I said, 'I have an apartment with two rooms where I run a beauty parlor. The rent's paid for another week — you go down there and stay.'

She commenced to cry. 'I'm scared; I'm jes' scared to death!'

She left the next morning; she was quaking in her boots. God knows what happened to her in the end. That woman was afeard of life.

Next I had to go and talk to the agents, Madison & Burke, to see what I could do about my rent. Miss Mumble paid a hundred and twenty-five dollars a month.

I told the man, 'I can't pay you that, it ain't in the cards. The place is empty, not more'n six rooms rented, and the dirtiest I ever seen. You come up and look it over.' He said he didn't have the time.

'Well, how much will you allow me for gettin' it back into shape?'

'Nothin', that's your affair,' he declared.

'I'll make it your affair!' I said, and I got up and slammed out. By gorry, the next morning I had a summons to move....

There was a restaurant underneath my place, called Westervelt's. Mrs. Westervelt owned the whole property, my lodging house and all. I got her address from the manager of the restaurant.

I took a street car and went out to her home. We had a long talk. I liked her, and I reckon she liked me the way she acted.

'Mrs. Westervelt, the people that has been in your place didn't make good. Miss Mumble wasn't much different from the others, from what I'm told. I can't pay the rent your agent is askin' and make my keep. No one else could.'

I told her the condition it was in. 'A hundred and twenty-five dollars is a lot of money,' I said.

'What do you think it is worth, Mrs. Jenkins?'

'My offer's this: I got a beauty business further down in the 1100 block. It's runnin' good, and I ought to be able to move it up to the lodgin' house without losin' my trade. I'll pay you a hundred dollars and improve the reputation of your house. I'll clean it up and fill it! I'll make a place outen it you won't be ashamed of, but I want six weeks rent free.' After some more talk she agreed, and I got a note from her to that effect. I went straight off to the agents.

'I'm here again to talk business with you — I got your summons to move off.'

'Have you moved?' He grinned, as much as to say, he guessed I had.

I said I hadn't. He looked at me in surprisement. 'What do you mean by that?'

'This will explain it.' I handed him the note from Mrs. Westervelt. Say, but it was funny! The expression on his face. Madison & Burke had the worst name of anybody in town for being hard. But it was mostly their manner. At bottom they wasn't no harder than nobody else. I got to know them well, and we become great friends.

Mrs. Westervelt give me a three-year lease; that was a few months after. Then I sold out for fifteen hundred dollars spot cash — to a German woman that done fine with it, better than me.

I heard about a place across on Taylor Street, and I took that over. I paid three hundred and fifty dollars for the lease, and assumed a mortgage of fifteen hundred dollars. There was twenty-four rooms, furnished up from Friedman's store with the best furniture anybody could wish for. But the woman didn't know nothing about running a lodging house and couldn't make a go of it. She sold it to me for half it was worth.

Now here comes a queer thing. Madison & Burke was the agents again for this house on Taylor Street. It was a place with a bad name — uproars all the time and the police getting calls every week almost. I made up my mind to clean out the gang in there when I moved in.

So I went to Madison & Burke once more. I told them what I planned to do. 'What's my rent goin' to be?'

'Eighty dollars, just what it has been.'

I always called this fellow Mr. Madison & Burke, as a josh. 'Why did that woman fail, that was in there?' I asked. 'The place has a bad reputation and it's me that will have to fight it down. All fair and square, and I expect the same from you, Mr. Madison & Burke.' I told him, 'I'll give you seventy dollars. Come the first of every month for your money and you'll get it — in a decent run place, too.'

Listen to what he said to me. 'How is it you take over our leases, and never say a word to us about it till after you move in? And then come in and dictate to us your terms?'

'Because I know what's good for us both.'

'You sure know what's good for Mrs. Jenkins!'

I cleaned out most of the boarders, and never had no occasion to send for the police. But it was a close call. One night I had to throw out a drunk. He come to call on a girl, but she locked her door and wouldn't let him in. Then he started to kick the house down. I put him out the front door and it was about all I could do. I didn't want no flat-footed policeman trampling over my carpets so I tended to that job myself.

May come down and visited me awhile. When she went back to Vancouver she let me keep little Billie for the rest of the year and a half I stayed in my Taylor Street place. I never was in business in San Francisco again.

I decided to leave for the north — but first I wanted to see the feelings that Madison & Burke had for me, account of the way they'd been after raising my rent all along.

So I called on them. I said, 'Good morning, Mr. Madison & Burke!' We both laughed, that was our little joke.

'I sold out my place on Taylor Street....'

'Then I suppose you come in to talk to me about another place you already rented!'

'No,' I said, 'I'm leavin' you in peace. I'm goin' away; but I thought, in case I ever come back to San Francisco and want to go into business again, it might be good to have a letter of recommendation.'

He smiled. 'You set down till I write it.'

Here's what it said: 'We know Mrs. Jenkins very well. She has been a tenant of ours in different properties. She keeps her property up and pays prompt. But she makes us do what she wants. She is the first tenant that ever come in and dictated her own terms!'

I put a notice in the Argonaut, the society paper of San Francisco, that I was retiring from the beauty business and that Mrs. Bibo had bought me out. She was a poor woman, with a drunk husband and three little kids.... I give it to her.

We left for Seattle one night in January, 1897. I was standing on the rear end of the ferry boat, holding Billie by the hand, and trying to have a last look at the town. The fog on the bay hid everything but the street lights on the hills.

Tears was in my eyes. I was thinking of that Sunday on the bench in the park, when Jimmy Reed told me San Francisco was a cruel place. 'You ain't cruel,' I said half aloud, 'you ain't hard on strangers. You treated me good.'

Chapter XXI

MAY met us in Seattle. She come down from Vancouver when I wrote her that I was planning to go to Alaska. We talked about the Klondike with gold laying all over the place, the richest the world had ever known. Then Harp Shea come out over the ice and brought me five hundred dollars from Jenky. That clinched it; Jenky'd been having a hard time, gambling and tending bar, it was the first good news.

We decided to go in the spring. We started off getting things together — underwear, and heavy wool mackinaw that we made up into pants and long overcoats, the same for little Billie as for us. We bought four kegs of whiskey, five gallons each. And granulated potatoes that was a good makeshift for mashed potatoes.

All rations was in cans. The butter in one, three and five pound containers — real butter sealed tight. Our only meat was bacon. Come to think of it, the flour and meal and sugar wasn't in cans — we guarded it with our life to keep it from wetting. We never lost nothing that way — the whole trip we lost only one sack of meal, when a man's horse mosied over to our cache and filched it. The next day he give us a sack of flour in its place.

I went to buying some stuff I thought I could sell, finery for the dance-hall and sporting-house girls that I knew was in there. Everything that a woman in that kind of business wears and uses: silk shirtwaists; and underwear, stockings and such like. Over a thousand dollars worth at wholesale prices.

We got us a sled, and then we scouted around to find some dogs. Jingle Weeden, an old sweetheart of May's, give her a curly, half-breed Russian hound, golden brown in color. I bought me two shepherd dogs, brothers, Scotty and Husky, for twenty-five dollars apiece. Scotty was the smartest so we decided to make a lead dog out of him. I ordered harnesses, and turned the three dogs over to a man in Seattle to train.

There was a Mrs. Rice, on Pike Street, whose husband had already gone in. She was about thirty years old, a hefty Swede, an honest woman all the way through. She aimed to join us.

And her friend Frank Hart was fixing to come along. We seen them many times, and talked over and planned everything.

I heard of some men that had just come out over the ice. We went to see them and they said not to worry about getting people to help — men to do your work for you. There was hundreds, working their way in on boats, and getting stranded at Dyea. Without outfits, and glad to work for anybody that'd fit them out and feed them.

Meanwhile Granville Merrill, from Henderson Bay, showed up and wanted to go. That suited me. I loaned him five hundred dollars to buy an outfit; he give me a mortgage on his Henderson Bay homestead for security. Paid me back in Alaska.

So that was our party, us three women — me, my daughter May, Mrs. Rice — and my grandson Billie, and Hart and Merrill. Six in all.

We sailed the middle of March, 1897. We had our stuff took to the boat. It was supposed to be put in separate by itself so's we could get it at Dyea. I never seen a mixup like that — dozens of outfits and dozens of dogs. The dogs all tied on the upper deck, barking and taking on. The confusion was terrible.

It was only a few days from Seattle to Dyea where the Chilkoot trail begun. Everything was unloaded on big scows — there wasn't no wharf at Dyea. Dogs the same way, and all of it jumbled on the beach.

Between the beach and the woods there wasn't more than a hundred foot of cleared space — you had to cut down trees to make camp, and you was lucky if you didn't have a stump in the middle of your tent. We made camp like everybody else; we set up housekeeping and done our cooking. A white city raised up there on the edge of the woods.

The very first morning I got news of Jenky. Billie was all

over the place, peeking about and acting growed up. Somewhere he run into a man that just come out. It was him said that Jenky was in Dawson, running the Sour Dough saloon and doing good.

Jenky had been in Circle City when the Klondike rush started. To get the lay of the land straight — if you don't know it already — Circle City is further up the Yukon river than Dawson is. I mean it's further north. That there Dawson place is in the middle of the Klondike diggings, and is in Canadian territory, while Circle City is in Uncle Sam's part of Alaska. Well, when the rush begun Jenky tore right out of Circle City and made for Dawson, sledding up the frozen river. He didn't look for no gold when he got there. That's the strange part of it. With all his looking for money the easy, gambling way — playing cards instead of working — once he got in gold country, with wealth laying underfoot waiting to be digged up, what's Jenky do? Rolls up his sleeves, puts on a bartender's apron, and goes to work! Figures out to settle down to business just when everybody else around him is gold crazy. Well, Jenky would.

Once our stuff was separated and piled up in what they called a cache, our next move was to head up the trail from Dyea. First for Sheep Camp, and then for the foot of Chilkoot Pass through a narrow canyon one hundred foot high, just going as far as we could and making camp, and finding out as we went along plenty that was plaguy and new.

I picked up another man at Dyea, making three in all. My crew was supposed to hitch up the dogs, load the sleds, go five or six miles, make a cache — pile everything up in the snow and cover it with the tarpaulin — and then go back for another load. May pulled a sled with fifty to a hundred pounds aboard. She was a husky woman them days — not that she ain't a fine specimen still. Caches was safe; you dasen't touch a cache unless you lost your own and was up against it.

Between Sheep Camp and the foot of the summit we had a stormy day that kept my men from going out. Late in the afternoon it cleared up, but they said it wasn't no sense working for the piece of the day that was left.

May was a little sore. 'I'm loaded,' she said, 'and I'm a-goin'!'

None of the men offered to help her, so she hitched the dogs and drove off.

On the way to the foot of the summit she seen a man stuck on the trail with a big load. He didn't know what to do. She couldn't pass him without one of her runners going into the soft snow and perhaps tipping. She walked over to see what he was waiting for.

He said his dogs wouldn't pull and he couldn't make them. She asked him, 'Ain't you got a switch or a whip?'

'No, I don't believe in whippin' dogs.'

'Me neither, but you have to scare 'em. Why don't you try a little cussin'?'

'No, I never swear, lady.'

So May told him, 'You'd better learn, or you won't get far on this trail!'

May picked up a switch in the snow, down the trail a piece, and straightened out his dogs for him. Between the two of them they got the load going.

She never seen him again until one day in Dawson in the Alaska Commercial Company store May went to the scales to have some gold dust weighed out for what she owed, and here stood this man, Charlie Debney. She thought his face was familiar but she couldn't place him. He asked her, 'Ain't you the lady I met on the trail?'

'Maybe,' she said.

'Well, ain't you the lady that told me to learn to swear if I wanted to drive a dog team?' She told him she was.

'I learned,' he said; 'I learned proper!'

We had three sleds in our party. The last thing was the camping outfit. When they got that up to the cache we pitched tent until the next start. We'd find a place for our tent and build a fire in the stove. They was little square-shaped affairs, called Yukon stoves, made out of sheet iron with two holes on top, set cater-corner, and a pipe to run through the tent.

In Alaska the dogs come first. We cooked their food in a

galvanized vat — boiled rice, and fried grease from squares of dog bacon, yellow and too old for people to eat. While it is cooling off the dogs is laying around, resting and coming up to their appetites. A satisfied dog, with a full belly, curls up in the snow with his tail over his nose and stays there for the night. The morning feed was dried salmon; every dog got half a salmon.

Scotty seemed to know what was supposed of him. We never had to learn him more than he was trained in Seattle. He got right into the gee and haw business — to the right and left. When you wanted to start him you hollered mush. Whoa meant stop.

You ain't got a chance without your dogs. Sometimes their feet get sore from traveling on the ice, all cut up and bleeding. Then you got to doctor them, and make them canvas moccasins. These malamoots is fighters. They don't fight much after they've had a hard day's work; the trouble starts when they're running around doing nothing, waiting for the next mush that might be days off. If it's a fight among your own dogs you can separate them, but if they tangle with a strange team, dogs from everywhere come running in to mix it. The dog that's at the bottom is in for it.... I was scared to death of a dog fight.

We was a month getting from Dyea up to the foot of Chilkoot Pass. Then we stayed there, I reckon it was close on to two weeks, until our crew got everything cached up on top.

One of them nights, very late, I woke up hollering for May. I was smothering! Lorda'mighty, yes! May jumped out of bed and lit the coal oil lamp. Then she started a fire in the stove and put some clothes on. I was crawled to the foot of the bed where I could see how the tent had mashed down against my head. It looked to May like the tent ropes come loose. She started outside to tighten up, but as she turned to go around the corner of the tent she run into snow. Up to her middle!... Well say, the way May screamed she'd have woke the dead — clambering over a mound of snow and hollering, 'SNOW SLIDE! GET OUTEN YOUR TENTS! GET OUT QUICK!'

I wedged outside and what I seen made my blood run cold. There wasn't a tent above us! All of them buried! Everything smooth in the moonlight — smooth, fresh snow. And people streaming from their tents below us, scurrying around for shovels....

In all that racket there wasn't no sign from them on the incline, above us. Everybody went to work digging — nobody thought nothing about the buried caches, only about the people that was covered up. It was horrifying. Some tents they got at easy, knowing where they was, but others they couldn't find in the hurry-skurry.

Once the tops of the tents was sticking out above the snow the people could help themselves. But further up there was nine tents completely covered that had to be located. The last tent full was farthest up the incline, they got it digged out at last. They did, they found them all; no one was lost.

A snow slide don't make a bit of noise. It slips and creeps, piling up and on, slow and easy, without no warning. It takes everything in its path, covering it up. Next spring forty people was killed by a slide on the same trail.

I told May: 'I don't like it so well here that I want to stay forever, but that's what I'm aimin' to do until I can ride out peaceful on a train!' And believe me that's what come to pass, though it didn't seem like it was possible when I said it.

The first day of May we broke camp and headed for the pass, me and May and Billie. We stuck to the trail but it was slow work. It was that steep they'd cut steps all the way up. There was a second trail along side for going back down but there wasn't much to it; all you had to do was double up your gunnysack, set on it, and slide. Climbing up though, the chance of slipping on the steps made it dangerous. The dogs was no good at all there. Of course, we didn't do the packing; my three men done it all, a hundred and fifty pounds at a time, caching it on the plateau on top, and sliding down for more.

A man named Burns rigged a sort of trolley on the top of the mountain to hoist packs up. It was a wire cable contraption that worked fine for them that could stand the charge. Fifty cents a pound! I forget what kind of power he had. Horse, I expect, because Burns used to rent out horses to haul for people between Sheep Camp and the pass. You could make longer hauls with horses than working the dogs — there was quite a few horses brought up on the boat with us.

Camping below Chilkoot everybody was hungry for fresh meat. Burns heard it said, and he offered to kill a horse if he could get customers for it. He was a bear for charging. I declare, I don't know how much we paid Burns per pound for the meat, but I'm certain he made five hundred dollars off that old cayouse! It was tough as leather and awful dark. We got away with it but nobody enjoyed themselves! That was the first and last time I ever tasted horse.

The weather was fine when we started up. May had the dogs harnessed and made Billie take hold of a rope tied on to the traces. Billie had a grand time, thinking he was driving them dogs. We trudged along, other people trudging along like ourselves, and men sliding down, lickety-split. It come on dark just before we got to the top and I didn't know if to go on or turn back. May was for going on. 'All we got to do is follow the dogs.'

'You run things,' I said, 'I ain't worth a durn!'

When we quit climbing we knew we was on the top — there wasn't no other way to tell; it was black as pitch. I don't know how big a space was up there — I never will know. And no trail. We punched around with our sticks for packed-down places, safe to walk on. We put Billie between us, and May took hold of the dogs because she could handle them best. Scotty led the way and he was sure wonderful, getting off from the trail but nosing back until he picked it up again. We went that thing alone, two women and a boy — and a dog that knew when he was right and when he was wrong.

It took us two and a half hours to get up, which wasn't bad going the way we'd been told. Half way across the plateau it cleared and was beautiful. Everywhere was caches, tons and tons of stuff.

My three men was ahead; they'd packed the camp outfit on to Lake Lindeman where we was due by sundown.

So the next step was to get down the mountain on the other side. 'Mush!' I said. But I changed my mind when I seen the slide in front of me. I couldn't make my feet step out. Plain balked! It wasn't so steep neither; not near so steep as climbing up, but slick as glass. Looking down made me sick. It sure did.

'May, I never can go down there!'

'You will have to!'

I took another look. What made it so slick, the men at the top would load their sleds up, cinch the stuff on tight and turn them loose. Imagine a loaded sled going down a mountain! You'd hear them holler, 'Look out below!' Down there everything was bustle, getting the sleds out of the way as they come shooting down. Well, it was a mountain of ice, that's what it was.

May was trying to coax me. She went over to our cache and took a shovel, and practiced me to sit down on it, holding the handle. 'Dig your heels into the snow,' she said, 'and hang on!'

Little Billie, he said, 'Nana, I can jes' set down and scoot!'

'Yes,' I told him, 'but you don't weigh no two hundred pounds!'

I decided to try that shovel business on a small knoll. May pushed me off. About half way I spilled over in the snow, backside up.

May went over to the cache next to ours and borrowed a tarpaulin off the man there. She took it and doubled it up so's it come over my lap. Meantime little Billie was at the bottom. He'd slid down. May tied a rope around my waist and got me over the edge.

'You hang on to the tarpaulin,' she said, 'and stop actin' up. We'll go down together.'

She started me off with nothing to brace her, but she told me later she had one foot under her and kind of held back to the edge with her other foot — away from the slippery part in the center. Knowing May was on the other end of the rope made it better. It didn't take us over three minutes. We sure sizzled and bumped.

Then come the long trek to Lake Lindeman. We had to get there by sundown. We hadn't no food with us; we knew we'd freeze to death if we didn't make it. We had a kind of iron contrivance to keep from slipping, fastened to the back of our shoes. We walked and walked, and stopped and rested, and walked some more.

It was getting night; we had to hustle. The dogs shifted for themselves; May'd unhitched them so's they could run separate. Then Billie spotted a faint light ahead. Oh, how tired and hungry we was, but we knew we was there.

It was pitch dark when we begin to inquire among the tents for ours. Mrs. Rice got in before us and had supper ready. We wasn't long piling into bed.

Next day we seen what it was like: no town, only what the tents had made. Spread out in front of us was a great lake of glare ice, six miles long — so beautiful I felt like I'd started life in a new world. Everything dark, dark blue and snow white. I loved it — but I couldn't stifle the terror inside me.

'If all Alaska's like this,' I said to May, 'I ain't sure I'll be able to stick it out.'

'Everybody feels like that.'

'It ain't easy to explain it in words....'

'You don't have to,' May said, 'it's a helluva place!'

I never knew nothing until I went to Alaska. That's where I learned — it will learn anybody. There was so much that I couldn't understand, I seen for the first time the nothingness of the small things. In Alaska everything is big....

Something happened to me that give me faith and made me stick it out. I reckon I never could have no other way — the cooped-up feeling that makes you want to pick up and run, and the hardships that all but kill you.

May done the baking on the trail. It was bread day, about three in the afternoon. When I went inside the tent to have a nap May put the loaf in the oven. She had it baked when I called to her — so it was an hour later.... It seemed like a dream, but I know it wasn't. Most people won't understand that, but there'll be some that will.

'*I had a wonderful experience,*' *I said,* '*I ain't been asleep at all.*' *May said,* '*You ain't? You sure been quiet.*'

'*I was quiet because I wasn't here! I got up and throwed them tent flaps back and walked out. Then I started up, up till my feet touched solid. I don't know where I was; I reckon I'll never know. Around me I seen people dressed in flowin' white, and all alike so's I couldn't tell the men from the women. Shiny lookin' people, like clouds with the sun a-breakin' through. They was singin', not the way you find down here, different from anything I ever heard. Nobody paid no attention to me at first — I felt terrible lonely. Then I heard a voice askin'* — "*Don't you want to rest with us?*"

'"*I would like to,*" *I said,* "*but it ain't right I should.... I got to go back; I can't leave them I love, like they're fixed... but I wish I could stay.*"

'*It come over me, when I said that, do I know what I'm a-sayin'?... I was studying on it, I couldn't get a hold on myself, I couldn't make it out....*

'*There was one figure standing over to the side, the face was covered up. I asked who that was.*

'"*You can't know unless you decide to stay. But we won't keep you. We will take you to your people.... We will help you through all your trials.*"

'*I stepped back into space and floated down. They was chantin'.* "*Fare you well! Fare you well!*" *fainter and fainter. When I couldn't hear them no more I was back by these here flaps of the tent.... It felt like I was being squeezed into myself, pushed into a small space, and I knew it was my spirit rushin' into my body — that I had been away.*'

I was sore all over and tired, oh, so tired. May tried to tell me that I had been dreaming. I made her feel of my hands and face — I was icy cold, not like no one that's been asleep under a blanket.

We was never in a tight place after that I didn't say — '*You don't have to worry, nothin's goin' to happen to us!*'

Chapter XXII

WE STARTED across Lake Lindeman on a sled, with the sail up. We went so fast that Merrill, out in front steering with a gee pole, couldn't manage it. So we hitched the dogs on — sprawling and slipping and sliding on the ice. Finally we got over and made camp on a portage between Lake Lindeman and Lake Bennett. There's a short stream linking them up. We could just see Lake Bennett, three or four times as big as Lindeman, with lots of mush ice on it, no good for sledding.

We knew we had to build a boat here like the rest of them was doing — to last us to Dawson. We was through with hoofing it. It was a serious business, with bad water and dark days ahead.

We moved our camp to the woods and put up a sawmill: a scaffold with cross pieces — one man on top and one man underneath, and a whip-saw to cut through the round logs, any length that was needed.

There wasn't no brains among my three men, and no leader. Greenhorns is called cheechakos in Alaska and there never was no cheechakos worse than us. I had scouted around Seattle among them that had been in, trying to find out all I could. Most important was to season your lumber. Someone told me, 'By all means, let your lumber dry out thorough. Everybody will be in a hurry, but you take your time.'

We all helped. Even Billie done errands, he hobnobbed with everybody; he thought he was as big as any man.

When I decided the lumber was dry enough they went to it, building a scow. It was thirty foot long, and twelve to fourteen foot across. It wasn't very deep — three foot, if I recollect right. Flat bottomed most of it and drawing mighty little water. There wasn't no place to sleep on it; nights we landed and pitched the tents. All it was for was to carry our supplies and us.

It was over a month before the scow was built, caulked and ready. We sledded her down to the water to see how she'd ride. She leaked. We repitched her but she still leaked some. We decided to keep her bailed out and let it go at that, though she sank until she wasn't twelve inches out of the water when we loaded her up.

Up to lunch time, that first day, everything went lovely. We stayed close in, account of me making them. 'Little boats should stick close to shore!' I said.

After lunch a stiff breeze sprung up and we put up our sail. There wasn't none of us knew nothing about water; I don't suppose we'd ever started if we had. We'd been told to look out for Caribou Crossing, where it come into Lake Bennett, but we lost our bearings. And maybe that wind didn't blow. 'She blowed, and she blowed, and bye'bye she blowed some more!' as the Frenchman said on Lake La Barge. A regular willywaw. Kept one of us bailing all the time.

It begun to go dusk like it was coming night. The wind was blowing across into the narrows and the first thing we knew, cachunk! we hit bottom sidewise, right on to a sand bar. Then there was a commotion! Out went the dogs, and the boat pounding up and down, and all of us tumbling over one another in the dark. I held a council of war to know what to do. Merrill wanted to stay there for the night; but May said, 'There'll be no stayin'! Put on your gum boots, and get out there with the pole till you find the channel!' Hart done that, while the other two shoved and pulled. At last the man at the bow struck deep water. We used the oars and in a few minutes we shot into the fast current and over to Caribou Crossing.

We was soaked wet from the splatter of the waves but there was lights ahead that cheered us up. One of them overnight camps. Next day we was up early with everyone else. We tried to keep in sight of the bunch to know where we was heading, but our scow was too slow. We had boats in sight maybe half the morning, then we lost them.

We plugged along down the river heading for Lake Tajish, dodging sweepers, and doing our best to keep off rocks and sand bars — very little rowing, the current carries you along most of the rivers. Then come Mud Lake — the only one of the chain with flat shores, the rest of them is set down among high mountains. Mud Lake is shallow all the way and about twenty miles long.

Drifting down the rivers, now and then you'd see an Indian camp. The Indians trailed along in their canoes until you put in somewhere; then they'd try to sell you moose meat and moccasins. Or trade you for your tea, sugar, and baked bread which they didn't seem to know how to make. They was crazy over tea and whiskey. Tea's the drink on the trail — you dasen't touch liquor when it's real cold, you feel too bad when it wears off. Tea, strong tea, until you turn in — there ain't no getting along without it.

We was out of fresh meat and the Indians had plenty. They liked May's bread, and cut out big pieces of moose for all the bread we give them. Of course, they wanted to know if we had any whiskey. That's where I blundered. I let them have some out of a bottle. There must have been twenty of them. After a while they got to feeling good. They was dancing. There was an old, old man that the young bucks said was the chief. I went over and made signs to him that I wanted to dance. The Indians played their tomtoms. They don't dance like the whites, just pounding a stick on the ground and keeping time with the music. I made the old chief dance my way! We danced until I was wore out and had to quit. They wanted another drink, so I give them a couple of rounds.

Well, they wouldn't leave. No sir. So I told my crew, 'We're goin' to clear out from here!' We loaded up our outfit — we hadn't put the tents up yet — and drifted on down the river for about two hours, until we pulled into another place that looked likely. We pitched our tents and all turned in. We was dozing off when a commotion on the beach started up and here was the same bunch of Indians!

It wasn't no joke. I opened up the tent flap and asked them what they wanted. 'More whiskey!' What I had in the bottles was getting low. I mixed some water in and commenced to dish that out. A young buck made me understand he wanted something strong for the chief so I give him the straight stuff. They hung around there until I told them that we was going to stay next day, and to come back at night, and I'd give them all they could hold. The first peek of day I had everybody up and away. I seen lots more Indians but I never give out no more drinks.

Some place along there we took the boat out of water, unloaded and repitched her. She was leaking bad. We hated to make stops because a dozen times a day boats and barges was passing us. We was all alike in one thing, making the best time we could, thinking of the gold....

The men got into some sort of an argument while they was doing this work on the boat, Merrill and Hart especially. That made it very bad on a small boat. In floating down the river with the stream, in place of using oars, we had a long sweep at each end to steer with. One day it seemed as though Hart was trying to pick a fight with Merrill, steering up in front. Hart wasn't doing his work; Merrill looked back and told him to get busy, that he couldn't hold the boat straight alone. Hart said something that riled Merrill; he started back over the load and there they went at it hammer-and-tongs.

The boat begun to slew around every which way. They didn't care; they couldn't think about nothing but fight.... A man made little Billie a toy wagon at Lake Bennett and they knocked this off into the water. Billie commenced to scream that his wagon was gone. In the meantime May piled in. She grabbed them somehow and flung them apart. The third man took to the front sweep and tried to hold us on our course.

I told Hart and Merrill, if they didn't straighten up and cut out their wrangling, I'd dump them on the shore at the next camp and pick up somebody else. They got to be pretty good friends again after we reached Dawson. I want to tell you there was many a split-up on the trail, among friends, too. Yokemates for years got so's they wouldn't speak. I think it was the hardships, and the strain of the rush.

Fifty-Mile connects Mud Lake with Lake La Barge. Half

way down you hit Mile Canyon. I reckon it's two hundred foot high; anybody looking at it would say men's hands built it — like the sides of a brick house, only with square stone blocks instead; perpendicular up and down, beautiful but very terrible.

We was there all day, all night, and part of the next day. The shore was lined with men and boats, making ready to go through.

The first day we made our load ship-shape, and covered it with tarpaulins so the water would run off. Us women and Billie walked around the gorge and it was sure a tough place to get through. We was watching off the bank about half way. The current is fairly fast above, where the river is about a thousand foot across; but between the walls of the canyon, where it gets down to a squeeze, the white waters race through, forming a ridge in the center at least six foot higher than the sides. Your boat has to stay on top of that ridge. A foot off on either side and she'll hit the rocks hard enough to cave a boat in two. I know, I seen it do it — two men drowned, boats wrecked, and a lot of others so bad damaged they had to build them over, even to whip-sawing new lumber. That's what broke your heart — them awful delays.

But my little scow went through perfect, the water rolling off her canvas and doing no damage at all. I give the men a drink then and there — hauled out a bottle, and how they did enjoy it.

Next come Squaw Rapids — bad enough. Then White Horse Rapids, an awful stretch twenty foot across, all foam and rocks. At the time we was there, in June, there's a shelf of ice running out that makes an eddy. We portaged across, with them wild waters running underneath.... Some of the boats wanted the experience of going through — I seen a dozen try it and five of them was wrecked and their outfits lost. You can't explain a senseless thing like that. People just won't believe nothing without they try it.

It took us four days to cross Lake La Barge, twenty-five miles below White Horse Rapids. The last lake in the chain, and the biggest of them all. And most times rough. We had it calm, but that meant lots of rowing.

The upper reaches of the Yukon is called Lewis River. We'd been warned against the bad rocks and the fast current. It kept us busy, keeping out of trouble.... The small islands and sand bars was full of wild fowl. May had her scatter gun handy but we hadn't no time for larking — 'cept once when May lay back on something and knocked down two geese. That night we had a good feed.

We drifted along, always now by ourselves. There was only one more bad stretch of water between us and Dawson, called Five Fingers, but none of us knew if it was a day or a week ahead. They told us what it looked like, and where and how to take the rapids through a very narrow place on the extreme right side, 'between the thumb and the first finger.' Like a human hand, five fingers outstretched, standing up, and clear across the river. A stretch of treacherous white foam, with the rocks rearing up — you couldn't mistake it. We slipped through without mishap. Goodbye to the bad places! The rest of it was just drift and drift.

It was soon after that we seen a town on the east bank, with people on the shore. We truly believed we was at the end of our journey. We called and asked them if this was Dawson. They hollered no, and my heart flumped down to my boots.... 'Louse Town!' And then, 'Dawson's round the point!' Well, that was better.

Everybody had been in days and days before us, and they begun to think we was lost. It was three o'clock in the afternoon, nigh on to the first of July, when we got in. There was hundreds of scows and barges pulled up, three and four deep from the bank. We couldn't see no way of getting in close enough. Men commenced to cross from the shore, jumping from one boat to another until they found out, asking who we was, and then somebody shouted to somebody else to fetch Jenky. A crowd collected in no time, plenty of them that had been on the trail with us, wanting to know where we'd been, and what we'd been doing to take so long.

'Look at the old tub,' I said, 'and you'll know why.'

Soon, here come Jenky rushing down. He was so mad when he seen me in pants, he shouted it out before even saying hullo: 'Why didn't you put on a dress?' That's the way he welcomed me to Dawson!

'I come the whole way in pants,' I called back.

When he reached the scow he said to me, 'You could a-put a dress on to land in....'

'Aw,' I said, 'shut up, will you?'

When Jenky spotted the load in the boat he thought he was seeing things. 'What in hell you got in there?'

'Some of it's mine,' I said, 'but the biggest part of it's things for sale.' I explained what it was, and that I wanted it put right up to wherever we was going.

'You come on out of the boat, Linney, and I'll send down some men to cart everything to the house. And the first thing you gotta do is take off them pants and put on a skirt.'

There was precious few buildings to see, but hundreds of shanties. Along Front Street there was maybe a half dozen log buildings. Jenky pointed out the Alaska Commercial Company and the others.

We walked up to the house he'd started to build for me. He heard that we was coming. He got busy, thinking to surprise me, but it was only part built with a half roof on it.

Jenky was making money, running the Sour Dough saloon. He'd made good money over to Circle City, too. Him and his partner bought a lot for fifteen hundred dollars and sold it two weeks later for four thousand. They was running a gambling house then, until the Klondike rush when he give it up and come to Dawson.

Chapter XXIII

JENKY bought him a lot on Second Street. There was a shortage of cut lumber so it wasn't nobody's fault the house wasn't finished. It had two rooms, with a partition out of canvas. May set right to work with boxes and made shelves and cupboards. Above the beds she laid boards for a kind of loft, to store the stuff I brought in to sell.

Working inside, trying to get things fixed for the night, I could hear the tinkle of the dance-hall music. 'That never stops,' Jenky said, 'but you'll get used to it.'

The miners paid a dollar for a drink and a dance — the girls got a percentage. The men down from the claims danced in their dirty mackinaws, and muddy boots and mukluks.

The girls was looking for suckers to buy high-price stuff — they hadn't no use for beer boozers. Thirty dollars was the price of a quart of champagne — they got five dollars out of that. Whiskey sold for fifty cents a glass. At Jenky's Sour Dough they didn't sell nothing much besides whiskey, though there was champagne for them that called for it. If there was gin in Dawson I never heard of it.

Jenky hadn't no dancing in his place, just a regular saloon with card games and faro. It run twenty-four hours a day, with three bartenders on the job all the time. Jenky joined up with his partner, Ed Fitzpatrick, in Circle City, after the split with Ace Blakey.

Our second day in Dawson come a big rain. It knows how in there. I had the table set and was getting dinner when it started, filling the plates and running all over the floor. I yelled for May, and between us we pushed and pulled until we got the trunks and boxes under the part where the roof was up.

I commenced to cry, thinking how everything might have been damaged. 'It ain't right,' I said, 'after the trouble we come through, a-fetchin' it in. I'll have a roof on here or know why!'

A friend of Jenky's stuck his head in the door to see how we was making out, and I asked him would he fetch Jenky. But Jenky sent one of his bartenders instead.

'The boss says he can't do nothin' about it. Burke, over to the mill, won't sell him no lumber. He was a-tryin' again this mornin'. Burke told him to go to hell!'

'Hell and Dawson is all one to me,' I said; 'I'm goin' to get me some lumber!'

I hied myself over to Burke's mill. Just a little piece down the river. There was half a dozen men clamoring for lumber. It wasn't much of a layout.

I asked Burke, 'Don't you think women ought to come first?'

'Always first with lumberjacks, mam! To tell the truth I didn't believe Jenkins when he said it was his *wife* that was a-comin' in. You'll have your lumber by tomorrow.' It come too, and Jenky put some men to work roofing.

The town itself was unsanitary. It's built on a flat in the curve of the river, all covered over with niggerhead grass. Everything under us was icy, except a few inches on top. When the warm weather set in, it melted into slop. Niggerhead grass, that turned sideways when you walked on it, gosh-awful slush and no sidewalks.

People sickened, and there was mighty few doctors. Dawson was British — you couldn't get a license without you passed an examination. That barred most of them.

There was a regular epidemic of scurvy and pneumonia, five to ten dying every day. We all helped. There wasn't no organization, only the Northwest Mounted police, just a handful. The Sour Doughs called them Red Coats.

Digging graves was as bad as the sickness. It meant thawing out the ground first — fetching up wood, and building a bonfire where you was fixing to dig. Burning and digging and burning some more, over and over. Let me tell you, Dawson made a lot of us forget the itch for gold.

Late that fall, before it froze up, there was a man took sick on one of the creeks. His partners brought him down the Klondike River and tied up to the bank in front of Dawson. There wasn't no hospital then. Jenky heard of it and went to see this man, Ed Craig, laying there in a red mackinaw, and not able to talk. His partners told Jenky how they was hunting to find somebody to take him in, and nobody willing.

Jenky told me about it. 'Bring him to the house,' I said, 'I reckon it's my work.' I didn't say nothing to Jenky, how I dreamed the night before of caring for a man, in a red mackinaw, that was very sick and needed help.

They carried him up on a stretcher made out of gunnysacks. He was a pitiful sight to look at, in his early thirties, and almost completely paralyzed. He couldn't speak, but I knowed by the way he looked at me how thankful he was.

May was up the creeks; I hadn't no one to help me nurse him. The doctor was in, but he didn't know no more about the case than me and I told him he needn't call no more. I took care of Ed Craig the very best I could, and he lingered on for a week. One night about ten o'clock he passed away.

Ed's partners come and give me the gold dust that was on him when he took sick. 'It's for you, Mrs. Jenkins, for all your trouble takin' care of him.' But I refused it. 'Send it out to his mother,' I told them.

In about ten days, they come to see me again, with more gold dust. They said they sent Ed's stake out to his sister, his mother was dead. This was their own and they wouldn't take no; they made me keep it.

Father Judge's business was saving souls, but he give it up to save lives. The sickness made him do it. He come up from converting Indians around Circle City and Forty Mile. It was forced on him — there wasn't nobody big enough for the job except Father Judge. He become the hero of the Klondike — not that he wanted it like that.

When Father Judge got in that summer, half of Dawson was sick. Scurvy, pneumonia, typhoid was killing people by the dozens, and nobody doing nothing about it. Four thousand people, hundreds of shacks and tents, and no hospital. Father Judge knowed what he had to do, and that he had to do it quick. Creeds didn't count with him, or breeds neither. He seen all men alike, the decent people and the sinners, the Indians and the whites.

He selected a hospital site and set to work — but he hadn't no funds. Wages was ten to twenty dollars a day, and lumber cost two hundred and fifty dollars a thousand. He got the lumber from the mill, though Burke knew the priest couldn't pay for it. The A.C. Co. give him everything he wanted, too — trusted him for thousands of dollars.

The ladies of Dawson wanted to help, and we started out in twos, raising money. On the creeks first. May and Kitty Spencer went up Eldorado and worked it for two days. Fifteen miles each way and they had to leg it, but they come back with twelve hundred dollars in gold dust. We done the town, too. May and Kitty had a block on Front Street, mostly all saloons. They worked at night so as to catch everybody. Their pockets was stuffed full of currency and gold dust, over two thousand dollars that one evei.ing.

We held another meeting and found we hadn't raised enough to clear the Jesuit priest. We voted to hold a bazaar in the Vanity Theater. Many of the merchants donated things to be raffled off. There was dancing every night for the whole week. Somebody got the idea of holding a contest and selling votes for the most popular woman in Dawson. May had a time talking Kitty into it, but she finally give in for the sake of the cause. Kitty had a saloon running there. Harry Spencer died the year before with typhoid fever but Kitty kept on with the business. She'd been inside since '95 and knew everybody.

Votes was fifty cents apiece. We sure had a lot of fun out of it. When it come down to the last few minutes of balloting May shoved in a batch of tickets and Kitty won by over a hundred votes. They picked her up and carried her all around the hall, shouting like crazy people. If I ain't mistook we made forty thousand dollars, more than enough to take care of all Father Judge's debts.

Back in 1891 he was an unknown missionary at St. Michaels. When he trudged up the Yukon into Dawson six years later he was still a strong, healthy man. Dawson made an old man out of him — killed him in two years. Wore out wanting to be a friend to everybody in the Klondike.

Every week we had dances in Pioneer Hall. That's where the respectability went. A man told a bunch of us, one of them dance nights, about a sick woman on the hill that needed somebody to look after her. There was a baby up there, too, the first white child born in Dawson. The mother's name was Schultz; she called the baby Dawsie. Next day some of us went up. The woman was laying in bed, a woe-begone sight to see. Her body was swelled twice its natural size, her lips was all purple-spotted, and the cabin was in a terrible dirty state. I asked Mrs. Schultz what her husband was feeding her. 'Mostly soup,' she said.

She asked us if we would clean her up. We got Schultz to go outside while we went to work. Then she said, 'I want you to look at what he has been tryin' to feed me.'

May took the top off the stew kettle, setting there on a table behind the stove — it had soured and was raised up like a pan of yeast. May run outside and dumped it.

Schultz bristled up. God, he was mad. 'Who give you the right to do that?' he demanded.

May answered him, 'You been tryin' to feed her truck a malamoot dog wouldn't sniff at!'

May come inside and Schultz followed her. 'I don't thank people for interferin' in my family!'

We didn't pay no attention to what all else he was saying. As soon as we got her comfortable we went to the barracks and told the captain the condition this woman was in. The Red Coats went up there and ordered Schultz to find a place to stay while his wife was sick, and not to come back until he got permission. It was scurvy.

Schultz was a quack doctor, and a preacher, too. He had some strange notions and was dosing his wife with his own concoctions.... The Red Coats ordered a doctor up to see her, and us women run things for three weeks. Schultz hung around and threatened to throw everybody out.

The woman improved wonderful with the medicine she was taking, and the massages and rubbing we give her. It wasn't long before she was able to set up. She went on like that until she was able to walk around. She had her heart set on going out in the spring, which she did. Her and Schultz and the baby. But she died on the way down.

I heard about Schultz later, that he was the best kind of a father and worshipped Dawsie. But he sure was mean to his wife.

There wasn't enough vegetables to go round, it was that brought on the scurvy. The first potatoes raised in the Northern country came from the Stewart River, about sixty miles above Dawson. Jenky paid fifty dollars a sack, and they was cheap compared to outside potatoes, quality considered. Cabbages growed in there was the best I ever et; they cooked up like summer squash, sweet and crisp.

Eggs was ten dollars a dozen and none too fresh. Someone got the idea of bringing in some canned eastern oysters, and Jenky bought a dozen and paid a dollar apiece — not a can. He brought them home as a treat, to surprise me. I made him tell me how much they cost. 'You're welcome to the whole lot,' I said; 'maybe you can swallow a dollar bill but not me!' Jenky done it; he et 'em all.

May lived in a tent until the cold come along; a tent warms up fast with a fire going in the stove. But when the real cold set in she had to build her a one-room house, using the back wall of our place for a side. The roof was made of slabs, loaded down with niggerhead grass and dirt. The next summer May thought she'd raise a garden up there. Every day I seen her going up the ladder with water. It's hard to believe how growing things come up in Alaska. But the hot summer nights makes an awful difference. In no time May had a vegetable garden up top of the roof.

Us that went through the shortage during the big rush learned to think about something else besides gold, and all kinds of vegetables was raised. For meats and such people had a cache in back of their house, eight to ten foot off the ground to keep the dogs and wolves out.

At a certain time in the winter caribou traveled from one range of mountains to the other, across the Klondike River, about twenty miles above Dawson. When they started coming and the word reached town, there was a regular stampede with sleds and guns. We got all the meat we could haul — like shooting a cow.

Caribou meat is tender and sweet — much better than moose meat, which is dark and coarse. We used to grind it up into hamburg steaks and season it. It would keep that way for three months. There was lots of moose meat et in there, but the female moose looked too much like mule to suit me.

We cached dried beans, too; boiled them ready for baking or for making soup, so it wouldn't take us long to get a meal up. Some used to keep their flour in the cache. One or two had provisions stole, but the Red Coats nabbed the thief and put him on the woodpile. It wasn't often I heard tell of anybody robbing a cache — no one liked that word woodpile.

Up or down the Yukon you had to stop at every station, and register, and tell them where you was bound for. When you didn't show up at the next station the Red Coats went out after you.

My first winter, three men, Olsen, Rolph and Clayson, disappeared on the trail. It was pretty sure they had gold dust on them. Springtime, they found the bodies on a little portage in the river near where they was camped — jammed under the ice, and full of bullet holes. A stranger by the name of Conklin, going out that same winter, hadn't registered regular and was lost track of. The Red Coats knew he had a black, outside dog along but otherwise was traveling alone. They picked up the dog on the trail. A loose dog was like an empty saddle — it meant trouble somewhere. That was a slick trick of Conklin's, turning his dog loose, but it didn't fool the Red Coats.

They kept the dog for future reference. Later on they found out how Conklin bought him a horse and sled some place around White Horse, on his way outside.

Two years went by and Conklin turned up at Dawson under another name. They took him in and tried him for Olsen's murder. He claimed he was innocent; that he wasn't Conklin, and hadn't bought a horse and sled at White Horse. They produced the outfit, and showed where Conklin had bored out the uprights in the sled and taken the stuffing out of the horse's collar to hide the gold dust. The Red Coats had a good case except that they hadn't been able to locate nobody in Dawson to identify Conklin. He insisted up to the last minute that he hadn't no dog, and wasn't guilty.

But when they brought in his black dog, and it picked him out of the crowd and climbed on his lap, Conklin broke down. He confessed, owned up to shooting Olsen and the other two.

There was a young fellow in Dawson that just felt like he wanted to pull the rope that would send Conklin to eternity. He offered them fifteen hundred dollars to let him do it. Conklin was hung in the barracks grounds, off the scaffold built a-purpose. The young fellow run the show and paid over his money. He actually paid some one fifteen hundred dollars for the right to hang a man. I think Olsen's widow got it in the end.

Right in the middle of winter, with the cold around sixty below, Dawson had its first bad fire. Burned up a whole block on Front Street — and blocks them days meant something. Started in a dance hall. A miner and his gal got into a scrap. Someone throwed a lighted lamp and the big fire was on.

Way back on the hill you could hear them shouting, 'Fire! Fire!' — and the malamoots sticking their noses in the air, howling along with the humans. The one small fire engine pumped away, down by the river — until the hose froze solid. They formed a bucket brigade but the buckets froze with the water in them! Then the wind rose, fanning the flames and making it impossible to rescue much of anything. They tried hard to save provisions, tearing down the buildings ahead of the flames. Provisions meant life to the shut-ins. What good's gold dust setting around in cans if you ain't et nothing?

Everybody was affected by the fire. Rations was already low — butter was selling at three dollars a pound, and fifty dollars a sack for flour. The stores sold you just so much of anything. If you was lucky enough to have any provisions left, the Red Coats made you sell to them that had lost theirs.

The big rush started in '98. It kept on into the fall months and it looked like we was all going hungry, the way them people come piling in. I begged for an extra case of condensed milk, to be sure to have enough for Billie — but I couldn't get it....

One day I heard some kind of commotion outside the house. I went to look and the whole street was filling up with people, a-standing out. I couldn't see nothing. I run to the middle of the street to see better, and behold! A man was coming along, leading a cow! She mooed; land a Lord, it sounded good to me!

I found out as she belonged to Joe Cooper. He'd been outside all winter gathering five scows full of stuff. Now he just got back, with provisions and liquor and goodness knows what all.

Joe was a buddy of Jenky's — he run the Dominion Saloon. Jenky knowed him all the time he was in there but he was a stranger to me.

I told Jenky I was aiming to get some fresh milk for Billie. That was the first thing I done next morning. I spoke to Joe Cooper about my grandson being with us. I paid Joe four dollars a quart for the milk I got off him — two quarts every day, one in the morning and one at night.

The Red Coats took charge early. They checked up on all the food in the stores, and made a tally of the floating population. It was decided there wasn't enough food for half the next winter. They called a mass meeting in front of the Alaska Commercial Company store. The public didn't know what it was for, but they was all there and they soon found out. Capt. Hanson, of the A.C. Co., was the speaker. He told them that two boats was leaving in the next few days, and that the new-comers would be furnished with free transportation to St. Michaels where there was plenty of food to take care of every-body. Dawson, he said, could take care of the women and children, but the cheechakos had to go.

The Red Coats was guarding the trails leading out of town. There was a rush to the creeks, but everybody was stopped and turned back. The day come to go aboard and there was hundreds that went. Most of them drifted over to Nome; some of the scared ones took steamers for the outside, having had enough already. It sure helped to have that mob go down the river. You could buy a few things once more.

Every store with something to sell had a pair of scales to weigh the gold dust. You seen mighty little silver, and not much paper money.

The stores had narrow fronts but run back deep, and their wood floors was covered with sawdust from the mill. When a miner got to feeling mellow there wasn't no way to tell how much gold dust he'd be spilling on the floor and counters. Everybody was wise to that. In the saloons, the bartenders had a piece of ingrained carpet to set the scales on. The gold dust got poured out into a little scoop and onto the scales. You could be awful careless about it. Particles of gold dust flew off and got lost in the nap of the carpet, easy as not.

But there wasn't nothing careless about the way a bartender shook out his carpet onto a piece of paper, when his shift was over. It belonged to him — by custom, you see. Vince Mc-Laughlin, that worked in the Sour Dough, called it a precious poor day when he couldn't fluff out an ounce; that meant about seventeen dollars.

Jenky noticed his sweep-out man piling up the sawdust in back and putting it in a sack. 'I'm usin' it round my tent,' he said, 'to keep the mud out.'

One time Jenky went after him, to where he lived; he wanted him in a hurry. By hang, if he wasn't down to the river panning the sawdust he'd swept off the floor!

Jenky come home and told Billie how he was going to have
the sawdust swept up and sacked, and that he could pan it
out for hisself. Of course the young 'un was tickled to death.
Jenky digged a small hole out in back where the melted snow
water would collect, so that Billie had water to do his panning
with. Water had to be carried from the river and paid for at
so much a bucket — Billie's claim couldn't stand the charge.

Billie went at it and panned until the fall, until it begun to
freeze up and May wouldn't let him work outside. Then he
tried to wheedle Jenky into toting the sawdust over to the
house and piling it up, so he could play miner again in the
spring. Jenky wouldn't, he told him he'd made enough. Well,
he had: Billie panned out six hundred dollars!

Everybody was hard at work — but me. I got to thinking
about something to do. I told Jenky I could make as good
whiskey as he was buying. 'All right,' he said, 'if you want to
ry, I can get alcohol from the A.C. Company.'

He went down and bought a fifty gallon barrel and had it
sent up to the house. 'I got this cheap, Linney; you'll make
a big profit outen it if you work it up right.'

'How much did you pay for it?'

He commenced to fumble in his pocket for the bill. 'Not
much,' he said. A few minutes later he throwed the receipt on a
shelf where he kept his things; he'd forgot all about my asking
him. I went over and picked it up.

'Thirty dollars,' I said, 'that's certainly cheap....'

'Thirty hells! Look at it again.'

Well I did, and honest to God, it's a wonder I didn't faint!
Three thousand dollars for a barrel of alcohol. Sixty dollars a
gallon. I set down and tried to think. How was I ever going to
get it back?

I got hold of the man that carried water up from the river,
and I ordered him to fill our two water barrels and to come
twice a day.

Then I went to it, making hooch — all the home-made stuff
was called hooch in them days, just like now. I guess it was a

fifteen gallon keg I first made up. 'It don't smell right to me,' Jenky said. 'No, and it don't taste like whiskey!' He knew I'd be wanting to make a profit, and he thought he'd put a damper on it by saying it wasn't no good.

'Well, taste this bottle now of your own stuff,' I said.

'That tastes like whiskey.'

Here's what I done to him. The first drink was out of a bottle off his own bar and the second was what I made! I told him so but he wouldn't believe it. Then he tried a drink out of the keg.

'Linney, this is pretty good stuff, I own up to it. It ought to sell.'

So he carted it over to the Sour Dough, and right off his customers detected the difference in taste. Jenky used to have a saying later on — 'Boys, don't drink too much, the old lady can't make only fifty gallons a day!'

I made him pay me spot cash, but after a while he balked. Whatever I asked him he said it was too much. Then I told him I wouldn't make him no more. 'You get your hooch somewhere else!'

I went over to the A.C. Company and bought me another barrel of alcohol and went to work. I hired Stud Kilgarry; I'd known him in Seattle. He was a bartender by trade, and I got him to sell this whiskey around among the different saloons. I charged seventy-five dollars a gallon and everybody was just crazy over it. I worked twenty hours a day, many days. I didn't used to sleep, just worked at that confounded stuff.

Whiskey was getting a little low in Dawson, that is barrel and case goods. Jenky wanted to know why I wouldn't sell him.

I said, 'Pay me like everybody else and you can have all I make.' He sure had to come through for every keg delivered at his place.

Later I give out, I couldn't stand the long hours of work; and when business eased up and the money quit rolling in so fast I decided to stop. I rested up a bit.

But loafing is worse than work in Dawson. I found that out.

You had to hustle to keep from thinking.... I thought I'd try my hand at the beauty parlor business, and I fixed me up a corner of my living room. I didn't have to put out no sign; in two weeks I had more business than I could handle. I give facial treatments and dressed hair — no hair dyeing. I got five dollars for face work, and two dollars and a half for curling hair. I had all kinds of trade, dance-hall girls with the rest of them.

Dance-hall girls was all ages and all sorts — even a few of them married and respectable. Kilgarry spoke to me about a young 'un he knew that was sad and ailing; he thought as how I might be able to wrastle her out of it. She was a hugsome lass; quiet enough to start in, but awful jumpy when she got going. Her story didn't amount to nothing — it never does, the part they'll tell.

I asked her, was she sick? No. Was it some man? No, it wasn't that neither. She wanted something but couldn't name it.

I told her about myself, trying to make her talk. But it didn't work.

She begun to mumble. 'Oh, I reckon I'm all right....'

'You ain't neither!'... I took hold of her hands. 'Honey, it ain't money? You must be makin' twenty or thirty dollars a day.'

'Some times twice that,' she said, trying hard to think. 'Jeez no, it ain't money! It ain't nothin' I'm missin'.... I'll tell you what it is,' she said, jerking up straight, 'it's this goddamn Dawson that's drivin' me nuts!' It seemed like she just thought of that. She begun to talk wild, flinging her arms around, cussing the Yukon country and everybody in it.

'Honey,' I went on, 'I don't blame you none. You'd better go out in the spring, the first chance you get. I'm clearin' out myself.'

A good cry might have done her good but I expect she'd forgot how. I give her a drink of hooch. Then I give her another. 'It's the shut-in feelin',' I told her, 'Dawson ain't no place for a woman.'

She said, 'You mean it ain't no place for a tart!'

She went out sure enough. But not the way I was telling her. There's a small bridge over the Klondike River where it runs into the Yukon, near Dawson. A man seen her, she jumped off that.

Chapter XXIV

I LEARNED to dance in Alaska. I learned the best I could, it wasn't much. I found out there's no harm in dancing, none in the least.

The minister was a good man, he meant all right. He come to me and asked me why I didn't go to church. I told him I didn't have no time. 'You'll have time to die, one of these days, you know.'

'Yes, and I want to go to heaven,' I said, 'and I expect to.'

'Your grandson tells me you take the time to go to dances and you have been to many of them since you're here.'

'That's at night,' I said.

'Mrs. Jenkins, don't you think that dancin' is wicked?'

'Is good people, keepin' time with their feet, dancin' on the floor, any worse'n good people in church keepin' time with their voices?' I got the old fellow!

I stood up and showed him how we danced the two-step and the waltz and the square country dances. And I told him, 'Your organist is a sinner if I am!

'I was raised different than what this is,' I said, 'but I'm a more understanding woman than I was then, and I'm a better woman, too. My people was hidebound, I was brought up your way. I was brought up to think that if you went to a dance, the door was open and you danced straight into hell. But you don't know what dancin' means to people.'

'No,' he admitted, 'I don't, but I reckon it has its place.'

Among the ladies we met at the dances in Pioneer Hall was a very beautiful woman by the name of Lou Jesson. She was medium size, with a lovely complexion and large brown eyes, and a pretty shade of red hair. She dressed nice but never flashy. She wasn't liked by the ladies of our set but she was a big favorite with the men.

Jesson was lots older than his wife and wouldn't mix with

her friends. Nobody seemed to care though. 'Jes' dumb,' they said. That was Jesson. They lived for a while near by and Lou would run into my place several times a day. I liked her, she was such good company — one of the few decent women in that closed in hole that hadn't forgot how to enjoy life.

The Jessons went up one of the creeks to do assessment work on their claim. When they come back to Dawson they stopped with a friend that run a jewelry store, the only one in town at the time. He had two little rooms — the shop was in front. Two bunks was built in the kitchen in back — just space enough to get from in between the foot of one and the side of the other.

I got to feeling bad about now and couldn't sleep. I tried to doctor myself but it didn't have no effect. At last I told May how it was, that my room seemed to be full of people. I would shut my eyes but still I could see them. It went on for two or three nights so I decided to send for an old doctor I knew. He examined me but he couldn't find nothing, only that I was wore-out.

Then I told him about the faces in my room at night. He knew about the seance meetings I had been holding there all winter. 'Perhaps,' he said, 'some of your spirit friends is tryin' to tell you something important. Have you tried to find out through them what these faces mean?'

'No, Jenky's against my spookin'. I ain't done it much of late.'

This night it was worse than ever. Jenky was working late shift and I was all alone. A dozen times I turned out the oil lamp to try to go to sleep, but the faces would come so close I had to put my hands up to ward them off. I even tried singing to get away from them.

I got up at six o'clock the next morning to unlock the door. I went back to bed for an hour and I had a terrible dream. When Jenky come in I fixed his breakfast; then I went into May's place to talk to her. Uly Gaisford, May's friend, was there.

'Something terrible is goin' to happen,' I said, 'and I don't know what to do about it.' I told them about my dream: 'I followed a man down the street and went into a small room, through another room that looked like a store. Right in the doorway a woman lay there in a pool of blood. In the room was two bunks, one lengthwise and the other crosswise of the room. There was a man on his knees by one of the bunks, with his head buried in his arms. The woman raised up and give him a terrible look. Then she dropped back dead.'

Uly's brother — Grunter by name — that run a restaurant up on Front Street, stopped in on his way to work. We went on talking, but I never said nothing about Lou Jesson though I knew it was her I'd seen in my dreams.

Grunter said he'd have to be off. He wasn't gone a minute until he come running back. 'Hurry quick,' he said, 'there's been an accident.' We run up the street and into the same room I seen in my dream. Lou Jesson was laying there, only she never come to life.

I asked, 'Who is that man on the bunk?' He looked up and I seen it was Jesson, and I felt in my heart it was him killed her.

Can anyone say why I had that dream?

Jesson said he was going up the creeks and had asked Lou for some heavy socks. That was at the inquest. She told him they was in a sack up over the bunk. He stepped on a keg to pull the sack down. He'd forgot there was a gun in the sack. It come down and hit the keg. Lou was combing her hair in front of the window. He heard a shot and as he turned around he seen her fall.

There was some holes in the sack; I stood there while they was looking at it. They couldn't find no powder burns though; couldn't even smell powder on the sack.

They didn't do nothing with Jesson; claimed it was an accident. He went outside early in the spring by the first boat.

If he cared he never showed it. 'Jes' dumb,' everybody said.

Wash Coggins was a well read man and very smart. But he never had no church affiliations; he didn't believe in religion that way, he said. I never met a better man in my life; everybody loved him, truthful, honest and upright. He was just barely alive a few years back — Ham Hart kept him going.

Ham was in Alaska there that same time, and poor as a snake. Him and Wash and Jenky was great friends. Ham told me about the three of them living their first winter on nothing but salmon bellies and whiskey. Ham made a lot of money later on — had a big house in Berkeley, California. He died a double millionaire.

All winter I had been holding what Jenky called spook meetings. At night, after the beauty parlor business was finished. Wash Coggins had a wife outside, expecting her to have a baby and knowing the time was up. He was worried. He used to come and talk to me about it, and once I told him I'd try to find out what he was after. I got the answer — she had her baby a few weeks already and everything was fine. Was it a boy or a girl? That come, too; it was a boy. Bye and bye he got a letter from the outside, all about it. Of course, from then on Wash was a believer, telling everybody. The old-timers come drifting in, asking their questions and seeming to get the homesick pains out of their hearts. I never took no money for it. I was agreeable and glad to help them lonely souls. Anybody that would ask me I would try to get a message for them. Until Jenky got sore.

I was getting breakfast one time, making hot biscuits, when Jenky come in through the front door, stood by me a minute and went out the back way. I set the biscuits in the oven to bake, when I seen Jenky pass me again and go into the front room. At least I thought I seen him. Pretty soon I called him but he didn't answer. I thought maybe he'd gone out the front door into May's, but her door was locked when I tried it.

The fact of the matter is that Jenky didn't come back at all. The whole time he was out in the privy, and when I went to look for him he was setting there sound asleep!

I wish somebody would tell me how that was. The way it has always seemed to me, it was in Jenky's mind when he went out there to come right back into the house for his breakfast. The thought was enough to form his image and materialize him in the room. Naturally, I told Jenky, and that's what made the trouble. He swore up and down I was crazy. Jenky hated anything he couldn't put his fingers on. He got so set against my meetings I never went back to it regular again.

Though Jenky kind of changed, too. There was a Mrs. Fairchild that he liked just as much as I did. She come over one night and pleaded with me for a setting. She knew Jenky was against it but Jenky wasn't home. She pestered until I give in.

Suddenly Mrs. Fairchild seen Jenky standing in the doorway. She tried to stop me. 'Let him come in,' I said, 'he's the very one I want to talk to!' And I commenced to tell Jenky things that happened in his younger days that I never knew nothing about. He set still with his head hanging down.

A few years later, in our San Leandro home down in California, while Jenky was reading his newspaper after supper and I was setting there sewing, he turned around to me and said, 'Let's spook, mama!' I was so stunned I don't know how I managed to answer him at all. After a bit we set down in front of the fireplace, me with my eyes closed and my hands flat on the table touching with his'n. I was singing soft... some hymn. The next thing I knew I was on the floor and Jenky was throwing water on my face. 'What's the matter?... Stop it,' I said, 'you're gettin' me wet!' Then I come out of it.

I asked him, 'What was it I said?' 'Oh, not much,' was all he answered.

To the day he died he wouldn't talk about it, though I asked him many, many times.

My beauty business sold the last stitch of finery I brought in from Seattle — I had it laid out around the room so that the girls could see it. It didn't take long to spread the news that there was dress things to sell up on Second Street.

I got wonderful prices, more than four times what it cost me.

I decided to send May outside — she wanted to go any-way — to buy some more things. All she could manage — underwear, kimonos and silk night dresses; silk shirt waists, too, and black cotton stockings.

Jenky fixed it for her to go out with the mail team, over the ice, down to White Horse. None of it was bad but one night, at a way-house — with the bunks full up, and men sleeping all over the floor, and no place for a lady. The driver thought she'd better stay out on the sled. May cuddled down under her fur robes and went to sleep — with one of the dogs on her feet. The railroad was built in from Skagway, so she rode out from White Horse in style. At Skagway she took the boat for Seattle. That was June, 1898, the first boat out.

May started back from Seattle with a whole caboodle of stuff, twice as much as I brought in the first time. I told everybody that come into my parlor how May was outside for more goods, and expected back soon. They just flocked in; it wasn't no time until everything was sold.

From the first day, when I said that hell and Dawson was one and the same, I hadn't changed my mind. I was wore out and homesick. Jenky was agreeable to going out, too. May was back and said she would look after his rents; if she'd known how he was going to act up she mightn't have been so obliging.

Jenky still owned our house on Second Street. Now he bought him a store building for fifteen thousand dollars, and leased them both — for bawdy houses. I knowed all about it; I can't say I didn't. I didn't like the idea, but when you're renting out places in Dawson, you can't be choosey.

He paid out twenty thousand dollars for a third interest in a claim, called '33-Eldorado.' It was a plain gift from two Swedes that liked him and wanted him in with them. Klondike friendships got you things cheap, nothing was on a business basis. When Jenky sold out later I mind his saying, 'I'm a-givin' it away, but I got it for nothin'.'

We went down the river on a boat called the 'Susie.' May let us take Billie. He'd been going to school in Dawson but

I thought he needed the change as much as us. There was a
nice jolly crowd aboard — dancing every night, and poker,
solo or whist, whatever you wanted.

When I went below deck to fetch something for Billie, the
first night, they asked me if I wouldn't come into the dining
room and hold a seance. I said I would if everybody promised
to behave. I set down, but someone rapped on the table and
I told them I wouldn't go on if it happened again. They all
denied it.

I pointed my finger at a young man across the table: 'You
done it, your Aunt Mary is here a-tellin' me!' I asked him
if he had an Aunt Mary and he said no.

'Well, you had?' He said yes; he did have an Aunt Mary
but she died years ago.

I asked him, 'How do you think I got this message if she
wasn't dead?... She wants me to tell you to watch your gold
dust every minute. She says to give it to the purser or you'll
be takin' off without it.'

'Not me, it's better where it is than gettin' mixed up in
some of the black sand down in the purser's cabin!'

A story was going around that the pursers got rich changing
dust for black sand, just a little at a time. It weighed near as
much as the gold. All the boats carried signs to leave your
valuables with the purser. He'd seal it up — but what was to
prevent his breaking the seal, taking out a little gold dust,
and putting in enough black sand to bring the weight back
to where it was before? And sealing it up again? The youngster heard that story like everybody else.

At St. Michaels we was transferred to the 'Roanoke' for
the trip outside. We was on board a couple of days when this
same boy missed his gold dust. Someone smashed the lock
on his iron chest and cleaned him out.

He was broken-hearted. He didn't know what to do and
nobody could tell him, though there wasn't much else talked
about. That night I had a dream. I seen the man that took
the gold dust — seen him plain....

A friend of ours, Dan McGilvray, was making the trip out,

too, and had the same cabin with this boy that was robbed. When I told Dan I believed I could pick out the thief, he said, 'We'll stand on the stairs leading to the dining room and let you try.' Dan was there by my side when I spotted him. He was waiting table. Dan said, 'Why, that's my cabin boy!'

Jenky was furious. He said I'd kick up a shindy, accusing an innocent man, and he told Dan not to say nothing. Dan said he guessed Jenky was right, but he was going to keep his eyes peeled all the same.

The next night I dreamed that a young girl come to me and said that she was going to show me where the gold dust was hid. We started below deck, down to the hold. As we passed along I seen a big vat seemingly filled with water, and I stopped to look in. 'No, not there.' she said. 'He thought of puttin' it there but he changed his mind.' We went on a ways until she stopped. All this was in the dream. 'I can't go no further,' she said, 'but I'll tell you just where it is.' She pointed to the bow. 'It's down among the ribs, covered with old sacks and sails.'

I mentioned my dream to Jenky and tried to get him to look below deck. He wouldn't. He went to cussing and calling me names.

When I got my clothes on I hunted up Dan McGilvray and told him. 'Well,' he said, 'it won't hurt no one to have a look, that's sure.' Him and two other men started off. They come back and Dan said, 'There ain't no gold dust that we could find, but the sacks and sails was there. *Something else, too! My cabin boy was down by the bow — he seen us the same as we seen him — and if he ain't a skulkin' land rat then I don't know one!*'

A storm was blowing up and I was worried about little Billie, thinking how if anything happened in the night I wouldn't wake him up. The old tub rolled and pitched higgledy-piggledy. Our strong box, full of gold dust, slid over the state-room floor, pounding all night....

Come morning, the water was much smoother and everybody was over their fright. I forgot all about the boy that lost his gold dust. I went on deck and the first person I seen was Dan McGilvray. Him and a whole crowd of men were standing around talking about something. Dan come over to me. 'Well, mama,' he said, 'I got some news for you! Aunt Mary's boy got his stake back! In his bunk; he stubbed his toe against it last night when he turned in!'

Dan said he guessed the cabin boy got scared and put it back when no one was looking. It must have been like that. I've thought about it all these years but there ain't no other way to explain it.

Chapter XXV

I LANDED in Seattle worse dressed than a Louse Town squaw. In a mother hubbard, made out of some colored canton flannel I got me at the A.C. Co. That thing, and an old check cloak. The Dawson girls bought the clothes off my back; I didn't even own a hat!

But I wasn't worrying none about my looks. My mind was on Jenky's strong box, and getting our gold dust changed into cash. They paid us fifty-five thousand dollars. Twenty thousand was mine.

We stayed in Seattle a few days. Jenky give me a pair of diamond earrings, and a diamond pin. Then he wanted to buy a house there. But I held out for a home in California. A lady friend talked so much about the little town of San Leandro and the wonderful flowers you could grow there, my heart was set on seeing it. And that's where we wound up.

First we went to Siler City, North Carolina, where Jenky's folks lived. He wanted to visit them, and I had been kind of anxious to know what they was like, too.

I was a Republican. Jenky told me on the train, 'Mama, don't let 'em know your party or they won't take to you; my people is all strong Democrats.' We'd been there only a few minutes when Jenky asked where his brother Joey was. They told him he was out making a speech; he'd just been elected sheriff on the Republican ticket!

Jenky had a great time teasing Joey. Joey was very stern with his servants. He had seven of them — they cost him five dollars a month apiece. One morning, when Eliza come in to build the fire, Jenky give her a stiff drink. At breakfast, passing the corn pone, Eliza slipped and landed on the floor. 'Eliza,' Joey said, 'I can't imagine where you got your dram this mornin'.' ''Deed you can't, sir!' she chuckled.

Me and Jenky went driving to see some of the family that

lived in the country. It was so desolate looking around there I told him, 'I never did think you had much sense but I changed my mind. You was smart enough when you pulled out of this place!'

We visited for a month; then we left for California. When I seen San Leandro I liked it even better than I thought I would. Jenky told me to go ahead and buy me a house. I got one too cheap to suit Jenky; he give the old lady that sold it five hundred dollars more than she asked.

I was content and happy, buying furniture and everything to make a pretty home. But we wasn't no more than settled until Jenky commenced talking about going back to Alaska. Grousing around, like a fidgety old hen. Well say, San Leandro wasn't much of a place for a Dawson barkeeper....

I done my best to talk him out of it but he just kept on with his preparations. At last he started off — for Seattle and Skagway and White Horse; the rest of the way was over the ice. Took all his money back with him, a wad of currency big enough to choke a mule.... Jenky went right to where May was. She'd bought her an interest in a restaurant in Dawson and was doing good.

Now, Jenky supposed he was getting three hundred and fifty dollars a month rent off his one house, and two hundred off the other. But that winter the bottom dropped out of Dawson; all the rents went down, and May wrote outside telling Jenky how things stood and that the real estate man advised her to lower the rents rather than to let the houses go empty. May didn't hear from Jenky so she lowered the rents.

Jenky had it all figured out, how much was coming to him. He wanted to know what May done with the money and she told him it was in the A.C. Co. store safe. He had the gold dust weighed out and it was two thousand short of what he thought it ought to be. Then it come out that he hadn't got May's letter. Whether he did or not I never found out, but he was still squawking about that two thousand dollars ten years later.

May thought Jenky was sore at her; anyway, she seen mighty little of him. She found out different after a while but she never let on to me. Jenky just plain went to the dogs! The minute he got loose of me he went to whooping it up. Gambling up the creeks. And getting hisself mixed up with a dance-hall flusie. He hadn't enough to keep him busy, for one thing.

San Leandro seemed to me like heaven after the Klondike. I had lots to do with housekeeping and my garden, and little Billie had to be looked after. I wasn't thinking about Jenky; I never suspicioned nothing.

Then one day I took sick. My heart was acting funny. I went to Dr. Bilbilker in San Leandro; my neighbor, Miss Jamais, give me his name. She was a Christian Scientist, but when she seen I was determined to go to a doctor she said that he was well spoke of.

Dr. Bilbilker told me I was liable to drop dead any minute. 'Your old ticker's wore out,' he said.

'Are you sure about that? I'm alone here with a young boy,' I said; 'I got to know the truth as much as you can give it to me.'

'I am. I advise you don't you walk up steps or drive a frisky team, or do nothing that will cause you no strain or excitement.'

I was scared all right. I went across to Miss Jamais and told her. One thing I said: 'If anything should happen to me, if I was to fall down dead, don't let no one touch my body but you.'

She answered me: 'Since you have made that request of me I know there is something about this that's queer.... You are carrying money,' she said, 'now ain't you?'

I said I was. On my chest, in different size bills. It was a heavy bundle. I kept putting my hand up there, sort of shifting it away from the pain.

'You know this little bank down here in the village is as good as gold. But if it ain't big enough to suit you,' she said, 'you can go to San Francisco; there's lots of banks over there that will pay you interest on it.'

I decided to take her advice. I was holding my money to buy real estate but I hadn't had no time to look around. I went across the bay and put my money, all they'd take, in the Hibernia Bank. The rest I put in two other banks. I felt so relieved that I could go home and not worry.

And I begun to find out that with the weight off my chest my heart quit acting up — it was the weight of the package. When the doctor come again, I was all right. He tried to hide it, but I always thought he acted disappointed!

I went over to the Hibernia Bank to have the interest entered in my passbook. That was many months later. I stepped up to the window but the teller ordered me away.

'Take your time; come when you are called!'

I went back and set down and I seen others going up — some of them that couldn't even write their names. He was insulting people right and left. I heard him say to one man, 'Why don't you learn to write?' To another he said, 'Stand back there!'

I thought that was terrible, him talking to his own class of people, people that he'd sprung from, that was taking their mite in to save it for a later day — humiliating them. I thought he ought to have said, 'Fine! you done good, you saved up some more!'

Then he called to me, but before I could get off the seat he bawled me out: 'Move fast, can't you, I'm a-beckonin' to you!'

'I set here,' I said, 'and heard you insult a half a dozen people, but you can't do that to me!' I was afraid I'd say something to be ashamed of. But when he got through with my passbook I turned around to a man standing near me and I asked him to show me to the head office.

I went in and walked up to somebody I suppose was the president — I don't know what he was.

'I been insulted by one of your high-sniffin' clerks and he's got to apologize to me!' I handed him my book. 'That's my name,' I said.

He turned and spoke to a man in there with him: 'I told you he wasn't fit for a window.... Put in somebody else, and send him in to me.'

When the teller come he told him, 'You can apologize to Mrs. Jenkins if you wish; it's between her and you. But you been bully-raggin' other clients of this bank. Now,' he went on, 'go get what's comin' to you; you haven't no more job here.'

Then I felt sorry. 'Don't turn him out, give him something else to do, please!'... I went away then, and I don't know what they done about it.

Something else happened a minute later. I went out of the bank, and just when I was down the stairs, out of the door, a lady come up to go in. She had a dark mustache, almost like a man.

She started by me but I touched her on the shoulder and asked her if she would mind stepping out on the street. 'You are a woman and I am a woman, we are sisters,' I told her. 'You have a blemish there on your lip that I know you will be very glad to be rid of.' I wasn't in the beauty business no more but I had some of my cards from the old days. I give her one and I told her to call on me in San Leandro. 'I will relieve you of that nuisance without a five-cent piece; I don't want no money, I don't need it.'

Well, she showed up bright and early. I had to take it off three different times, but it always come out each time a little fainter.

She got so stuck on herself, so proud, she asked me would I sell her the recipe.

'Why no,' I said, 'it ain't for sale. I might get broke-up sometime and want to go back into business.'

She was a smart woman, a business woman. She told me, 'I won't interfere with none of your plans. I want it; I know where I can make some money with it. I ain't rich, and this is a good chance for me. If you will let me have the privilege of selling it, only in three counties in the southern part of the state, I'll pay you fifteen hundred dollars cash!'

I took it, but not just then. I hesitated, but eventually I took it.

She made thousands of dollars with it. Southern California was full of women that had a terrible lot of hair on the face. I don't see them much down here no more — perhaps they died out. There was lots of Spaniards in California and their women was mostly dark. They intermarried, I reckon, but there was lots of them in the old days.

That was a curious way of making money, wasn't it — accidental like?

I was homesick for May. Besides I was having some dreams about Jenky I didn't like. May wrote from Dawson, wanting Billie. So I got myself ready and started with him for Seattle. I said San Leandro was like heaven after the Klondike, and yet there I was heading for Dawson again. Nobody made me go; I just had to be on the move. I left the San Leandro house in charge of little Bella, my Portuguese girl. Meanwhile, May, without letting me know, pulled up and started down from Alaska. She figured to surprise us in San Leandro — it was just the biggest piece of luck the way we run together at the hotel, in Seattle. May went to register and the clerk told her I was upstairs!

We stayed in Seattle a week, and then we went back to San Leandro. I was so glad to see May that Jenky went right out of my mind. I still had the idea of going to Alaska, but it was put off.

One day in San Leandro we was visited by a friend of ours that was in the hardware business in Dawson. He said he had a proposition to make to me. He heard I was leaving, and he was going back, too, shipping in a lot of hardware. He didn't see why we couldn't pack a few barrels of whiskey in with his stoves and tools. His proposition was for me to go in with him on the liquor deal. He was sure he had everything fixed at Dawson with the Canadian customs, so's not to have no trouble. I was to finance the whiskey and split with him on the profit.

I bought the whiskey off the Crown Distilleries Company, in San Francisco, and had it delivered to a warehouse where my partner packed it in with his hardware. I went up to the warehouse to see what was going on and I got so enthusiastic the way he managed things, hanged if I didn't go back and order more whiskey!

May and Billie, myself and my partner on the 'St. Paul,' out of San Francisco bay, headed for St. Michaels. We waited at St. Michaels several days for the river boat to take us to Dawson. At last it come. We got our freight transferred — pretty near a boatload. On board was a Mr. and Mrs. Younghusband. He commenced kidding me about Jenky hell-raising in Dawson. I never let on that I didn't know all about it — just kept him talking until I realized it was true. The wife told me more: Jenky was going with some woman called the Rough Rider; she'd taken him down the line for all she could get out of him.

We got to Dawson at night. Jenky was waiting on the river bank in the crowd. I never got over the way he looked — in dirty yellow mackinaw pants and coat, like an ordinary barroom stiff.

Jenky told me as how he'd bought a building on Front Street, and had fixed the downstairs to live in. He said he left it to me to attend to furnishing it.... I wanted to know what business he was in and if he'd made any money. He said he'd started working the claim, but I reckon he never seen it only when he needed cash.

'No,' he said, 'I ain't been doin' nothing much to crow over.' I told him to get some decent clothes to wear. Then he come out with it and owned up he was broke.

'Where's all the money you took in?'

'Hell, that was only chicken feed to what I'm loser!'

So that's the way it was.... I let him alone; he was feeling bad enough, and I had a little thinking to do on my own hook.

I begun again in a day or two. I asked him had he been going with any woman. 'My God, mama,' he confessed, 'I might as well tell you the truth, before someone else does.'

He was full of remorse. 'I been mixed up with a skirt and she was a sure enough hellion.' He told me how she'd badgered him, busting in on his card games and walking off with hundreds of dollars of his chips. Used to stand treat — buy wine for the crowd with Jenky's money....

'Now you know it all,' he said, 'and I don't blame you any way you feel about it.... But I'll try to get to doin' something to make it back.' He meant the money he'd lost.

I was heart-broken. I didn't let on though, only that I never went near him. I tried to make a decent home for him, but nothing more.

The whiskey was hid away in a house and locked up safe, Jenky didn't know about it, and I wasn't ready to say nothing. A month later I told him. 'If you listen to me, Jenky, we'll both make some money. I want you to open a bar right here, downstairs.'

We talked it over, and he agreed to my proposition. He had some partitions put up on the second floor to make sleeping quarters, and me and May fixed it up. Jenky bought a big stove for the saloon; the pipe run upstairs and kept us nice and warm. If I ever wanted Jenky all I had to do was to rap on the stove pipe.

We went to work getting things ready downstairs. The whiskey had to be bottled, labeled and sealed. Jenky scoured the town and bought barrels and barrels of empty bottles. We stuck on all kinds of labels I had brought in. I told Jenky he had to close every night at twelve o'clock, and no gambling.

We had a wonderful opening. Jenky took the old name Sour Dough as Ed Fitzpatrick was gone out of business. The receipts was big right from the first night. One day Jenky asked me if he could put in two card tables. I said, 'Absolutely no!' Then he argued with me over it and showed me why it would be good for the house. I seen he was right so I told him to go ahead — I said he would have to pay me ten dollars a table, and the first time I heard of Jenky playing, out they'd go. He turned over my share of the profits every night, and the twenty dollars for the two tables.

I kept a watchful eye on him. I was nice towards him but cool; I never made a fuss over him as had always been my habit of doing.

Christmas Day, when Billie come home from church, he asked me, 'Nana, what is Christmas for?' I tried to explain to him it was the day our Savior was born — a time to forgive your enemies.

I no more than said it when a voice spoke to me over my shoulder: 'Are you practicin' it?'

I answered, 'No, I ain't!'

Billie wanted to know what I said. 'Nothing much, honey.' But I knew in a flash what I was going to do. And when Jenky come home to our Christmas dinner I put my arms around his neck. I wanted to cry a little but I didn't.

Jenky was liked by everybody, and he was doing fine with the saloon. Oftentimes we heard stories of a bunch drinking in another place and somebody saying, 'Let's go over to the Sour Dough for some real whiskey!'

Along late in the winter bottles begin to get scarce so Jenky told Billie he would give him a dollar a dozen for all the quart bottles he'd bring in. Billie got busy after school hours. He found plenty of bottles the first week. After that it wasn't so easy. He figured in his own little mind a better way. A few days later Jenky went out back and seen half a dozen boys with sacks and Billie paying them off for their bottles.

'What's all this about?'

'I pay twenty-five cents a dozen. Let 'em make a little money, too,' Billie explained.

'That boy has a head on him!' Jenky said to me. 'He'll get by in this world.'

When spring opened up Jenky was so busy he couldn't get away to the claim so he sent May. When the second clean-up come along Jenky took charge. A clean-up means taking out the gold dust from the sluice boxes after the dirt has been washed away. Jenky's share was forty thousand dollars that year.

After Jenky got back from the claim we decided to sell out

everything we had in the northern country and leave it for good. I had been inside eighteen months this time and I didn't like the hurdy-gurdy stuff no better than before. We'd sold all the whiskey I smuggled in; the money I made was more than I bargained for and I was very much delighted with my venture.

Times was bad when I got into Dawson that second trip. I'd bought a piece of property on Front Street for seven thousand dollars, a grocery store building, a few doors below our saloon. In the summer Dawson boomed again, and I sold out for twenty-one thousand dollars. Three times what it cost me.

Jenky sold his two houses first, and then the saloon building where we was living upstairs. We had close on to a hundred and fifty thousand dollars between us that we changed into paper money before we left Dawson. There was a bank there now.

Chapter XXVI

WE BOARDED the up-river steamer and took the train at White Horse. Us and May and Billie. Charlie Thiebold, that run a regular butcher store in Dawson, had a brother George that wasn't doing nothing in particular, just trying to make a clean-up like everybody else in the Klondike. He was on board with us. A very likeable fellow and good company. Full of hanky-panky — a great one to paint things in bright colors. He heard how Jenky had a lot of money. All the way out he was talking cattle business to Jenky and trying to get him to go to Payette, Idaho, across the Snake River from eastern Oregon. George had a little bunch of cattle in there and he told Jenky what a great opportunity it was.

It turned out George was on the square — he was boosting for Idaho cause he loved it there. He told Jenky the cattle business was good right now and cattle men was making money. Jenky decided to take George's advice and head for Payette. He was anxious to settle down to something legitimate. He was through with bartending and mining, and he reckoned he was through with gambling, too.

But first I wanted to see my son, Ollie, over on the Pend Oreille River, out a ways from Spokane, in northeastern Washington. It was always hard for me to imagine Ollie growed up; yet he had a wife and five young 'uns. On May's first trip out from Alaska they was living in Oklahoma, a hand to mouth existence. But May sent Ollie money and moved them from there to Spokane.

I bought them a whole trunkload of clothes and drygoods, knowing how sure they was to be needed. Ollie was having a hard time trying to make a living cutting railroad ties. Now, when I got there and seen how things stood, I talked to Ollie and said that we intended to buy some place, maybe in Idaho, and that I wanted him to come along. Naturally, he was willing.

My other boy, Will, walked in the second night of our visit to Ollie's. Nobody was expecting him. The last I'd heard he was in Texas. Will was glad to see us all, but in twenty-four hours he was off again. Had to meet some hobo friend, and he acted like he was late for a date with Lillian Russell.

The minute I seen him I said: 'Will, when did you have a bath last? You look kind of lousy to me!'

'Shucks,' he answered, 'they boiled me and my Prince Albert in Seattle.'

I offered to set him up like Ollie, but no, he didn't want it. He had a dollar in his pocket when he come and a dollar when he left. Jenky bought him some chewing tobacco and that's all Will ever needs to keep going. He can travel a thousand miles on tobacco, and a little cheese.

Will don't care what started the last war or who's going to be the next president. I never seen him open a newspaper or read a book. 'I ain't interested,' he told me once. 'If you read you get to worryin' about things; an' if you write you have to answer letters.'

I have had my share of life but I wouldn't be afraid to try it a second time, if I could knock about and see everything like my boy Will. I reckon he gets his gypsy ways from me. I used to look at him and think it was just too bad me and his father ever met. But I don't know. Will humps along and asks no odds of nobody. That's more than most can lay claim to.

We went from Spokane to Payette, Idaho, and stopped at a small hotel there. We drove over to Ontario, Oregon, to look about but run into one of them eastern Oregon wind storms. You couldn't see nothing. We was thoroughly disgusted with the Oregon side and went back to Payette. After a few days we drove back to Ontario for another look. This time it was nice and calm, a really beautiful day.

We went into the First National Bank that had our money

we'd transferred from Seattle. Charlie Emison, the cashier, told us his mother's two hundred acre place was for sale. I questioned him about how far it was.

'Seven miles,' he said, 'let me take you out and show it to you.'

I was enthused from the start. 'There's my white and green house!' I whispered to Jenky. We talked a while with Mrs. Emison, and if it hadn't been for me Jenky would have made a deal then and there. We left saying as we'd be back next day.

'Let the old lady wait,' I told Jenky. 'You'll be savin' money every day you stay away!' I had a hard time holding him down; but I was stubborn, I made him wait.... A week later we went out and bought it. Furniture and stock, chickens, turkeys, all just as the place stood, for seventy-nine hundred dollars — against the ten thousand she was asking.

There was a three room house, down the road a piece from the big house, and Mrs. Emison asked us to let her have it for a few days until she could get located in Ontario. We missed a lot of stuff right off so I thought I'd go over and have a talk with her. 'Well,' she said, 'you know, I was supposed to have my personal belongings.'

Then she begun coming over after this and that, like a bake pan and other things her boys had bought her. She done that many times a day, and always I give her what she wanted until she had me run ragged.

'Don't let her have no more,' May said.

Pretty soon she come over again. There was two pictures on the wall she claimed her daughter had painted and she wanted them. May told her, 'You cadged a third of the things that was in here. Now don't come no more because it won't do you no good!'

It seems like mostly I was hard, but once in a while somebody would come along like this Mrs. Emison that knowed how to get around me. Then I would call May in. When May said no she meant it. How she got that way is beyond me — not from her father, Williamson Page. And not from watching Jenky do business!

After it got around that 'them Klondikers' was in town three or four parties come over to sell us farms, and the same day that Jenky bought the Home Ranch from Mrs. Emison I laid out three thousand dollars to Si Qualey for the Upper Ranch — a hundred and sixty acres about three miles west of the Home Ranch.

It was just as good land, with a big orchard that was better really than anything on the Home Ranch. But there wasn't no improvements — just a shack, without a floor even.

What I had in mind was a place for Ollie's family — they moved in with us while I built them a five-room house. They stayed on the Upper Ranch until I sold it. Then Ollie moved to town and went to building and carpentering. He's been at that more or less ever since.

George Thiebold got Jenky to buy a thousand head of cattle. I was against it, but as things turned out I was wrong. So Jenky got busy having his brand recorded, and venting the cattle, which means putting on a small brand to show a change of ownership. They was many days branding.

I didn't want them critters wintered on the Home Ranch and I said so. To satisfy me, Jenky bought an eighty acre place, three miles north of us, and herded them in there. That was late in the fall of 1901. It was known all over the country as the Boneyard — account of the grass being sparse and the cattle looking so poor.

Pretty soon we decided to go and pack up our furniture in the San Leandro home and ship it to Oregon. May took charge of the Home Ranch. My boy Will showed up and said he'd stay through the winter, with May and the hired man. May tells the story, how one morning it was snowing and blowing until it got to be a regular gale, with great snowdrifts everywhere. As she got breakfast she noticed a bunch of cattle on the back road, drifting with the storm. It's the courtesy of the country if any stray cattle come by your place, to turn them in and feed them until you can get word to the owner. May couldn't see if this bunch belonged to Jenky or not.

Stock won't face a storm, they always move with it, and May was afraid they'd all die in the cold. So she ordered the hired man to ride across the field and take along a wire cutter to open up the fence and let them cattle in.

The hired man said he wouldn't ride out in no storm for nobody's cattle.

'All right,' May said, 'you go out and saddle my horse!'

He went to the barn, but he saddled his own horse and cut the fence the way he'd been told.

Before he got back, Will come in from somewhere, and he said to May: 'I'd a-done it if he hadn't; but first I'd a-give him a hidin' for actin' contrary like that!'

May was still hot. 'Seein' how you is so willin', you go hitch the team and take our extra stove over to Ollie's! I'm thinkin' them kids of his'n will freeze with their old stove.' Of course, after Will's big speech, there wasn't nothing but for him to go. He started, but it took him till sundown to make them three miles. The snow was up to the top of the fences, and the team, big as they was, had to lunge and keep lunging every foot of the way.

Next day it was fine and clear but awful cold. About eleven o'clock in the morning Will got back from Ollie's. 'Tell your hired man to unhitch the team. I'm headin' south for some place where it don't snow!' That's right. Left without waiting for his dinner.

In the early spring we come back from California. Jenky sent through everything in a freight car: all the furniture, and a mare by the name of Nellie, and Fanny, a greyhound. I wasn't able to sell the San Leandro place so I rented it out on a long lease to an undertaking parlor. That same trip I bought a house in Oakland. It was rented and I bought it as an investment, but later I lived there. I sold both them places at a good profit long after, especially the Oakland house, as the city had moved down that way and real estate was having quite a boom.

Now, about them two animals we shipped up. Nellie was a fine driving mare — that wouldn't drive! Jenky worked

on her all one morning until he was so mad I thought sure
he'd have a stroke. Lunch time one of the hired men come
by with a hay rick. Jenky told him to get a rope. 'I'll make
this damn mare go or I'll choke her to death!' Jenky said.
They tied Nellie to the back of the wagon but she braced her
front feet and let them stretch her neck. Then she leaned over
trying to break the shaft. I declare, she was a mean devil!
They put her between the team but she wouldn't pull a
pound. Jenky even started a fire under her and she just
stumped up and down until she put it out. So he give it up.
Later he broke her to the saddle and she turned out his favorite horse.

There was a boy in San Leandro that thought a lot of
Jenky and he give him this Fanny, a half-growed greyhound
bitch. Jenky wanted her for rabbit coursing, the jacks was
so thick around the ranch. Every farmer that could spare
the money had his place fenced in with wire netting about
three foot high. As it was the jacks got away with tons of
alfalfa; I seen fields et off a hundred foot back from the road,
just as clean like a mower had been over it. They was worst
along at dusk. Crawl out from under the sage brush and make
for the fields by the thousands. We had a rabbit-proof fence
around the Home Ranch, but there was a place to let them in
when Jenky wanted them for coursing.

Fanny growed big, and Jenky took her to the best greyhound there was in that locality. She had pups three times,
and we kept out two male dogs twice. So now we had four
dogs besides Fanny. Watching from the porch I seen her
catch three jacks in one run. She could move that fast.
Fanny's pups was all fast but not as fast as their ma.

Jenky kept one bitch pup out of Fanny's last litter that
was a ringer for Fanny, only that she wasn't full growed.
But he couldn't make her obey right. He was trying to train
her away from running jacks as he was using the dogs now for
coyotes. They'd start out and this bitch puppy would sidle
off after jacks. Jenky told one of the farm hands if she didn't
tend to business he'd give her a load of shot with his scatter

gun. 'I won't kill her,' he said, 'but if I do it can't be helped; she's spoilin' the rest of 'em.'

We was setting around the stove one night — all of us but Jenky — when I remembered I hadn't seen Fanny. 'I wonder why she ain't been scratchin' about,' I said.

'Good Lord, I don't think Fanny will be around no more.' May said that.

Now the cat was out of the bag! 'What's the matter, what's happened to Fanny?'

Nobody would open their mouth or say a word. I jumped up and went into the bedroom after Jenky. Before I could speak he said, 'I heard May.... Mama, I didn't know it was Fanny. I thought it was the bitch puppy. I put up the gun and meant to shoot over her, but I got her. I pretty near cried in front of the men....'

Next morning I told him: 'Every greyhound leaves this place. I won't have no more dogs to love and get killed!'

I made him give them all away — just kept out a collie. Do you know what he done? He give them to Bill Stennett. Bill used to work for us and was an awful good hand. Bill was over in Ontario living there. Jenky give him all the hounds, everyone of them; but sakes alive, two weeks later he went and hired Bill for another year so as to get them dogs back! That was Jenky's way of getting around me. The truth is he loved them dogs too much.

That first night, after Bill was back with the dogs, Jenky come in to supper. 'You know,' he said, 'I was jes' thinkin', I never seen a man I thought so much of as a dog!' It was a long speech for Jenky — he wasn't smiling neither, he meant every word of it.

There was a sheep camp right close to us, and this spring they run out of hay and had to feed their ewes on corn. The ewes was pretty near to lamb. When the time come they died off something terrible. There was an old sheep lying there dead, with her poor little lamb next to her. Jenky come along on horseback and put the lamb in a sack. He brought it home and layed it on the porch. He hunted me up and he said, 'Mama, I got a present for you. It ain't dead but it's mighty close to it — it's come a week before it ought.'

I worked on that little lamb until three o'clock in the afternoon before I got two drops of milk down its throat. It was four hours before it got to breathing natural. I wanted to save it so bad I was willing to do anything. I set up at night with it, trying to get it to sleep.

May had a beau there. She asked me, 'Ain't you goin' to bed?'

'No,' I said, 'I ain't; if you two've something to talk you can go on outside. I'm a-settin' up with this here lamb!'

I fooled with it for three weeks before it could waddle. I propped it up in a little contraption I made to help it along. It looked to me like it would never learn to walk. I told May, but she said, 'It will go all right when it gets stronger; you'll learn it.'

It was four months old when I took a trip to California. May said, when I went away, she thought in her soul my lamb would never stop running places, looking for me and bleating. When Jenky seen that he said, 'There's a couple of lambs up there that won't go with the herd; I'll bring 'em down for company for this 'un.' But my lamb didn't take to them at all, it wasn't used to its own kind, it had a human feeling. You see what wonderful things there are in this world that we create ourselves. Life was nothing to that lamb, you might say, but I wanted it to live.

Ten weeks later, when I come back, everything was fine. It was following Jenky with the dogs all over the country. You could see Jenky going down the road with the lamb and all them greyhounds following after him. People said, 'Here comes Dad Jenkins!'

Me and May went up to Seattle to visit. And my God, Jenky, without saying nothing, killed it.... I couldn't no more have done that. It was human. It was part of me; I made a trick lamb out of it. Jenky and the ranch hands et it.

I was thinking, ever since we visited Jenky's people in North Carolina, how I wanted to see some of my folks. There was only my brother Alfred left in Indiana; and my two sisters, Betty and Mary, down in Texas.

Since he was a youngster Alfred lived around Crawfordsville and never had a week off in all his life. I wrote him and his Rebecca, would they like to have a vacation and a trip out West. Well say, it didn't take them long to decide: out they come, and stayed with us two months. They had a fine time, except that Rebecca kept fussing about things back home in Indiana. Like when she said, 'Hanged if it don't seem as if I can hear old Prince, stumpin' his shoes off in the barn — right after gettin' new shod, too!'

Alfred was smart about hogs and mules, but our Oregon layout had his eyes popping out. It was all new like, and he sure had the time of his life. He'd never seen nobody before like Jenky — he thought he was the most wonderful man in the world.

Jenky was a great hand with jack rabbits — he had anybody beat I ever seen when it come to cleaning them. A cut, and a squeeze up the middle — then he'd hold the jack by its back feet, bang it against a tree or a fence post, and there wasn't nothing left but good meat. All the insides popped out like a bursted balloon.

When he showed that to my brother Alfred nothing would do but for him to go out and try it hisself. Alfred sneaked off alone, but I seen him coming in. His shirt and pants was full of blood and mess, and his face was all smeared up. He owned up later, there was pieces of jack down his pants leg and in his ears!

Then I got the idea of going to Texas and having a family reunion. Besides I wanted Alfred and Rebecca to see some city life. Rebecca was willing, but we sure had to drag Alfred off. I made the arrangements and we had a wonderful time the whole way. We stayed in San Francisco a week and didn't miss nothing. We went out to the old Chutes, near Golden Gate Park, a regular Coney Island. We took in all the side shows and finally landed up in a little vaudeville theater. There was an act with some trained hogs climbing ladders and doing tricks. Alfred went into raptures, thinking how marvelous they was and how much sense they had. When he should have knowed a hog ain't got a lick of sense.

'You jes' wait till tomorrow,' I said, 'I'm goin' to take you to a real show!' I asked around for the best play in town. They sold me tickets to 'When Knighthood Was In Flower,' with an all-star cast. We was thrilled, me and Rebecca, we talked it over way into the night.

We'd forgot all about Alfred, setting over in the corner of the room, smoking his corn cob. He was listening to us gabbing for two hours. I asked him, 'Wasn't it grand?'

'I reckon it was good play actin',' he said,' but I liked them hogs the best!'

After the trip to Texas Alfred and Rebecca come all the way back to Oregon and visited some more. I don't know how long Alfred would have stayed away from home if it hadn't been for Rebecca remembering that her prize speckled rooster had to be groomed for the County Fair.

Brother Alfred lived until 1914. He wrote me just a week before he died:

Crawfordsville, Ind.
January 16, 1914

Dear Sister —

Was glad to hear from you and glad you are feeling good. I would have answered sooner but I had just received a package of medicine from a specialist of Detroit Mich. on stomach troubles and thought to try it a while before writing you to see if it helped me any. This is the 6th day Ive been using it and the gas dont bother me near as bad as it did. Only I and you of the whole family is alive and we have got to take care of ourselves. The 4 girls lived to a good old age they would average a little over 80 years.

The connections is all well as far as I know. Bell's man is dead been dead over a month killed hisself with booze. Bell's girls is all married but Kate the one that has fits.

We are getting along fairly good. We have anything we want to eat and wear and thats more than lots can say. We are only milking one cow now but will have a heifer fresh soon.   The old woman has 3 dozen hens — eggs this winter is 30¢ per dozen.

Say, Sis I was looking over some of your old letters the other day. I found one you wrote me when you was in Seattle. You was lecturing me on thought. The theorys all right if you can make it work. You said think health and youd have it think wealth and youd have it. But the trouble with me is how can you think you have good health if youve got the cramps colic or cholera morbis rite bad or how can you think you is wealthy when you know you aint. It wont work in my case.

I want to see you all so bad I feel like coming out some Sunday and taking dinner with you. I dont think we could have such fine dinners and fine times as we had on the Home Ranch. Just think of the spare-ribs backbones and fine turkeys we youst to have. WHOA it makes my mouth water yet. Such things has got so high now we have to jump up to smell them. Well we are trying to live as happy as we can considering means and ability.

With fond love to all. By by as ever

Your loving brother
A. A. PLUNKETT

Chapter XXVII

WE SUPPOSED we was settled down for good. We lived a very quiet life, riding the ranges after cattle, raising alfalfa hay, and grain, and doing all the farm work in general.

I commenced to talk to Jenky, advising him to get rid of his cattle. There was a buyer come around from Yakima, Washington, paying high prices. That was 1905. Jenky finally decided to sell and the deal was made. He had thirty days in which to deliver to the stock yards in Ontario. So him and May and the hands started for the hills. They put in all daylight in the saddle. Sometimes they wouldn't get back until ten o'clock at night, tired as bull cats. They got all the cattle but a half a dozen strays that showed up later. The buyer told Jenky he was lucky selling when he did as beef took quite a slump. As long as we lived there prices never was that high again.

Soon after that I moved to Oakland with Billie to give him some good schooling; I took Ollie's Jenny and Alfred along. I stayed there two years while Jenky run the Home Ranch in Oregon.

May was visiting in Seattle. She run into a cattle buyer from Kansas City by the name of Archie Dickson and they fell in love. They married at my Oakland home. Archie used to buy cattle and hogs in the Northwest and ship them down to his Kansas farm for fattening. May went back with him to Kansas City, but not for long. They moved to Idaho, and Jenky and Archie went into the hog business. All Archie give was the experience; Jenky put up the money.

They had some kind of a disagreement and Archie quit. Said he was going back to Kansas. May tried to argue him out of it, but he was too sore to listen. May went to packing up. But she changed her mind and told Archie that she'd join him later. He said no, she'd have to come now or stay where she was for good. No one can talk that way to May. She stayed. Archie went to Kansas, but only for a little bit. He telegraphed May from Salt Lake City asking her to meet him there, but he didn't mention travel money. May wired him, 'Walking not so good from this end.' She never seen him again; a few years later she divorced him.

May kept her troubles to herself. When I found out what was going on I packed her off to Seattle for a vacation. *That's where I seen a race track for the first time. There's a lot coming about horse racing from now on....*

My back wasn't hardly turned when Jenky bought the Boise Ranch. Now we had three ranches — he'd sold the Boneyard. Pretty soon I was going to buy me another, too.

Jenky's new ranch was six miles out of Boise, Idaho, and about sixty miles from the Home Ranch. It cost thirty thousand dollars, half down. Later Jenky made May a deed to it. I told him, 'Perhaps that's your idea of a gift but it ain't mine, with a fifteen thousand dollar plaster on it!' He bought it because some old dry bones said it was cheap. Three hundred and ten acres — Jenky sold off eighty acres for a good price, the rest he give to May. She's owned it ever since, raising alfalfa hay and clover seed — principally clover seed — and paying interest on that mortgage.

I went through hell trying to make my money, but once it started coming it seemed to slather down. Jenky used to get mad because the first thing I done when I got to a new place was to loan out money. And when someone figured out that my income was a dollar an hour I thought it was too small!

In the end I always bought real estate. Jenky was a gambler at heart and I knowed he would bet out all our money if he got the chance. I told him the only way for him to hold on to it was for me to buy land that he would be so crazy about he'd buy it from me! I wanted to protect him. Many a piece I sold Jenky. But he didn't sometimes pay me nothing. A note, but maybe I'd never see no cash. I didn't care; he was like a baby....

Pretty soon I bought the Idanha Ranch. I had my eye on it a long time. There was lots of prune ranches round us but none as big as this one. Ninety-nine acres was out in prunes, except one little corner in alfalfa hay. I bought it from a Hollander by the name of Van Gilsie. He homesteaded it. Now he wanted to sell out and visit back home, to pay the money he owed his people and to show them he'd made good in America.

Jenky come in one day and told me, 'The Dutchman's place is for sale.' I called Van Gilsie on the phone and asked him how much he wanted.

'Twelve thousand spot cash.'

'If we buy it it'll be spot cash.'

I heard him tell his wife, 'Mama, I think I got it sold.'

'You have,' I said, 'if you'll take ten thousand.'

'Not a penny less than twelve thousand!' he answered.

'Listen here, Mr. Van Gilsie, my husband will be around tomorrow. I think he may take it.' I put it that way because I wanted Jenky to handle it. I wouldn't live with a man that could say I wore the breeches. I was too proud for that. Jenky done all my business for me, whatever I told him to do.

The next day Jenky went over with twelve thousand dollars. 'Buy it cheap,' I said.

'How much?' I asked him when he got back.

'Twelve thousand,' he said, 'and next time you do the dirty work!'

A year later I done the harvesting and sold the prunes for ten thousand dollars. Then come two years when the prunes brought twenty-seven thousand five hundred dollars and fourteen thousand. But I had my mind made up — enough was enough. With property sky-high it was time to sell. A man bought Idanha from me for forty-eight thousand dollars. I thought I done good. Shucks, in six months he sold it to an Italian from Philadelphia for ninety-nine thousand dollars!

It was all a lot of money for everybody. As a consequence

it didn't last me long. It come too easy. I lost it at the races. It went like snow on a hot stove, but say, the sport I got out of it!

Well, I done it with my eyes open. I didn't forget the lean years. I had fun with my money, but I knowed how much to spend and how much to save. I never touched my stake. But that's all another story.

A few months went by and Jenky sold the Home Ranch for fifty thousand dollars — twenty down, and the rest on part payments. But the man couldn't go through with the deal and Jenky got it back a couple of years later. It was mighty lucky for Jenky he got that much out of it, because he finally lost the Home Ranch in a poker game.

It wasn't all money they give me for Idanha. I took two Boise houses in trade, one that I give to Billie later on, and a place I kept to use. I was tired of ranching and thought I'd like to live in town.

I had to furnish up the Boise house; it was brand new. That's where I met Joe Pugh, and got the family into business. I went into a furniture store where Pugh worked and seen a bedroom set and a dining room set that I own to this day. I didn't want neither as they was too high price — but I bought them. And I said to myself that anybody that could talk me into buying Caucasian walnut furniture was smart enough to start my grandson on his first business venture.

Billie was about twenty-two and just out of business college in Oakland. My idea was to begin him in a small way in Boise in the second-hand furniture business. There was pretty near enough stuff from the ranches we'd sold to stock him. But Jenky was crazy over Billie and wanted to do something big for him. He never told me nothing until the day he walked in and said how he'd bought the Daley Brown Furniture Company for Billie and Pugh! Paid down so much, and they was to pay off the balance monthly.

Maybe I wasn't mad! 'You've ruined that boy,' I said. 'You've put him so in debt he won't never get out.' It took

Billie many years but he did finally clear it up. The name was changed to the Jenkins Furniture Co. Jenky used it as his bank — whenever he wanted money he'd draw a sight draft on the store.

Racing horses kept me alive. It don't make no difference what your ailments are, it makes you forget. And as long as it does that it is worth what it costs in money. I won with my string of horses; I run them square and I had good jockeys. Any other way horse races ain't meant to be beat. Playing them with your own horses is a business, but trying to beat them from the grandstand — nothing doing, it can't be done. I found that out like everybody else that's tried it. It's a great sport — for the rich enough and the poor enough. For the millionaires and the bums. It ain't intended for the rest of the people, paying off on radios and washing machines.

I get tired of this luck talk. Did you ever notice it's the thinking people mostly has the good luck? Take somebody you know that's got the reputation of being lucky; he's smart, ain't he? But people say he's lucky. What they mean is he uses his head. It's the lazy man that's unlucky — everybody shakes their heads and feels sorry for him. Shucks, it ain't bad luck that's pulling him down, it's bad brains. Most luck is inside you, and the trouble with us all is waiting for something lucky to happen instead of digging it out.

Horse racing is supposed to be crooked. Well, it is. There's a crooked side to it, and plenty that's honest. It ain't half as crooked as some of the wise 'uns make out, and it's a lot more crooked than the trusting common people has any idea. Stop to think of it, ain't that true of all things? I don't set up as no smart business woman — I'm just a trader that can get along — so I mustn't be saying too much. But from my experience, swapping things and ideas, it appears to me like all ways of making money is crooked or straight, depending on who's running the show.

What I object to in racing is the crookedness that hurts the poor man. When the crooks put their heads together. And the poor man with his one or two horse stable — eating his heart out for his horse, living with the critter like his own child, waiting for his spot — gets robbed out of the purse by the gamblers and their bribing ways.

I was just learning what horse racing is like, up in Seattle about twenty-five years ago. One day a man whose name was Bunkus come to my room and told me about a woman that was fixing races. She owned a fine restaurant there in Seattle, but once the races started she didn't bother about nothing but bribing horseowners and jockeys.

Bunkus was the go-between. He told her I was the biggest bettor at the track so she sent him over to see me. He wanted to know how much I'd stick for — would I put up some money to fix a race? Then I was to bet something for her, and a thousand for myself, and I could win maybe five thousand dollars.

'No,' I told him, 'I would scorn the idea of such a thing. I don't hire no one for the lust of money.... No, absolutely no!

'And you tell her for me,' I said, 'she put that over a couple of days ago but it won't do her no good. Tell her I'll still be settin' in the grandstand and wearin' my diamonds years from now. She may be successful for a spell but it will get her in the end. She will be sorry she ever done such a terrible thing; she'll be down and out. Tell her I said she'll learn to hate crookedness and regret that she ever stooped to it.'

I hadn't heard of her for five years when she come up to me at the El Paso track. 'You don't know me but I know you,' she said. She stood there like she wanted to shake hands. 'I am the woman you sent word to once in Seattle, for fixin' a race, that it would get me. Well, it has.... I'm out here cookin' for the swipes.[1] You said I would learn to hate crookedness; I hate it now, I hate it above all things in the world.'

My heart went out to her. I grabbed her by both hands. 'I'm proud to know you!' I told her. She's working at Agua Caliente right now — still cooking for the swipes. And she does the same thing at Belmont when she goes East. To this day I like her and we're good friends.

[1] Men at the barns; stable boys.

I become acquainted with Billy Blaylock in Seattle, in 1908. Blaylock was a horse owner, and before I got through with him I was a horse owner, too. Blaylock was all right, dead square; but Allen, his partner, was the other kind. Allen got them both in bad.

Blaylock went broke, because of Allen, but he managed to hold on to two of his horses, and his trainer, a young fellow by the name of Bert John. It was through Blaylock that Bert John come to work for me.

'I'm wantin' my own stable,' I told Blaylock, 'and one of these days I'm goin' to buy me some horses.'

I went back to the Home Ranch — about the same time that Boise opened up with regular racing. Blaylock turned up in Boise, with his two horses, On Parole and Internacion. He was up against it — no money and the railroad wouldn't let him unload. So he hunted me up at Ontario and come out to the ranch. He needed sixty dollars; he said he'd give me his note.

'I don't want your note, I'll see you out at the track.' I give him the money and he went on after Bert John and the horses. When he left he told me, 'I'll be payin' you back, or you'll be havin' that stable you was a-wishin' for!'

I done pretty good at Boise. I knowed the horses better than some of the boys that was making book.[1] But Blaylock couldn't cash a bet. When he got ready to leave Boise he asked me for another loan and I give him a hundred dollars.

We moved down to Oakland and Blaylock come to me there, along the tail end of the racing season. 'Mrs. Jenkins, I don't believe I'll be able to redeem them horses.'

'Well,' I said, 'if you need some more money you can have it.' I give him another hundred and I told him not to worry. 'If you win a race, you'll be able to pay me off.' But his horses didn't round to form. Finally Blaylock went off, and I owned a racing stable that cost me two hundred and sixty dollars!

It was over at the barns, before Blaylock left, that he said to me, pointing to Bert John: 'My stable's broke up, but over yonder is more'n good horses. He's been in charge of every

[1] Bookmakers. Called here, bookies, layers, chalk-writers.

thing for a year now and I ain't paid him a dollar in wages. The clothes on his back is all he's got and he's washin' dishes for his board.'

That didn't humiliate Bert in my estimation; I thought it was grand. I was very glad to hire him....

Everybody around the tracks knows Bert John and nobody has a word to say against him. Bert can't say no to nobody; he'd give every cent he had in his pocket — and that ain't much — to anybody that needed it. Most men around a track gets their loans squared one way or another; generally by borrowing when they need it — going broke and making a touch, the same as they loan it when they're flush. Bert's different; that's the only fault he's got. He loans so easy people don't seem to think of paying him back.

Bert trained for me, beginning with Oakland, and trained my stable up to the last day I owned horses. From 1909, until me and Jenky quit racing two years ago.

He's not married and I guess he never will be. He says he don't want no woman supporting him and he can't afford to take care of nobody but hisself. That's so, the way money runs through his fingers. He's forty-five about; he don't drink and he's very moral. He hasn't no bad habits at all — except I don't know whatever he's aiming to do when he's old, and no money put by. Gives it to anybody....

I never did pay him regular wages. He wouldn't set no price. That first time, I asked him, 'What do you work for?'

'Blaylock ain't paid me nothing. It was all right, I wanted to get his horses ready. He never had nothing to pay me — I'll take whatever you think I earn.'

I bought Bert a rig-out, a suit and everything, and when I got him dressed up he looked dandy. He sure was a pretty gentleman in his new clothes.

I knew he was a wise bettor, and a good money maker — if he wouldn't give it all away. He used to clock horses before he worked for Blaylock and he understood form. I'd ask him if he needed any money. If he did he'd take it, and if he didn't he'd say so. That's about the way we worked it all them years.

Chapter XXVIII

RACING got into my blood. Two horses wasn't enough, I wanted more. Tom Williams owned one of the best stables in the west but he was selling out. A horse called Tom Haywood was in the lot. I went to a friend and asked him would he bid Tom Haywood in for me.

'I want him for myself,' he said. 'He's a distance horse, and where you're fixin' to race there ain't no good takin' a slow-startin' horse like Tom Haywood.

'Jes' the same,' he went on, 'maybe I can make you win a piece of money. Tom Williams has a horse by the name of Roalto that I seen run. He looks good to me if he'll stand up. He can go three quarters but that's about his limit. He's fast as lightnin' but was broke down three years ago.... He's been got ready on the sands and they say as he's sound.'

Thursday, the first day of the sale, my friend bought Roalto for me. And Sunday we went down to the track to give him a workout — me and Jenky and Bert John, the three of us with watches. The boy only worked him a quarter but he run it in 23 flat.

Roalto was entered the next day and Bert got Borrell, the best boy at Oakland, to ride him. It was the last week of the meeting, in fact the last time they ever raced in Oakland. I got to the track and I seen that Roalto was 100 to 1. I bet three hundred dollars against thirty thousand. The bookies took all I give them. They knowed all about Roalto breaking down and they didn't figure him an outside chance.

I was setting in the grandstand, my lap full of five and ten dollar tickets, counting how much I would get as I was expecting to win a fortune. Jenky was over in the paddock with Bert, talking to Borrell.

'Feel that horse out,' Jenky said, 'and see if he's worth a bet.'

Borrell asked him, 'Ain't you playin' him today? Mr. John says he can win.'

'No, I ain't. I've a race picked out for Thursday, if you say he can run. I haven't no money along now.'

Then Bert said, 'Mrs. Jenkins is bettin' on him, but I don't know how much....'

Jenky went off half cock. 'She ain't bettin' no real money. Roalto's 100 to 1; the way the wife plays 'em, he'd be 20 to 1 by now if she was a-bettin'.'

That sounded reasonable. But Jenky overlooked one thing. Them chalk-writers hadn't no use for a broke-down horse that hadn't started in three years; they couldn't figure Roalto no chance on form.

Jenky might have sent word to me to see what I was doing if the time hadn't been so short. Anyway, he didn't; Roalto was saddled and the race was coming up. 'You pull[1] him!' Jenky said to Borrell, and walked off.

After the race Borrell told Jenky he could have gone to the front any time and won by ten lengths. 'I couldn't hardly keep from showin' up what I was doin'.'

'So much the better,' said Jenky. 'You ride him Thursday and I'll have a bet down for you.'

Bert was furious when he found out I had three hundred dollars on Roalto. 'I'm a-goin' to tell Jenkins what you was cheated out of! It's a crime!'

Jenky come up to the grandstand, pale as a ghost. Well, so was I, and almighty near to crying. 'You ruined me,' I declared, 'and I ought to kill you!'

'Mama, don't take on that way. I'll bet it back for you. You'll get a better price on Thursday. You'll win forty thousand in place of the thirty thousand you might a-win today!'

Gracious me. Thursday there was too many horses entered in Roalto's race and the Jockey Club scratched him — him and a lot of skates that didn't figure to be in the money. Then we entered him Saturday, the last day of the meet. It was the same thing — get-away days and big fields, with everybody wanting to race their nags to pay feed bills. Roalto's entry was thrown out Saturday, too.

[1] Illegal method used by jockey to restrain and defeat his mount.

From Oakland we shipped to Victoria, in British Columbia. I was still counting to make a clean-up. But things was different in Victoria. We had to train Roalto on the track in plain view of the railbirds; there wasn't no other place to work him, and Lord have mercy on my soul, he burnt up that bullring! The books made him favorite first time out! Sure, Jenky put up the money like he said he would. And Roalto toeroped his field. I won three hundred dollars instead of thirty thousand.

Jenky had the racing fever worse than me. Stayed out to the track, and had a tent put up as a cook house to feed the Oregon-Ontario outfit — the name of our stable. He done the cooking for a while, until the swipes nailed the griddle cakes against the side of the barn and throwed rocks at them!

Jenky come to me one day. 'You can make a lot of money if you listen to me.' I was always suspicious of Jenky when he talked like that.

'I am a good listener,' I said, 'till I get where I want to talk.'

'It's like this,' he explained. 'They want us to lump together with the rest of them and play a long shot. All of us but one is goin' to pull our horses. Roalto will be one of them pulled if you'll agree.'

'Dad, would you do that?'

'You bet I would! It's done every day, it's part of the game. Why not make all the money we can?'

'I won't,' I said, 'it's plain stealing!' I tried to talk him out of it for fear he would do it anyway.

He asked me, 'What shall I tell 'em?'

'You tell 'em to go to hell! I ain't pullin' my horse!'

They let me win just one more race. The next time Roalto run, a good friend, a life-long friend to this day, come to me and said, 'I don't believe I would bet on Roalto, Mrs. Jenkins.'

I jumped up off my seat. 'What's the matter! Has he broke a leg?'

'No,' he said, kind of snickering, 'it ain't that bad, but he needs a rest, he's had an awful lot of racin'.'

I was stubborn about it. I never even asked Bert John. I bet five hundred dollars on the race and lost it. Roalto got beat way back. Brooks, that I thought the world of, and a mighty good jockey, rode him. I felt sure that they done something to my horse but I never peeped. What was the use, it wouldn't have done no good.

We shipped to the new Brighouse track, near Vancouver. I started Roalto and he run last. Absolutely last. I begun to ease up on him — I thought that maybe Brooks hadn't pulled him after all, that day in Victoria. Maybe he wasn't feeling good.

I felt pretty bad about the money I'd lost — but much worse, worrying that my horse was going back. There wasn't nobody I'd listen to but Bert. I went to him now and asked him.

'Mrs. Jenkins,' he said, 'Roalto loves a pasteboard track so's he can hear his feet pop. He runs in a crump, and he likes to hear his feet under him. He can't do that here.'

It went on this way nigh on to a month. One day Bert showed me a picture of Roalto on a hard track, all humped up, sort of in a knot, ready for another jump. 'On this here new track,' he said, 'the dirt breaks under his feet. It makes him nervous; he's got no confidence in hisself.'

By now I was desperate. I was afraid Bert was wrong and that Roalto had really gone back. 'Bert,' I said, 'why don't you give Roalto some stimulants and make him have confidence in hisself?'

He answered me, 'If you mean dope, I don't believe in it. It's against my ideas.' Bert don't allow no drugs, he never has.

Well, I got to thinking about this confidence talk, and how a man I knew give his horses hop. About two weeks before I met Benny Tilyou for the first time. He come to me, out to where I was living, and wanted me to bet some money for him on one of his mares. 'She's had trouble with her forelegs,' he said. 'I jes' give her a little stimulant, nothing that will hurt her, something to give her courage so's she'll go on.'

Tilyou's mare won that race. That's how I come to think

of Tilyou now. I sent for him without telling no one. I asked him if he could make Roalto run; that he was scared of this new dirt track at Vancouver.

'Hop won't make him run faster,' he told me, 'but it will make him stay — and stayin' wins more races than speed.'

'He'll pay an awful price and maybe I'll get a good bet down. You can make a bet for yourself, too,' I said.

Tilyou went out to the barns but Bert John abused him and run him off. Tilyou come back and told me. I wrote Bert on a note: 'If you value your job, let this man do what I told him.'

That was the last I knew about it. When the race come up I started betting. I had my money there, nearly all in hundred dollar bills, and I had Ian West, from Henderson Bay, placing my bets. Roalto opened at 20 to 1. I got up five hundred at them odds. The balance was from 15 down.

The race was six and a half furlongs, with a pretty good field of sprinters. I was afraid, the way Roalto had been running....

Roalto broke in front but he wouldn't go. They all passed him. It went like that the first quarter until he must have been ten lengths behind the last horse. Petey Clark was the caller. 'Roalto way back,' I heard him. I dropped on the bench with my hands over my face! Oh, I guess this must be wrong, I thought, God ain't a-goin' to let him win. Something said to me, 'Since when has God anything to do with a horse race?'

Then I heard Petey Clark calling out, 'Roalto comin' fast on the outside!' I jumped up and run into a stranger's box so's I could look down the stretch. I seen all them horses in a bunch but one — a horse by the name of Hush Money was five lengths in front.... Over there, a little on the outside, I seen my pink and blue colors. Roalto was running like them others was standing still! Never in all my days have I seen a horse travel that fast. Next he'd collared Hush Money.

I forgot all about everything. The jockey's name was Goggle. I jumped out in the aisle yelling, 'Goggle! Goggle!

Goggle!' I was running around in a circle, crazy as could be, in front of everybody. I was truly — but nobody was looking at me, they was all watching the finish. Petey Clark was hollering something about Hush Money — but I didn't care. Roalto was coming like blazes, with Hush Money running a little wide. Roalto passed him the last jump. Talk about your Snapper Garrison finish — that was it!

I thought I won, but I didn't know for sure until I seen the numbers go up — then I let out a scream....

Here then begun to come in the money. I just stuffed it down — my purse and my pockets was jammed full. A friend asked me, 'How much did you win?' 'I don't know,' I said, and I didn't. May wanted to help me. 'Let me be,' I told her, 'I don't need no help!'

We went home and May got supper. She wanted to know how I come out. 'I ain't counted,' I said. No sir, I hadn't. The next day was Sunday, I knew I had plenty of time.

I put the money in the bottom drawer of my bureau, locked it and stuck the key under my pillow. Then I went to bed.

Next morning I stayed in my room late. May come and rapped on the door but I didn't answer. She done that three or four times. She went to pounding on the door. 'Mama, ain't you goin' to get up?' I'd been setting on my bed, spreading out the money, laying a gold piece on top of each bundle of greenbacks. May hollered, 'I want you to let me in. I believe you went nuts!'

I come over to the door and opened it. When she seen my bed she just froze stiff, she was overcome with awe.

'God,' she said, 'you ain't nuts!'

Chapter XXIX

GOGGLE was one of Bert John's finds. Picked him up when he was down and out. A bum around the bushes; getting no mounts, though he was a good rider. After Bert straightened him out I seen him win as high as five races in a day.

Goggle double-crossed me a year later at Butte, Montana — him and that same Benny Tilyou. Bert fired him after the race.

A few months ago a woman come to me over to Agua Caliente and asked me did I remember jockey Goggle. She told me she was married to him three years. I said, 'You stood him longer than me!'

We set down and talked all afternoon about the old bullring days. She put me in mind of a race at Victoria that first year, something I clean forgot.

Roalto was running and I took out two hundred dollars to bet on him. But when the Roalto race come up I hadn't no money left; I'd lost my two hundred.

I set thinking what to do. I commenced unscrewing my earrings — held one in my hand and then I unscrewed the other.

'Billie,' I said to my grandson, 'take these to the Judge and tell him I want five hundred dollars.'

Back come the check. I bet it all, at 4 to 5. Roalto won easy; he always won easy if he won at all.

Another one like that, at Victoria. I drawed on my bank back home for a thousand dollars. The First National Bank at Ontario, Oregon. But the money didn't come. I thought to myself, maybe I overdrawed. So I sent a telegram to send the money right away, that my note was following in case there wasn't no money to cover it.

I didn't hear nothing. There was a big race coming up

and I hadn't no money. I went to the best bank there was in
Victoria and I asked for the manager.

He invited me into his private office. 'I am Mrs. Jenkins
from Ontario, Oregon. I run a string of horses here. I drawed
on my bank for a thousand dollars but the money ain't come.
I'm expectin' it, but I can't wait no longer.

'There's a horse in today,' I said, 'that is goin' to win for
certain.' Roalto again — but I didn't want him to know. I
opened my purse and took out a blue-white, five carat diamond
that was in a pin. 'Look at this and see if you could let me
have a thousand dollars on it.'

He was awful surprised. 'Do you aim to bet that on a
horse?'

'Every dollar of it.' He begun to get nervous. Not about
the money, because he knew he wasn't risking nothing on the
diamond. But he was an old time banker, the kind that don't
like to take chances. No, and he couldn't imagine such a
thing, that I would bet a pile of money without it was going
to be on something good.

'Would you mind tellin' me the name of the horse?' He sort
of cleared his throat.

'All right,' I said, 'you come out to the track, and I'll tell
you in plenty of time.'

There ain't nothin' as scarey as money, and this banker was
having a hard time making up his mind....

He looked at me like I was wearing a halo instead of a hat.
'I don't bet on horse races,' he said, 'but I am confident you
know what you are about. I'm a-goin' to follow that thousand
dollars!'

'When I'm done bettin' you bet all you please' was the way
I put it. 'Come up to the grandstand jes' before the third
race.' Roalto was entered in the fifth race but I didn't want
him to try any of his tricks.

He took my pin as security and I left with the thousand
dollars.

Somehow it got around, it had preceded me, that I was
not going to bet on Roalto. Petey Clark asked me if my money

come, the day before in the evening, and I told him no. That was the truth. So he got the idea I wasn't betting. Roalto was always around even money — up to now — but this time he opened at 2 to 1, and then he went to 2½ to 1.

The odds was too good, it kind of scared my banker friend. 'Say,' he said to me, 'you ain't changed your mind?' I didn't answer him, I showed him my ticket, two thousand to a thousand.

'He's 2½ to 1 now,' he said.

'You'll be jes' that much ahead of me. Go on and bet all you want to.' He done it. He played Roalto down to 6 to 5!

He had his wife there; he brought her over. She bet a hundred dollars. Bless me, I don't know how much he bet, but he was shaking like a leaf when the race was over.

Roalto went out in front and stayed there. He won eased up. Never did I see nobody so scared looking as that banker. He tried to shake hands with me after the race. He said, 'Congratulations, Mrs. Jenkins, you never will know how I enjoyed myself!' He must have bet two or three thousand dollars. He could afford it, I guess.

The wife come over next. 'Lord,' she said, 'the way you two was bettin'! It like to scare me to death.'

I told her, 'I hope I didn't get him in no bad habits. Bankers ain't allowed to bet on the races, you know.' She believed it. She thought I meant it.

Roalto was just fed and took care of until he got awful fat. Bert was getting him ready, on the Home Ranch, for the Salt Lake meet.

We started him three times but he run absolutely last, the same as he done on the Brighouse track. The gamblers was watching him because he was a very much liked horse — they knowed what he could do and some of them was laying up to win a barrel of money.

I didn't play him his first two races at Salt Lake. He wasn't ready — he was fat as a butter ball. The third time he come out prancing. Say, he looked so good I told Bert, 'He looks like he might be able to run some today.'

'No ma'am, I wouldn't advise you to bet on him.'

'I'll throw twenty dollars away, it won't hurt me.' I got 3 to 1 to show.

About ten seconds later, it seemed like the whole place was betting on my horse. It was just five minutes before post time. We couldn't understand it. They went crazy in the betting ring, trying to get their money up. Men rushed up to the grandstand to ask me. I told them the truth, I couldn't figure it. Roalto was backed from 15 down to 6. He closed even money to show.

Well, he finished second and never went to the post again. He'd been doped right in our own stable. Made to run when he wasn't ready for a race. Was that terrible or wasn't it?

He didn't drop dead; I'd have been glad if it had been that way. No, Bert telephoned me to come over quick — Roalto was sick. Poor old horse, he was all drawed up, and suffering so terrible. I told Bert to chloroform him and let him die. We was all crying, me and May and the swipes. We went home, I couldn't stand it.

Bert never suspected no crooked work among our own boys. He never thought about such a thing. Just the same we was double-crossed; somebody made a killing because money was bet on him all over the country — away from the track. Salt Lake City was betting on him in the Chicago poolrooms, and everybody knew about it except the two people that should have known — Mrs. Jenkins and her trainer.

When Bert come home that night I asked him, 'What do you think about it? Was we framed?'

'I think, but I don't know whether I am thinkin' right or not.... I know what I think; but if I knowed for sure, I would kill him before mornin' if I hanged for it!'

Chapter XXX

I LAID off racing to go home and look after the prunes. Meantime May went into partnership, racing with her friend, Jim Hall, and I let her take Bert for trainer.

Jenky was hanging around Boise. Wouldn't come home maybe once a week. I got lonely and decided to join May in Salt Lake.

I got tired of that, too; I wasn't satisfied to sit in the grandstand at Salt Lake and watch May's gallopers. Then I heard through Bert how Tol Cobbledick, that owned the little mare Lady Macy, was selling out. I seen Lady Macy win a lot of races and I liked her.

Bert said to go ahead and buy her, and Charlie Getz, a gelding, from the same barn. Tol wanted fifteen hundred dollars for the two of them.

Here come up the bitter and the gall. Tol wouldn't do business except I'd hire Mace Sharp, his trainer. Sharp had Tol under his thumb. I hadn't no trainer, now with Bert working for May and having his hands full. But Sharp had the reputation of being a crook.

Finally I sent for Mace Sharp. 'Do you know,' I said, 'you have the name of being the biggest crook in these parts?' He turned red and said he didn't know it was that bad.

I looked him in the eye. 'Mace, I'll tell you something you can depend on. I won't stand for no crooked work — no hoppin' of horses, and no pullin'. If you throw me down and I find it out I'll kill you quick as I'd shoot a cat. And not hang for it, neither!'

That's what I said, and he answered me, 'I never will.'

Sharp was dishonest, but he was a wonderful conditioner of horses. Some say as a jockey's more important than the horse under him. Well, maybe, but I'm one that thinks the trainer is most important of the three.

Sharp's weakness was his wife. He was wonderful to her. Mary Lou was fifteen when he married her. Nothing was too good for that girl, always trying to give her money to buy clothes, always wanting her to look pretty. Sharp was a fine trainer and a good husband, but that's all.

One afternoon Sharp rushed up to me and said that we would all be ruled off the track unless I'd give him the money to pay for a mare he'd claimed.

'Claimed! I don't claim horses, I don't believe in it.'

'Well,' he said, 'you'll have to take this one in — I claimed her in your name.' I was pretty bad crossed up; I give him the money before I had time to think it over.

There wasn't a man in Salt Lake I could trust to ask, so I wired Jenky what Sharp done and how I wanted to get rid of him. Jenky wrote me he'd be down soon, not to do nothing until he got there. I had another talk with Sharp and he promised me all over again everything I wanted, and that he wouldn't do no more claiming.

I started my horse Shooting Spray, and by God, Sharp pulled him on me! Mr. Wilson, that owned a big hotel in Butte, was track judge. I went to him and talked it over.

'You know the horse can win,' he said, 'and so do I.'

I asked him, 'Do you think I knew anything about it?'

'No, I know you didn't.' He said he knew me when I started racing and that everything I done was on the level. 'But I don't want to see your trainer around this track no more,' he declared. 'I don't care what he does for you — that's your business — but put somebody else's name down as trainer. Sharp can't train where I'm judge!'

I was sorry for Mace Sharp's wife — a fine little woman, and I couldn't help thinking of her. Every time I wanted to fire Mace I thought of Mary Lou. I asked him, 'Will you take the curse off Sharp when he leaves here?'

'I will,' he promised, 'I'll do it for your sake.'

From Salt Lake we went to Juarez. Me and May lived in El Paso and crossed over the Rio Grande every day — it wasn't much of a river that time of the year. Villa was on a rampage and Juarez was all shot up. Everybody was jumpy, not knowing when Villa would turn up next but nothing happened; we wasn't molested.

Barney Forsythe was the first jockey I ever owned. I bought his contract the same time Mace Sharp come to train for me.

Barney, before that, tried to kill his boss. He'd been awful cruel to Barney; used to whip him with a bridle, and one day he beat him up with a martingale.

'What's the matter, Barney,' I said, 'you don't look like a bad boy.'

'I ain't,' he said, 'but I don't know what it is for no one to treat me right. I never could do a real wicked thing, but I got a temper, and when people blame me for something I ain't done, I fight back.'

I told him, 'You behave yourself, and everything will be all right.' I aimed to get him a room at my hotel but he didn't want that. 'I don't want no room in no fancy hangout. I'd like a place, if it's the same to you, so's the boys can come in nights and play cards. I won't do nothing to shame you, Mrs. Jenkins.'

I never seen a better boy, and I learned to love him. I treated him like he was a human being. They would do anything to boys them days; it's no use talking, it was something terrible.

Barney's a big man on the ships now, got too heavy to ride. He worked hisself up to first mate on a boat and every time, for about ten years, when he come ashore, he hunted me up. The last time was a few years ago, right here in Chula Vista. But I ain't seen nor heard from him since. I can't understand that — I hope he's well and prospering.

One day Barney come to me and begged me to listen. 'Mother, Mace is doin' something to your horses. I don't know what, but I work 'em faster than they run their races.... Anything I say against Mace you don't believe me. Gee, I wish your husband was here, or something!' No, I wouldn't say anything against Sharp to the boy.

I never seen a gamer horse than Charlie Getz that Tol Cobbledick sold me. In eight starts at one meet he wasn't out of the money once. A little black horse, but stronger than most big 'uns. And this time I'm telling about he won but he just staggered in. Barney come to my room that night and he could hardly keep from crying. He told me what Sharp said after the race — 'Huh, you must-a tried to win for the missus the way you was ridin'!' 'Yes, I did,' said Barney, 'but it was the hardest race to win I ever was in.'

My, but I was wishing for Jenky to come down from Boise. He kept writing he was coming, and naturally I thought it best just to wait for Jenky to get there and see for hisself. But I was sure worried.

Then up come Shooting Spray a second time. I knew he was good and could go a mile. Sharp told me to play him. Shooting Spray finished fourth and I lost a thousand dollars. I walked downstairs to where Sharp was and I asked him what was the matter. 'He should a-win,' he replied. 'I think it was Barney's fault.' 'Well, I don't!' I said. 'You leave the boy outen this. You're up to your old tricks, doin' something crooked to my horses and bettin' against 'em!'

'Why mother, I didn't do nothing. I wanted to bet on him, myself, but I didn't have the money.' If ever I seen sin in a man's eyes... but what was I to do?

I went back to the hotel that night and all the people was standing around talking in whispers. There was something going on that I didn't know. Someone said, 'Mrs. Jenkins, you're goin' to win with Lady Macy tomorrow, ain't you?' You could have knocked me over with a feather. I'd raced Lady Macy twice and she'd got beat way back both times. I hadn't raced her since. And here was a stranger telling me she was entered tomorrow. It was all news to me.

I went next morning to the track about eleven o'clock. I hadn't no idea of betting on Lady Macy because I didn't think Sharp had her ready. But I kept thinking of that fellow's remark: 'You're goin' to win with Lady Macy tomorrow.' I didn't go near Sharp. What was the use, he'd only lie to me.

The race come up and I said to May, 'I can't let the mare run loose. Maybe I am superstitious, but you bet a hundred for me, to win.'

May come back with the money. She told me she couldn't get near the books. 'Everybody's on Lady Macy, wavin' their hands in the air and bettin' their heads off!'

That made me sick. 'By God,' I said, 'if Mace Sharp is up to something so is mama!' I tramped down to the paddock and I told Sharp: 'Lady Macy don't win today! She ain't been in the running nor nowhere near it. You tell your friends to tear up their tickets!'

'How can I hinder it?' he asked me.

'You say that? You go to Barney Forsythe and tell him my money ain't down!'

Even then I wasn't sure. Sharp would double-cross his best friend and laugh about it. I better finish this myself, I was thinking. I waited there in the paddock until Barney showed up for the race. And I told him plain, just one short sentence: 'You keep outen the money, boy!'

I reckon that was the meanest thing I ever done. Lady Macy finished fifth. Sharp stood to win a fortune. His crowd bet away seven thousand dollars for him — in Chicago, at O'Brien's pool room and other places. He was getting my mare beat right along until the price was right — and playing me for a fool. When he was ready to turn her loose Lady Macy was running for his money instead of mine.

And them was Sharp's friends, betting for their own account, that May seen in the ring. Sharp would have busted O'Brien's wide open if Lady Macy had come down in front. But he took his medicine like a man. Never let on that he knew what it was all about. After the race, he said, 'I reckon you was right, Mrs. Jenkins, she wasn't ready.'

I made up my mind, as long as I was waiting for Jenky to come down from Boise, to try once again. That's hard to explain, only that Sharp was a wonderful trainer and it tempted me. I bet five hundred on Shooting Spray that could run a mile in 1:40 and he got beat five lengths by a horse that

never run it in better than 1:41. Barney told me he couldn't
get my horse out. 'It's the same old story,' he said, 'Mace is
trimmin' you!'

I asked Sharp. 'He lose to a horse that couldn't beat him
again in a year,' he said, 'it's jes' the breaks in racin'.'

I wasn't satisfied; I wanted to know what other people
thought about it. I went over to the barns and asked the
boss of the swipes.

'What did you think of that race, Pat?'

'Sure,' he said, 'and that goddamn skunk's been double-
crossin' us all. Shooting Spray run with tea lead under the
bandages! How Mace done that without somebody a-seein'
him, faith, and I don't know. 'Pat had a thick brogue and a
pair of hands like hams. 'Mrs. Jenkins,' he asked me, 'would
you mind much if me and the boys had a talk with Sharp?'

'Go as far as you like,' I said, 'and the Lord give you
strength!'

The whole stable bet on Shooting Spray. When Sharp come
back to the barns Pat and the swipes was laying for him with
pitchforks.

I raced Shooting Spray right back two days later. Little
Barney told me, 'Bet every dollar you got!'

It made my heart ache. He won just the sweetest I ever
seen. Then I was called into the judges' stand; I knew I would
be. 'Mrs. Jenkins, can you make any explanation about the
way your horses has been runnin'? I believe you're all right,
but there's a crook in your stable. What makes you think
Sharp is any better workin' for you than for other people?'

'I know all about it now, Judge. I been waitin' for Mr.
Jenkins to fire him. But you can forget Mace Sharp,' I said,
'the swipes run him out of town!'

The judge laughed and so did I. It was the first **good
laugh** I'd had in a long time.

Chapter XXXI

WE TURNED the horses out on a big blue grass pasture and settled down to raising colts. It was going to be many years before we raced again.... Yes, it looked like racing was going out, gone. They closed up all over the west, and the eastern tracks, too. We had a pretty lot of horses and didn't know what to do with them.

Them years we still had the Home Ranch and the Upper Ranch. May run the Boise Ranch. We lived just natural, like folks in any home. Raised a lot of alfalfa, hay and grain. There was men and horses to tend, and different kinds of stock, chickens and turkeys. The furniture company was going along steady, and Jenky was putting in his time betwixt the store and the ranches.

Then he got mixed up in some gold dredging scheme away up in Warren, Idaho. Jenky was always looking for big nuts to crack; this was another proposition he was fixing to make a million dollars out of.

They was having a barbecue celebration in Boise. My grandson, Billie, was helping with the work — been at it all night roasting beeves.

'Mother,' he said — that's what he always calls me — 'I want you to look your best. To please me, you wear your wine-colored silk and your hat that goes together. I'm a-goin' to drive you to where everybody can see you!' We just got a big new automobile and he was trying to show me off.

I told him, 'I'll mind you till it comes to that; but if you ain't proud of me now I ain't goin' to start, at this late date, a-makin' a show outen myself, and havin' people a-hatin' me that I want to love me.'

Billie drove us over and went off to tend the carving, and running the barbecue. I dressed like he wanted; and while nobody was there hardly I set in the car, for it was a pretty spot and a nice place to look around.

Then the four hundred come — there's a four hundred everywhere, oh yes! 'Come on, May,' I said, 'let's get out and walk
among the real people.' Ain't it strange how them limousine
riders feel their importance? They get a little bit heady, don't
they? Bumptious! It makes me want to fight!

When dinner was ready everybody went over with their
paper plates. Just as May went off to get us something to eat
I seen three men walking my way. I knowed the middle man
— it was Governor Alexander of Idaho, smiling and talking.
The other two was strangers.

They come up and Governor Alexander introduced us.
'This is my friend, Malinda Jenkins, that crossed the Chilkoot
Pass in '97. You're meetin' a lady that has done things!'

Well say, them was the governors of Washington and
Oregon! 'Now,' he said, looking at me, 'with your permission,
we'll have our dinner with you.' I et, setting between three
governors! Outdoors, on a bench. And what a grand time
I had!

I was visiting in Vancouver. On the train coming home, a
man set down by me and started talking. 'Ain't you hump-
back Jenkins' wife?' You see, Daddy got to be very stoop-
shouldered. 'I know him well,' he said, 'and I think he is a fine
man.'

I said, 'How come? Where do you know him?'

'I played poker with him times on end.'

'Yes,' I said, 'but do you think that's a cause for braggin'?'

'Even so, lady, you got something to be proud of, and I'm
a-goin' to tell it to you now. I seen Jenkins set down and play
cards and lose a wad of money. And get up and leave the
game before it was half over. "I'm out of luck," he said.
"You'll get paid in the morning." Walked out in the middle
of everything.

'One of them asked — it was a stranger in the game — was
Jenkins good for it? Said it to the man that run the place. Do
you know what he answered him? "The squarest gambler I
ever seen!"'

I didn't let on to nothing; I pretended I was proud and pleased. 'Thank you,' I said, 'I'm much obliged your comin' over to tell me.' Jenky was famous in five states for his poker. 'You'll be settin' up with my corpse, a-playin' on the coffin lid,' I told him once.

Well now, I come back to Boise and his royal giblets had fixed up three rooms over the furniture company's warehouse, intending to use them for a gambling place for him and his friends. I went to see it without being invited, and I bragged on it to the family how he had it arranged real nice. I didn't let on I knowed what it was for.

'Gee, Dad,' I said,' that was sweet of you to fix this up. I like it better'n the hotel. All we need is a cook stove. Go on up to the store and get us an electric one.'

He said, 'No, you go.' I'll be durned if I didn't. It's the one I'm cooking on still.

Jenky didn't say nothing, and I unpacked and fixed up for housekeeping. Jenky went to the store and told Billie. 'Goddamn, the old woman put it over on me. I was goin' to have it to gamble in, but that's all off now!'

When Jenky worked that gold dredging out of his system I got him to go to Los Angeles for a spell — us and my granddaughter Pearly, Ollie's Pearly.

Jenky was playing cards in Los Angeles. It wouldn't take him long to find a place to gamble in. He come home one night and asked me, 'Could I have a poker game up here?'

Maybe I shouldn't, but I answered, 'Are you aimin' to make a gambling hole outen your own house next?'

'Mama,' he said, 'our club was closed by the police. We been playin' out to people's houses, and it's my turn to give the party.'

I don't know why, now — I was a little curious, I reckon — anyway, I give in.

'I wouldn't ask you,' he said, 'but everyone of them is a gentleman. You'll get acquainted with some right enough millionaires.'

By gorry, I did, too. The men sent their wives to call on

me; nice women, but land sakes, the questions they asked —
all about me and Jenky, and Alaska and the gold rush, and
most about my being married three times....

Jenky said to buy a big spread of food — to get it anyway
that I wanted, but plenty of it. I'll tell you what they done,
to show you the character of the men that Jenky played with.
They come there and played from ten o'clock at night until
four o'clock the next afternoon, and never left the house!

Jenky said it was stud poker. I can play this common old
poker, but I don't know stud. There's a difference. All I
know you can lose plenty at stud. We had two big rooms.
Me and Pearly was fixing to sleep in one of them; do you think
we done it, with them men in the next room? We kept the door
open and set up the whole blessed night!

There was a man that sold the chips — it was a regular
gambling lay-out. I was tickled to pieces; I was so excited.
These men was buying chips by the thousand dollars worth. I
never seen nothing like it, what them chips stood for in money.

I would go and set down by Jenky a bit and he'd throw some
chips in my lap when he won. But as soon as his luck changed
I'd get up and take my chips into the bedroom.

Pearly had been standing by one of the other men. When he
started to losing he told her to come back and bring him luck.
Gamblers is awful superstitious, ain't they?

This last fellow, when he commenced winning, give Pearly
some chips, and it went on that way for a long time. Directly
the man that was in charge of the chips said there was something wrong — I went and beckoned to him on the side. I
took him into the other room and showed him the chips we
had.

'Hey,' he said, 'so that's where the chips are! Count 'em
and I'll pay you off.' Well, I counted them all alike; I didn't
know the difference, that the different colors meant different
values. But he straightened me out. My chips come to over
five hundred dollars and Pearly's was a hundred. I never spent
such a night in my life, and I thought it was the grandest sport
in the world.

Jenky lost a thousand dollars. I went up to him after they all left. 'Dad, I have something to tell you, it ain't as bad as you think. I got five hundred of it!'

'Gee,' he said, 'did I give you five hundred dollars last night?'

'Sure, you threw the chips in my lap and I kept them.'

'Well, it's lucky for you I ain't hard up....'

'No,' I said, 'it's lucky for *you*, you ain't!'

For all his high gambling, Jenky could be awful stingy. But against that, right in the middle of a mean streak, walking along with nothing more than ten dollars in his pocket, and not a five cent piece in the bank, he'd hand a five dollar bill to a little colored boy to go buy him a pair of shoes. Not once, but a dozen times, I seen him pass out money to some friday-face he didn't know and wouldn't see again, that hadn't asked him — just account of Jenky deciding he needed it.

He was close-mouthed, Jenky was, like most true gamblers. And you couldn't interest him if it wasn't gambling. He wouldn't even listen. He'd come into the room and no matter how many people was there, or what the talk was about, in ten minutes he was asleep. Lived in a world of his own, all aces or deuces according to his moods.

If I asked him to set down because I wanted to talk to him, the only way I could hold him was to talk something with a gamble in it. I'd say, 'Now, Dad, you listen to me, this is important!' But the instant I was through telling him the exact particular thing I had in mind, his head dropped and he was asleep.

It used to make me so mad I'd yell at him and shake him — 'Can't you listen to me?'

He'd open his eyes and smile. 'Honey, I can't help it, I reckon you hypnotize me!'

I never set down and had a half hour's talk with him in forty-three years — and nobody else, neither.

Chapter XXXII

BOISE had a fair coming on. With racing. After laying up for years we was spoiling to go — Jenky the worst. He picked out seven of the colts and fillies and fixed it with May so's Bert could train them mornings, over the mile track at the Fair Grounds.

Bert left the ranch sun-up and was back at noontime. But Jenky stayed with the horses and never hardly seen home for a month.

I didn't like it, a respectable citizen of Boise living with the swipes, and I told him so.

'May can't spare Bert,' Jenky answered, 'and I dasen't trust them two year olds to nobody else. There ain't nothin' to do about it.'

Jenky just pitched in hisself. Hired three or four niggers, and the wife of one of them for cook. Most of the time he et with the niggers — a cup of coffee or something, him and them in a tent he rigged up. I stood for it because I had to....

Jenky won several purses at the Fair Grounds and had the racing bug bad. Went and shipped some colts down to Mexico. To Tia Juana race track, across from San Diego — without no trainer even.

Jenky raced through the Tia Juana and Reno meetings. Then he come home — left his horses at Reno to freshen up. He was thinking about going into the racing game strong. Every night we set around, talking horses and jockeys and ways to make it pay.

I was for it if May would give us Bert John to do the training. Bert didn't see how he could possibly leave. 'To hell with the ranch,' said Jenky, 'we can win more money offen one race than May here can make in a year!'

Sometime about then I heard of Ivan Parke, a brother to the jockey, Burley Parke, and how he was an extra good boy.

Ivan had been booting around the bushes and rode plenty already. It was getting late in the fall when I wrote Ivan's people in Declo, Idaho, asking them for a contract on their second boy. Jenky went to Declo and signed the papers, though Ivan come a little higher than any jockey after him.

You hear of a boy like that in different ways. Somebody will tell you, or you run across him yourself. A boy with small bones, small all around for his age, and smart acting. As a rule he's got more brains than anything else. Seeing as how he's small, it's a whole lot easier for him to learn to race than to get out and hustle for some other work. He can make plenty, and his people, when they hear that, if they're at all inclined, will give you a contract.

Ivan Parke come to Boise, and him and Jenky started for Mexico in a new Ford, sleeping out and doing their own cooking. Jenky done a lot of walking on the way. He was scared of the car — when they come to steep places Jenky made Ivan let him out. Ivan could drive fine but Jenky didn't trust the brakes. Sometimes Jenky hitched a log to the back to hold it from going too fast down hill!

Ivan told him he could manage all right. 'I don't want no log back there — come on, let's go.'

'No, by God!' said Jenky, 'I ain't takin' no chances runnin' over them grades and killin' us all!'

I followed on the train. We raced at Tia Juana all winter, living in San Diego, on the American side. When May come down we moved over, a few miles south, to Chula Vista.

Jenky was very seldom at home. Bert took charge of the stable, training the horses and learning Ivan Parke the way he wanted him to ride. Sometimes Jenky wouldn't see none of us in a week — he played cards all night in San Diego and slept at the track in the day time. I told him to stop playing cards and pay attention to his racing stable. But Jenky was like a dog with fleas — couldn't concentrate on but the one thing.

All the thinking Jenky done was strictly private; he never trusted nobody enough to talk out loud. Regular old froze-

face. Take his gambling — mighty seldom I'd know if he won
or lost. To show you how he was, he never missed an hour's
sleep over the biggest loss. I'd have gone crazy over some of
the things that man done. I know.

One Saturday night we drove down town to buy supplies
for the week end. I made out a list of what I wanted and I
told Bert to hand it to Jenky who was out of the car, by this
time, walking up and down with Ivan, nipping off ripe grapes
in front of the fruit stand.

I seen them talking and soon Bert come back. 'What do
you think,' Bert said, 'he ain't got but a dollar to his name.'

I just broke down. 'Good God,' I said, 'when he went out
last night he had seven thousand dollars!'

I was hurt so bad, I set down to talk to him quiet like, when
we got home.

'Dad, what in the world's it all about?'

'Mama,' he said, 'I'll tell you jes' exactly how it happened.
It was a gentleman's game in the hotel, not a gambling room,
and they was playin' stud and they got to playin' high stakes.'

That was Jenky's idea of a good explanation....

Bert had Ivan Parke in training six months when he give
him his first chance. That's awful soon but we wasn't risking
nothing; Ivan knowed plenty about sticking on before he come
with us.

Two weeks after that Ivan broke his maiden on Blanche
Meyers. A raw kid and one of our cheap ranch fillies, but they
come down in front at 20 to 1.

The horsemen around Tia Juana tried to buy Ivan's contract, but Jenky held out for big money. For a while he talked
twenty-five thousand. Bert told Jenky to take Ivan to Kentucky and he'd get it. He would have, too. Jenky took him
to Kentucky but he sold him too quick. Sold him to Harry
Payne Whitney for nineteen thousand dollars and Parke become the riding ace of America, for two years in succession.

I went back to ranching with May on the Boise place. It
was along in the summer because May, I mind, was cutting

hay. I was just settled and comfy when I got a telegram from Jenky to meet him at Winnemucca, Nevada. I left in a hurry. Jenky found out, before he could sell Ivan's contract, Whitney wanted another year added on. We had to go back to see Ivan's folks in Idaho and Jenky told me to do the talking. I got everything fixed up easy. Settled with them about their cut, too. Then Jenky stood treat and we traveled to Kentucky in style.

I was walking out of my room in the hotel one morning in Louisville when I heard a horse's name. There wasn't nobody there in the hall but me. I wasn't going to the races regular but I knew where I could get hold of Jenky down town. I telephoned him to bet fifty dollars for me.

'Who give it to you?' Jenky wanted to know.

'No one, it was whispered over my shoulder.'

He said, 'It's a wonder you don't make a real bet!'

The horse won, though it didn't pay nothing much.

Next morning I told Jenky I dreamed of five horses that was going to win. 'Hell,' he said, 'I dreamed I was King of England — that don't make it so!'

But after breakfast he remarked, 'I suppose you're playin' them five winners of your'n.'

'I reckon I'll have to.'

Jenky telephoned the pool room. Two was long shots so that sort of cooled my hanker.

I give Jenky five dollars to parlay [1] the five of them — I wrote down the names.

'They can't all win!' he said.

'And I can't lose no more'n five dollars, can I?'

Jenky was going over to the track. He got around among the bunch and played some horse in the first race and lost his money. He never give a thought to the paper in his pocket. Jenky went through the day, playing four races, and lost two thousand dollars. Coming home, him and Digby Short was setting together.

---

[1] A combination of bets, cumulative in effect, made on any number of horses, that pays only if all bets win.

'By gum,' he said to Digby, 'the old lady give me a five horse parlay and I clean forgot it! Let's look to see what they done.'

Every horse won! Then they begin to figure it. The second horse paid 30 to 1. The third horse something like 10 to 1. It figured out to pay about thirty-three thousand dollars.

When Jenky come in I asked him what had happened. 'They all win,' he said, 'but I forgot to bet it....'

'Jenky, why do you treat me like that? Why didn't you play them horses for me?'

'*The same goddamn thing that give 'em to you kept me from playin' 'em!*' Them's his words.

I didn't talk to Jenky for a week. The only thing that made me forgive him was knowing I should have gone to the track, myself; there wasn't nothing to keep me.

Of course, I didn't lose all that money. No bookmaker ever lived would have layed me thirty-three thousand dollars against a five dollar bill. But Jenky certainly cost me plenty.

Another time I had a dream about a horse — at Juarez. Jenky didn't like the horse; he said it was outclassed. His saying it didn't phase me. Anybody that's been around a race track knows that one person's as bad as the next, picking winners.

At the track I give Jenky two hundred dollars to bet, a hundred to win and a hundred to place.

'I think I'll lay you that myself and keep the two hundred in the family,' he said.

'You better not; I dreamed this one!'

He went off muttering to hisself. Down in the betting ring he seen that my horse was 5 to 1. He figured sure I'd lose. Poor Dad, he hated to see that two hundred get away; he stuck it back in his pocket.

My horse won in a gallop. Jenky came climbing up the stairs to the grandstand, his head hanging down. He took a big roll out and commenced to pay me off — seven hundred, eight hundred, nine hundred....

'Dad, did you get in on that?' I figured, maybe he followed my nudge.

'Sure,' he declared, 'I got mine!'

A month later he owned up. The seven hundred I won, I won off Jenky!

Back in Boise in the fall a meat buyer come to the ranch to buy hogs from May. He told us about a boy, Dick Johnson, that lived in Caldwell. He said he was small but wiry, and had done some bucarooing around the state. Dick hadn't never rode in a regular race. He thought we could contract him and that it would be worth our while.

Jenky went to see Dick's mother. He couldn't make much headway so I went to see her several times and talked it over and told her what it would mean to her and Dick — supposing he had the stuff in him.

Dick was set on going; it was that, more than anything I said, that made her give in. She talked to me again when I was getting ready to bring Dick down to California. 'I inquired about you,' she said, 'and they tell me you are a good woman with children — that you took two little orphan girls and raised 'em.' That was true, though I ain't mentioned it here.

'Dick,' she said, 'is my baby; his father died when he was small.'

'He ain't very big now from the looks of him.'

'No, he's always been delicate. His temper's the biggest thing about him — he ain't never had no boss.'

I told her, 'He's got one now.'

Dick told me he had a pal that was a good rider, but just a little bit bigger than him. This was Arthur Mortensen that lived at Homedale, Idaho.

Jenky made a few trips up to talk to Mrs. Mortensen and she was very favorable inclined as long as Arthur was all for going. The contract was signed, legal and proper.

Bert shipped to Mexico with a new lot of colts, stopping off at two or three towns for the fairs. Jenky took the two boys ahead. I went down alone to Chula Vista — that was 1924 — and bought this house I am living in now.

Besides housekeeping for eight people, and going to the races six days a week, there was always some youngsters around that had lots to learn about riding. But it kept me young — Dick and Arthur, and the rest after them.

The other day, out to the track, old Backy asked me how I done it all. 'Jes' done it,' I said, 'I don't know how. The hard part was with the boys. Some was willin', others shaped up stubborn — and all of them was green as weeds.... I showed them on a four legged kitchen chair — to cross the reins and get off flyin'.... And soft hands and the whippin' in stride, I used the settin' room rocker for that.'

May rigged me up a wooden horse in the back yard — with a regulation saddle on it. 'I taught them to tread the saddle, standin' up,' I told Backy. 'And when they done it good I'd tell them a story. Like the one about the Brooklyn Handicap that took ninety minutes to start — the time Winnie O'Connor hooked his foot around the rail, holdin' his mount steady and keepin' his weight in the air. Started fresh, against a lot of wore-out horses, and win on a 100 to 1 shot!

'Last,' I said, 'I taught them pace. Good jockeys keep a watch in their head. There ain't half a dozen in the whole country really know pace. Mortensen and Johnson learned it because they was born with it in them.'... Gosh, I get dizzy, just thinking about that old wooden horse.

Jenky was down to two horses. There wasn't enough to keep Bert busy so he went to training for J. W. Marchbank's stable and left with that outfit for Chicago. He took Dick Johnson with him.

Jenky kept Arthur Mortensen — went bushing with him through the fairs. Jenky picked up a few nags and done good with them, seeing as they wasn't much. Arthur was a great rider — he had to be. Jenky started him too soon, but he was lucky and come off without a tumble. What Jenky didn't know about training jockeys was plenty.

Arthur stayed a little ahead of Dick Johnson that way as Bert wouldn't risk letting Dick ride in Chicago. They got back to Chula Vista and Dick was crazy to ride. That little Swede wanted to start right off and if he'd had his way he'd have done it, too.

'Dick,' I told him, 'the Lord won't let you kill yourself more'n once....'

To show you how people is and what they teach their kids, Dick said — he talked kind of through his nose — 'I got only two years to live and do all my ridin'.'

'What!'

'Yes, two years.'

'We have a contract on you for five years. What about that?'

'Why,' he said, 'you know the world is comin' to an end in two years, don't you?'

'Who told you that?'

'My mother. Don't you believe it?' he insisted. He was very surprised that I didn't know it.

'I should say not!'

'Do you think my mother don't know? Do you think she would tell me if it wasn't so?'

'Now wait a minute, Sonny,' I said, 'how does she know all this?'

He straightened up and throwed back his head and drawed a big, long breath. 'Her and Brother Pig set and talked about it every night almost. Now, do you think she don't know?'

'I never talked to your mother enough to know what her idea is,' I replied, 'but that there Brother Pig worked out at our ranch and he didn't have enough sense to know to be a farm-hand.' Brother Pig belonged to a Bible class, there in Boise; he got hold of about twenty men and women and they was the only ones going to be saved in the town. He was a white man, white outside, but I think, inside, he must have been black as tar. He was awful ignorant, but somehow he was able to make other ignorant people believe in him.

'Poor little Dick,' I said, 'listen to what I'm a-tellin' you. Many times there has been people crazy enough to set the time for the world to come to an end, and lots of scared people has committed suicide through fear of it.... It comes to an end for us all but your time's way off. That's all the comin' to an end you'll ever know.'

Yes sir, that's the same Dick Johnson rode four and five winners a day and was the leading jockey at Tia Juana a few winters ago. I had told Bert to see what Marchbank would pay me for Dick's contract. Ten thousand was my price and I got it. But unbeknown to me, Jenky had borrowed five hundred dollars off Marchbank months before. Hanged if Marchbank didn't hold it out when he made out the check. It was for ninety-five hundred!

Perhaps I wasn't mad. May told me to forget it; it was just like picking up the money, that I'd never been out a penny on the boy, and more of the same kind of talk.

'Why, Dad will give you the five hundred,' Bert said.

I said, 'Like hell he will!' And like hell he did.

Chapter XXXIII

JENKY was hard up; he'd been more or less that way a long time. It seems like he borrowed twenty-five hundred dollars off Mr. Shimp, owner of the International Stable, and give the Arthur Mortensen contract for security. And now when the Kentucky season started up Jenky traipsed off to Louisville and sold Arthur to Mr. Shimp; he got six thousand dollars out of it, more.

Jenky come back all dressed up and I was tickled pink. 'Daddy, you look like you looked when I married you!' I told him. He must have blowed in plenty because a clothes trunk come to the Tia Juana track, along with the horses. Kept it across the border a while — I didn't know the stuff he really had.

Jenky fetched the trunk home but nobody opened it. When he took sick he called me to his bedside and asked me to open it for some papers he wanted. He thought I'd squawk about all them suits he never put on, but I didn't, he was too sick....

Once, back in Boise, I got so disgusted seeing him going around like a tramp that I went to Governor Alexander's store and hunted up a clerk that was one of Jenky's card-playing friends.

'Listen Sol,' I said, 'you put in a call for Jenky at the furniture store and get him up here. Make him a present of a suit of clothes. Some that fits him. Turn him around and let him see hisself; then shove him out the door! You can send the bill to me.'

They was good friends; Sol said he was ashamed of Jenky, walking the streets like that. Sol thought so much of him, it ain't unnatural Dad swallowing the whole thing.

Well now, he would take them spells. Wear out everything that he had. The last time I talked to him about it I reckon I hurt his feelings. 'You humiliate me to death,' I said. 'It

near kills me the way you act. You ask me to look pretty, and
when you go to show me off you tell me to wear my diamonds.
How do you think I feel out to places, the way you go around?'

'Don't you know, mama, that's the reason I never come up
to the grandstand, where you are. But I feel good this way.'...
Then, to show how slick Jenky was, he said, 'I was readin' a
piece in the paper where a man had a smart wife. Somebody
said to him, "How come you mopin' around like this and lettin'
your wife run everything? Jes' like you ain't got no sense?"
"I ain't," he said, "my wife's got it all!"'

Jenky was a swell when he come a-courting. He had enough
suits to stock three men, and he wouldn't wear the same one
twice without he'd send it to have it sponged and pressed.
That was saying a lot for them days.

My, how he changed. Got so's he'd walk down town in
Boise, where everyone knew he had two or three ranches over
on the Oregon side, looking like a tramp. But he didn't care.

One day a bum asked him for two bits and Jenky said, 'You
go on to the other side. I'm workin' this side.' He believed it
and went across the street!

Another time Jenky took two loads of cattle down to Portland and sold them. Him and a man named Butler. On the
way back they got off at Pendleton. A tramp braced him.
'I seen you comin' from the hotel,' he said, 'how's pickin's?'

'Pretty lean!' Jenky told him. Jenky had four thousand
dollars in his pocket when he said it.

Me and May went to Boise to pack up our furniture and
things to ship them to Chula Vista. It was a big job. Jenky
showed up before we was half through. He had a terrible cold
and was a pretty sick man. I tried to talk him into going to
the hospital for a while. It come pretty close to pneumonia —
the doctor kept him in bed ten days. After that Jenky left
for California and we went on with the work of packing.

There was so much stuff, May wrote Jenky to build us a
storeroom back of the garage. When we got to Chula Vista
Jenky took us out to see it, and say, he'd built two rooms

instead of one. 'By God,' he said, 'I'm tired of your bill-of-fare way of livin'! This other one's for me to do as I please, and I won't have nobody mussin' around, neither!' Jenky slept out there; it's a cute little room.

While we was still in the north I signed up Tommy Spencer that lived in Kuna, a town about twenty miles out from Boise. Tommy's old man told me, 'He's a ridin' fool!' He sure was.

Tommy Spencer ain't his real name. I tried hard to make a jockey out of him and he tried hard to be one. He lived here under my roof for two years. He was about fifteen, but awful little for that. Didn't weigh over eighty pounds, and all the looks of making a rider. A nice, honorable and truthful boy that everybody liked. He's a fine boy today.

I wasn't feeling good that summer, working and cooking for the crowd. When I set down to meals Tommy always went into the parlor for a cushion and put it behind my back. You couldn't keep from loving a boy like that.

Tommy got to looking sick. He wasn't eating nothing. I wanted to take him to a doctor, but no, he wouldn't go.

Every morning the men and boys cooked breakfast and went over to the track before me and May was up. But this time Tommy was setting here in the parlor and hadn't eaten no breakfast.

'Tommy, what's the matter? You're goin' with me to the doctor right after I've had my coffee.'

He started in to cry then — and got up and put his arms around me. 'I'm goin' to tell you the truth,' he said, 'I might jes' as well. I ain't sick. I'm yaller, yaller through and through! I'm scared to death of horses, yes, and I jes' might as well quit and go home to my father.'

'Oh no,' I said, 'we're goin' to try some more. I am willin' to take time with you. You're too small for a horse. I'm goin' to get you a pony to ride.'

I was patting him and talking to him. I said, 'We won't give up yet. You love horses, don't you Tommy?'

'Yes, I love 'em. I love to rub 'em down and feed 'em. But as soon as I get up on a live one I has a pain right here.' He put his hands on his stomach to show me. Bless his heart, he begun to tremble all over. 'I get so sick,' he said, 'I can't hold the reins in my hands.'

He went on to tell me what happened a few days before. 'One of Irwin's horses broke outen the barn. He was runnin' away from me but I couldn't have been more scared if he'd been comin' at me. I run into the stable. I fell down on a bed and stuck my head in the pillow. Will you tell me what was the cause of that?'

'Tommy,' I said, 'I think I can explain it. You been marked. Your mother maybe was awful frightened of a horse when she was a-carryin' you. Or it's something else no fault of your'n. I reckon, Tommy, you won't never get over it, but we're goin' on to try.'

That poor child, he stuck right to me. I bought him a small horse and he was riding it all the live long day, laying on its back like a jockey and pretending it was a race horse. Watching him start in the morning I had real hopes he was going to get over it. But he never did. Just found out the same, when he got on the back of a racer he wasn't no use.

Even now he tells me that whenever he gets money enough he's going to buy him a race horse and see if he can't kill that out. He don't aim to be a jockey but he wants to kill out the fear.

What I loved him most for was that he had to humiliate hisself; to own up and say, 'No I ain't sick, I'm yaller!' What a terrible thing that was for anybody to do. An ordinary boy would have lied out of it and made excuses. But Tommy ain't ordinary.

Delmar Trivett was our last boy — a local boy. Jenky loved him so much he turned down four different chances to sell him. Delmar's a wonderful rider that's had his share of spills and been hurt bad in some of them — but he's always game to go back to riding again. Norman W. Church, that Bert's with now, has him under contract; Delmar's one of the best booters in America.

Jenky was racing a small string of platers, but he wasn't feeling none too good. Not that he'd tell you, but he looked bad. I knew that he was taking insulin shots for diabetes. When he got too much they'd make him awful dopey.

One day he stayed at home — him and Delmar. When the rest of us come back from the track, Delmar met us at the front door.

'Bert,' he said, 'you better look into Dad's room; I think he's took bad. He fell off the bed and I jes' got him back in.'

May telephoned the doctor. He come in five minutes and hurried out to Dad's room. It wasn't maybe ten minutes more before he was back in the parlor. 'Don't feel bad,' he said, 'or take it too hard, folks, but he will be gone in an hour — he will be past all suffering.'

'Oh God,' I said, 'is it that bad?'

Bert come in and he told us, 'He ain't conscious, I don't know what to think.'

The Catholic priest was passing by; he lives up this way. He seen the lights lit so late, he come in. He went out to see Dad and stood by the bed a bit. When he come in to where I was he said, 'I am awful sorry, your husband is near gone, ain't he?'

'I don't know,' I answered. 'It might be so. I ain't been out there at all. They say as I can't do nothing and I don't want to break down.'

I am a coward all right, in some ways, because death takes an awful hold of me. When they are going, or after they are gone, I ain't no help. In my child days, back in Indiana, I seen too much of it under white sheets; I reckon that's it.

The priest stayed until midnight. Dad wasn't no Catholic, he wasn't nothing. 'I'm a-goin' out there now,' the priest said, 'and see how he is. Then I must go home.'

May said, 'Even if he can't speak, Father, maybe he is conscious. Could you take hold of his hand and ask him how he is feeling? Tell him to squeeze your hand. He won't do it for me, but he might for you.'

He done it, and Dad said, 'Father, I feel pretty rocky.'

May was up early next morning and come in to me. I was awful anxious and hadn't slept much. 'Is he better?' I asked.

'Sakes alive,' May said, 'he's over to the track two hours already!'

Jenky took the horses to Canada and Delmar went along. They made the circuit through eastern Canada and back down Vancouver way. Jenky come home looking fine; he gained forty pounds. But along in the winter he begun to go down again — in 1929, two years ago.

About April Delmar broke a bone in his foot and couldn't make the second trip to Canada that Dad was figuring on. I begged Dad not to go but it seemed like he just had to keep moving. He went to Toronto and Calgary. All through them parts they had county racing and fairs, a week at a time. When Dad come to Butte he was so sick his friends made him sell his horses and go home.

He looked bad. Finally he took to his bed. In the place he'd built hisself out back.

I asked the doctor would he suffer.

'He never has,' he said.

'Ain't there something you can do for him?'

'He wouldn't let me if there was,' the doctor said. 'He ain't tryin' to get better.'

Late that same afternoon Bert drove over from the track. He come in and give me a kiss. Then he went out back to see Dad. I set there thinking. Finally I went outside to see what was keeping Bert. He was standing by Dad's little room, talking to May. I seen it in their faces. It was Bert that told me. 'Mama, it's bad news.... Dad's hanged up his tack for keeps....'

May was alone with him at the end. She'd just give him a drink of water. 'We've had a good time,' Dad told her, 'but good things don't go on forever.' Dad knowed he was going. May said he sort of smiled... he didn't seem to mind much.

THE END